THE
**HOLOCAUST
DIARIES**

כָּל זֹאת בָּאַתְנוּ וְלֹא שְׁכַחֲנוּךָ
(תהלים מד:יח)

All this has befallen us
yet we have not forgotten You
(*Tehillim* 54:18)

The Holocaust Diaries

THEY CALLED ME
FRAU
ANNA

CHANA MARCUS BANET

P·U·B·L·I·S·H·E·R·S

New York · London · Jerusalem

Published and distributed
in the U.S., Canada and overseas by
C.I.S. Publishers and Distributors
180 Park Avenue, Lakewood, New Jersey 08701
(201) 905-3000 Fax: (201) 367-6666

Distributed in Israel by
C.I.S. International (Israel)
Rechov Mishkalov 18
Har Nof, Jerusalem
Tel: 02-538-935

Distributed in the U.K. and Europe by
C.I.S. International (U.K.)
1 Palm Court, Queen Elizabeth Walk
London, England N16
Tel: 01-809-3723

Cover credits: Yisroel Golding
Book design: Ronda Kruger Israel
Typography: Leah Langleben

Cover illustration reproduced
from original painting by Francis McGinley

ISBN 1-56062-0293
Library of Congress Catalog Card Number
90-82060

PRINTED IN THE UNITED STATES OF AMERICA

לזכרם הקדוש של סבי
רב אהרן מרקוס ז״ל
הורי יהודה ורחל מרקוס ז״ל
וכל קרובי משפחתי היקרים
קרבנות השואה הי״ד

Table of Contents

BOOK ONE

🌹

My Illustrious Grandfather

BOOK TWO

Before the War

BOOK THREE

My Shattered World

BOOK FOUR

In the Lion's Den

BOOK FIVE

The Aftermath

Publisher's Note

The Nazi holocaust was arguably the greatest tragedy ever to befall the Jewish people not only in terms of the number of people killed or in the cold-blooded savagery of the killers but also in terms of the astounding variety of forms and the myriad geographic locations in which pain and suffering were visited upon the victims.

If there is one archetypal holocaust experience in the common perception it is internment in Auschwitz, but there are countless other holocaust experiences which combine to create a totality far beyond the scope of the human imagination. Kristallnacht. Poland. Auschwitz. The Warsaw Ghetto. Babi Yar. Belgium. Holland. France. Czechoslovakia. Hungary. Extermination camps. Labor camps. Ghettoes. False papers and hideouts. Flight. Fear. Heartbreak. Despair.

Death. The images crowd in upon each other in an endless tragic litany, each with its own particular brand of horror, and it is our duty to commit as many as possible to the collective memory, both in deference to the victims and to immortalize the heroism, courage and faith of the survivors.

In compiling *The Holocaust Diaries*, we have tried to assemble a wide sampling of memoirs which would collectively convey the broad scope and the diversity of the tragedy. The highly-acclaimed *Late Shadows*, by Moshe Holczler, the inaugural volume in *The Holocaust Diaries*, concentrated for the most part on the Hungarian experience, although by its singular nature it was also a microcosm of the entire holocaust. In *They Called Me Frau Anna*, by Chana Marcus Banet, the second volume in the collection, the milieu moves to Poland.

When the German armies conquered Poland at the outset of the Second World War, the fate of its Jews was sealed, although no one could possibly imagine the extent of the coming holocaust. The Nazi net closed slowly around the Jews of Poland, impoverishing them, demoralizing them, enslaving them, isolating them in ghettos and finally herding them into concentration camps. Millions of Polish Jews were caught in the monstrous Nazi trap, while thousands more fled into hiding in the cities and the countryside. For the desperate fugitives life was also a continuous nightmare, with agonizing days and terror-filled nights, never knowing if the next day would bring starvation or discovery.

They Called Me Frau Anna is the personal statement of a survivor in whom the holocaust brought out profound spiritual qualities, who emerged from this terrible crucible victorious rather than crushed and defeated. For the most part, this book is the breathtaking account of a valiant Jewish woman and her struggle to save her two small children in the midst of the blazing inferno that was consuming her family and her people. With false identification papers, she wanders from town to town seeking shelter and food for herself and her children, always in fear of discovery and betrayal. In episode after hair-raising episode, guided by an unmistakable *hashgachah pratis*, she manages to elude capture, only to find herself back on the street in search of a new hiding place. Finally, she finds refuge in Krakow as a housekeeper for Dr. Helmut Sopp, a high-ranking Nazi official who is eventually imprisoned as a war criminal. After earning the respect of Sopp and his wife Toni, she is allowed to bring her children to stay with her, but her harrowing experiences continue, taking on a new dimension as she must constantly deflect the suspicions of the numerous Nazis with whom she comes into contact in the course of her duties.

Through all her tragedy and heartbreak, she finds in herself deep reservoirs of faith and fortitude that help her keep alive a tiny spark of hope and sanity in her darkest hours. In her struggle for survival, she is strengthened by the memory of her illustrious grandfather Rabbi Aharon Marcus, a brilliant scholar from Hamburg who came to live among the *Chassidim* of Poland and became an important historian of the *Chassidic* dynasties, and she repeatedly writes that she is sure it was only because of the merit of her grandfather that she and her children were saved from destruction.

Moreover, the author gives the reader a panoramic view of the world that existed in Poland before the holocaust, as well as of the holocaust itself and its aftermath. The first section of the book is a fascinating and illuminating portrait of her grandfather and his times, including a number of stories and anecdotes that involve the Rebbe of Radomsk, the Rebbe of Husiyatin and Rav Shimon Sofer, the *Rav* of Krakow. The second section describes the author's immediate family and their life before the war. The third and fourth sections record her experiences under Russian and Nazi occupation and her struggle for survival, and the final section describes her efforts to rebuild her life in Eretz Yisrael in the aftermath of the holocaust.

All in all, in keeping with the avowed theme of *The Holocaust Diaries* collection, *They Called Me Frau Anna* is permeated by the noble spirit of the author and the indomitable faith that helped her rise above the horrors of her experiences and emerge stronger and more inspired than ever before. It is the testimony of such survivors that we must hear and record for all future generations. Their priceless words, and the exalted spirit with which they are infused, are the ultimate legacy of these dreadful times. In the darkest moments of history, the faith in their hearts shone perhaps more brightly than ever before, and it shone with such a powerful light that it will still illuminate our world long after they themselves have passed on to a better world. Out of this faith there also emerges a wondrous hope that even in the midst of a holocaust one is never beyond hope, that the *Ribono Shel Olam* hears the prayers of the individual and performs miracles for him. And indeed, even as she is still surrounded by mortal danger, Chana Marcus Banet repeatedly acknowledges the incessant miracles of which she is the beneficiary and thanks the *Ribono Shel Olam* for them from the depths of her heart.

The publication of this distinguished book less than a year after *Late Shadows* is particularly gratifying to us at C.I.S. Publishers, because as the second volume in the collection, it establishes *The Holocaust Diaries* in the public eye as a dynamic project. The quality of the final presentation is a fitting tribute to the concentrated efforts and dedication of all the editorial and graphics personnel involved in the production, with special recognition to Administrative Editor Raizy Kaufman, coordinator of *The Holocaust Diaries* project. May the *Ribono Shel Olam* grant us the ability to achieve the same standard of excellence with the other holocaust manuscripts now in various stages of preparation so that the project in its entirety may bring glory to His Name and comfort and inspiration to His people.

Y.Y.R.
Lakewood, N.J.
Iyar 5750 (1990)

THEY CALLED ME
FRAU ANNA

Preface

How can I repay unto the Lord
All His bountiful dealings
Toward me?
Psalms 116:12

This is my first and only book. For the most part it
deals with the tragedies and horrors that I lived
through during the time when the Nazi beasts ruled Europe.
But in order to understand where I found the spiritual
strength to bear the hardships, the dread and the dangers
that beset my life at every turn, how I did not break down
despite the storm raging about me, I must begin my story
with a description of my deepest roots in the homes of my
parents and my grandfather. These people bequeathed to me
the generations-old heritage of a proud and faithful Jewry
that put its trust in the Holy Blessed One, Creator of the
Universe. My forebears implanted in me a deep faith in the
One G-d. They taught me never to despair but always to take
heart, believing and hoping for the best. And they taught me

that the divine commandment, "You shall love your neighbor as yourself," the supreme moral injunction, must serve as a guiding light for me wherever I go.

Thus my story encompasses my entire life—my youth and young adulthood in Poland, as well as my life as a free woman in my homeland. But the most dramatic point in my life occurred during the Holocaust, especially during those two years that I spent masquerading as a Christian Polish house-keeper, the mother of two young children, in the home of the Nazi army doctor, Colonel Hellmut Sopp, a personal friend of the notorious Hans Frank, the Governor General of German-occupied Poland.

I could not write this book immediately after the war, when the experiences that befell me were still fresh in my memory. For many years, I was unable to relive all the trepidations and anxieties of those dark days. Everything remained buried inside me; some things had not even reached the threshold of consciousness. But now that I have reached the age when it is fitting for a person to make an accounting of his life, it seems the right time to relate my life's story, for the benefit of present and future generations.

I affirm that all of the incidents and experiences related herein are entirely true. I have invented nothing; I presented the facts as they are. Nevertheless, my purpose is not merely to relate facts; it is rather to draw a lesson from them. It is this lesson that I wish to transmit to my readers, especially to the young people among them.

I give thanks to G-d for granting me the strength, patience and ability to fulfill this task.

Chana Marcus Banet

BOOK
ONE

My Illustrious Grandfather

A New Way of Life

My entire family was marked by deep religious feeling. Not only were my parents strictly observant Jews, as are my children and I, but Jewish religious observance was implanted in us by earlier generations. The model for a lifestyle that joined firm strong faith with a thirst for general education was my father's father Rabbi Aharon Marcus, a highly unusual and fascinating personality.

Aharon Marcus was born on the twelfth day of the Hebrew month of *Shevat* in the year 5603 (January 13, 1843, according to the civil calendar) in Hamburg, Germany. In his youth he was described as a *Wunderkind*; at age four he already knew how to read complete sentences, and at five he had begun to study Talmud. As a young man he learned to read and write French, English, Italian and other modern European languages, in addition to Hebrew and his native German. He was also well grounded in Latin, Greek and Aramaic.

This was most extraordinary for young Orthodox Jews at the time. When my grandfather was young, the Orthodox Jews of Hamburg were carrying on a fierce struggle against the Reform movement, which called among other things for Judaism to take note of the findings of secular learning. The most extreme among the Orthodox adamantly opposed any form of secular study, for fear that this would lead to assimilation and intermarriage. The greatest rabbis, known for their saintly lifestyles, strictly forbade reading modern literature of any sort, especially *belle lettres*.

My grandfather was a deeply religious man, but at the same time he had a thirst for general knowledge. He would make do with little sleep, spending the better part of his nights over books. He took an interest in philosophy, linguistics (especially Semitic languages), archaeology, astronomy and mathematics, for which he demonstrated an exceptional talent that would serve him well throughout his life.

One day, a famous rabbi, Rabbi Baruch Lifschutz of Danzig, came to Hamburg. The rabbi was both a learned Jewish scholar and well versed in the general sciences. He was also a gifted speaker; in the synagogue, speaking in classical literary German, he stressed the great moral values of the Torah and Talmud as they related to the values of modern learning. His personality and his sermons made a powerful impression upon my grandfather, who saw in him a model worthy of emulation.

In private conversation with the rabbi, my grandfather made known his wish to put an end to his studies in Hamburg and to move on to one of the great academies of Jewish learning in Eastern Europe. His dream was to get to know the world of the *Chassidim*, the pietist Jews of southern and eastern Poland, and their great leaders, about whom he had learned with fascination from his study of *Chassidic* literature. Rabbi Lifschutz understood the young man and advised him to go to Krakow.

At that time, the Jewish community of Krakow was getting ready to choose a rabbi, and Rabbi Baruch Lifschutz was a leading candidate for this most exalted post. Were Rabbi Baruch to be chosen, he would be able to serve as my grandfather's mentor. In the end, however, the community chose another candidate, Rabbi Shimon Sofer, son of the famous Chasam Sofer of Pressburg. The main reason for his selection over Rabbi Baruch was that Rabbi Baruch was known for seeking to build a bridge between Jewish and secular learning, whereas Rabbi Shimon believed in cultivating traditional Jewish religious learning alone. Most of the governors of the community feared that too great a rapprochement with secular culture would alienate Jewish youths from Judaism.

Despite this, though, and despite strong opposition from his sister, his teacher and his closest friends, my grandfather determined to proceed to Krakow.

The journey by train was a tiring one, and for part of the way he had to travel by horse-drawn post coach. He was able, however, to meet many people on the way and to obtain from them valuable information about possible contacts in Krakow. Among those he met was a follower of the Rebbe of Radomsk who was touched by my grandfather's story and impressed by his personality. He gave my grandfather the address of the place where the Radomsk *Chassidim* in Krakow gathered to study and assured him that there he would find someone to help him get started. He also gave him the name of one of the most important of the Radomsk *Chassidim* in Krakow, a certain Reb Shmelke Blitz.

Hungry, tired from the journey, tied down with a heavy suitcase, my grandfather arrived in Krakow and walked through the bustling streets of the city. Somehow, he managed to find the address he sought. As it turned out, he was in luck, for he arrived at the place where the Radomsk *Chassidim* studied on the evening marking the anniversary of the death of a great *Chassidic* teacher. According to *Chassidic* custom this was an occasion for great celebration, with food and spirits mixed with words of wisdom and *Chassidic* lore and with song and dance, all in order to honor and exalt the spirit of the late teacher. It also provided an opportunity for the poor and passersby to enjoy the refreshment, which was distributed to all comers. When my grandfather entered carrying his suitcase, all those present gathered around him, observing with curiosity this strange young man dressed in Western European clothing. They asked him where he had come from and what had brought him to this place. My grandfather replied that he wished to study Torah and to get to know the *Chassidic* way of life up close.

Immediately, they gave him a shot glass filled with especially strong vodka, which he was to down in one gulp. My grandfather, the straight-laced German Jew, who was not used to drinking that way, swallowed the contents of the glass all at once. Of course, he turned white and lost his breath.

When he regained his composure he was invited to join the group at the table and to participate in the festive banquet. He was delighted to accept, for he was quite hungry. He had not expected such a hearty welcome. The stories about the *rebbe* and the discussions on Torah immediately won him over to the *Chassidic* way. Even though he had already read much *Chassidic* literature, the spoken word influenced him deeply. When those seated at the table heard him quote from memory the holy *Chassidic* works, there was no end to their amazement. This "*Yekke*," this young German Jew, whom the *Chassidim* had suspected of being altogether ignorant of *Chassidim*, could suddenly take part in their discussions and debates that lasted until the very wee hours of the morning.

When the question arose at the end of the banquet who was to be host to the guest for the night, the most prominent member of the group, Reb Shmelke Blitz, announced that he was prepared to put the young man up in his home for several days and to take care of all his needs.

Reb Shmelke Blitz was a well-to-do man, though hardly rich. He sold prayer shawls, large, heavy, hand-made ones with silver ornamentation that he imported from the Orient and that were famous throughout Eastern Europe as "Turkish *talleisim*." These were much in demand, especially among the ultra-Orthodox. Those who dealt in them could become quite wealthy if they were able to maintain just the right inventory. But this was not an easy thing to do. The field was highly competitive; everything depended on the merchant's ability to produce the goods, for which demand exceeded supply.

The largest supplier of such prayer shawls lived in Constantinople, but he could not keep up with the orders from Krakow, since he himself had to import the shawls from Arab countries. When he had enough in stock, he would write to his customers in Krakow to let them know. The correspondence was conducted in French, and once a price had been agreed upon, the Krakow merchants would journey to Constantinople to inspect the merchandise, pay for it and arrange to bring it to Krakow. Such a trip would usually take ten or more days, as the railroad system in Eastern Europe was still not well developed, and in Turkey itself it was often necessary to travel by horse-cart over roads plagued with highwaymen.

The major difficulty lay in handling the correspondence in French, since the *Chassidim* of Krakow barely knew any Polish, let alone French. Even the Reform Jews, who could rarely be prevailed upon to help the *Chassidim*, were unfamiliar with French, having concentrated instead on the study of Latin and Greek. As a result, the Jewish merchants of Krakow were at the mercy of two Christian lawyers who were fluent in French and English. These lawyers demanded the exorbitant sum of one gulden, worth two gold francs, for the translation of a letter. Nevertheless, the Jewish merchants competed for the time of these translators, with the ones able to send off their replies most quickly usually gaining the advantage in the market.

One day, a letter in French reached Reb Shmelke Blitz while my grandfather was a guest in his home. My grandfather asked to see the letter, and Reb Blitz handed it to him with a disdainful laugh. To his amazement, my grandfather instantly translated the letter and offered to compose a reply on the spot. There was great rejoicing in the Blitz home that night.

From that time on, my grandfather became a permanent member of the Blitz household, and Reb Blitz no longer had to bear the crushing translation expenses, for my grandfather would answer the letters from abroad quickly and in an excellent style. In addition, being used to German order, he installed a precise accounting system for his benefactor, thus helping him avoid the nagging visits of the tax authorities, who were especially vicious toward the Jewish population and extracted from it high taxes, as if the Jews were a cow to be milked freely.

My grandfather's education and his knowledge of foreign language remained unknown to the rest of the *Chassidim*, for Reb Blitz had asked him not to tell about any of this at the place where the *Chassidim* studied. This was for his own good, for such a discovery could have harmed him.

Aharon brought real joy to his benefactors; he actually brought them good fortune. Their economic situation improved inestimably, just like the story of Joseph in Egypt. Reb Blitz's competitors did not know what to do. They simply could not understand why their own incomes had fallen so drastically, whereas that of Reb Blitz had grown great. Reb Blitz travelled abroad frequently, and his assets grew steadily. His competitors would get together often in order to figure out ways to get over the difficulties that beset them. Many of them believed that Reb Blitz's prosperity had come to him thanks to the *rebbe's* blessing for taking in the lone stranger.

The more the guest came to know the *Chassidic* way of life, the more he liked it. The willingness for mutual assistance, the blurring of the barriers between rich and poor, the good nature and joy for life, the deep faith and the confidence in G-d's good grace—all these opened before him a new world that until then had been altogether foreign to him, different from the hard, formal world typical of the Jewish community in Germany.

Thus, my grandfather adopted the way of the *Chassidim*; he would go to the ritual bath every day before breakfast, study the holy books day and night and read *Chassidic* literature often. Reb Blitz got him new clothes, dressed him in a long cloak and a round fur hat. These changes put my grandfather through a difficult struggle inside himself, for in Germany a man's external appearance was a matter of great attention, while here the most important thing was internal spiritual values.

Reb Blitz noticed my grandfather's emotional turmoil and advised him to make a personal visit to the *rebbe*. This way he would get to know the real picture of *Chassidim*, a living picture of Judaism (although everything he had learned of *Chassidim* until then was also real). The *Chassidim* knew how to express their innermost feelings in communal singing; they understood the great educational value in melody and communal singing, which exalt the religious man and raise him to the highest levels of the divine creation, which help him free himself from his material worries. The soul of a man entranced in a spirit of exaltation can even reach divine levels of happiness.

The Rebbe of Radomsk

he *Yamim Noraim* were drawing near, and the
Chassidim got ready to travel to the *rebbe*. In the
study house there was much discussion as to whether it was
time to take the young German Jew to the *rebbe* and whether
he would know how to behave in the *rebbe's* court during
these holy days. Nor was it known how the *rebbe* would
receive the young German who had grown up and been
educated in an altogether different environment and did not
know the local customs.

Reb Blitz, who had adopted my grandfather as his son,
took upon himself the responsibility for his behavior. My
grandfather wanted with all his heart to be able to get to
know the *rebbe*, who was known as a holy man with a sharp
eye that could discern one's innermost secrets. Thus he

immersed himself in mystical and pietistic literature and learned from them that all of man's daily activities, such as eating and sleeping, are not only physical activities meant to supply his bodily needs and personal pleasures but also had a heavenly purpose in allowing him to be healthy and whole so that he can serve our Creator.

Thus my grandfather set forth with a large group of *Chassidim*. He spent many hours walking with them, crossing the border between Galicia (in the Austrian Empire) and Congress Poland (in the Russian Empire) secretly at night, for he did not have the necessary identification papers to cross the border legally. He reached Radomsk weary and exhausted from his long journey.

Chassidim, not only from Poland but from other countries as well, would come to the court at Radomsk for the holidays. Only rabbis and the most venerable of the *Chassidim* were allowed to sit up close in the *rebbe's* shadow. The masses and the young people regarded the *rebbe* with extreme awe and maintained the proper distance.

When the *rebbe* saw young Aharon Marcus among the masses of the *Chassidim*, he asked the people standing next to him who the young man was. After being told, he called my grandfather to him and gave him a hearty blessing. Not only my grandfather but all those around him expressed their delight at this step of the *rebbe's*, which had singled out the guest for special favor.

From the time of that first visit to the *rebbe's* court, Aharon clung to the great man with all his heart and all his might. He would travel to the *rebbe* almost every holiday until the *rebbe's* death in 1866. My grandfather, possessed of deep religious feeling, found spiritual balance here; here he discovered the serious essence of the Jewish holidays, the religious fervor that allows the soul to pour itself out. The *rebbe's* pleasing voice as he walked past the holy ark and the hearty melodies he would sing enchanted him. Here in the *rebbe's* court he understood that during prayer one must concentrate all one's thoughts and intentions upon the content of the prayer and banish any extraneous thought or intention.

Such great and stalwart people who take care to perform the minor commandments in the same manner they perform the central ones, who sought to become joined to their Creator through maximum isolation and concentration, were privileged that their prayer was so deep that through it they could reach the heights of actual prophecy. My grandfather saw such spiritual depth in the Rebbe of Radomsk. My grandfather would reach the greatest heights of fervor especially during the *Unisaneh Tokef* prayer on the High Holidays, which the *rebbe* would recite himself and which stirred my grandfather to the depths of his soul.

In contrast to the heavy seriousness that characterized the High Holidays, the joy of *Sukkos* and *Simchas Torah* was great. My grandfather joined the *Chassidim* in dancing with the scrolls of the Torah with fervor and spiritual exaltation until past midnight. Here, in the *rebbe's* court, my grandfather discovered the secret of the holy spiritual pleasures, which are devoid of any material aspect.

He recalled the holidays in Hamburg, the city of his birth. There the worshippers would come to the synagogue in a rigid mood, wearing elegant clothing and top hats. Here, on the other hand, the *rebbe* would sing religious poems in a melody that allowed one to feel their entire depth and the spiritual exaltation of their contents. In this way, he would give expression to the collective longing of the entire Jewish people, of the whole people's soul, for the Creator, for redemption from the darkness of exile and from physical and spiritual slavery, for the revelation of divine light on earth, so that the peoples of the earth might understand that He is G-d, the One and Only, beside whom there is no other. In such an atmosphere a person can remove his daily material exterior. Through such genuine happiness, as is expressed while dancing with the Torah, the source of human morality, a person can reach the highest levels of spirituality.

This world, which was entirely new to him, this way of life

so different from everything to which he had been accustomed until then, the image of the *rebbe* infused with spirituality, fascinated my grandfather so much that he began to consider whether he should not relinquish altogether the synthesis between Torah and general knowledge in order to devote himself entirely to the *Chassidic* way. However, on *Shabbos*, while eating the festive meal at the *rebbe's* table, the *rebbe*, who as usual spoke words of Torah and morality, turned suddenly to young Aharon as if reading his thoughts and asked him, "Can you translate the Torah into the German language?"

The *Chassidim* seated at the table were astounded. They knew that the *rebbe* did not say things for no reason and that in every word that issued from his lips there was some hidden meaning. But this time they did not understand what the *rebbe* meant.

Aharon, however, understood that this great man had read his thoughts and that from his words he was to understand that he was being ordered not to give up that upon which his heart had been set.

My grandfather was sometimes given the great honor of serving as the *rebbe's* assistant when the regular assistant had to be absent from the court for any length of time. At those times, he would receive those people who had come to the *rebbe's* court for a blessing. He would take the slip of paper from them together with their contribution, known as a *pidyon*, a redemption payment. My grandfather, the educated, critical man, who was not dominated by delusions and who was privileged with such a rare opportunity to reside in the *rebbe's* company during all hours of the day, did not doubt that the *rebbe* was one of those who could see the future, and casting doubt upon his ability would be regarded as sacrilege.

Sometimes, Chabad *Chassidim* would come to the *rebbe's* court on their way to see their *rebbe* in Lubawicz. On one of these occasions, my grandfather met one of these *Chassidim*, a rabbi in a small village, who was well-versed in the teachings of the Chabad version of *Chassidim*. This man struck up a conversation with my grandfather and quickly discerned the breadth of his learning in science and philosophy. He explained the basics of the Chabad teaching of *Chassidus* to my grandfather as the founder of the Chabad movement, Rabbi Shneur Zalman of Lyadi, of blessed memory, had taught him.

My grandfather admired the Rebbe of Radomsk with all his being, and he wrote of him in his book, "Every word he spoke, even the simplest one, was magical; his intellectual acumen was brilliant, his singing was beautiful, but most magnificent of all was his prayer, which touched every string of the heart."

The *rebbe* treated my grandfather with exceptional kindness as long as he remained in his court and did not object to his fulfilling the function of assistant when his regular assistant was gone. The *Chassidim* looked upon this as a great honor.

Once an elderly *Chassid*, who had never before been seen at the court, came to the *rebbe*. His face and clothing indicated that he was a man of position and wealth. When he asked to be brought into the *rebbe's* chamber, he left on the table, in addition to the *kvitel*, a hundred-ruble note as a deposit, a sum equal in value to two hundred and fifty gold francs.

Most of the monies taken in would be distributed by the *rebbe* among the poor and needy, of whom there were many. The *rebbe* himself lived modestly and made do with little. Nevertheless, this time the *rebbe* looked into the face of this generous *Chassid* and returned his money, even though he had never done such a thing before. He asked my grandfather to bring the elderly guest a chair and asked him to sit down.

Then he told him a story:

Once there was a man of many possessions who held estates far from Jerusalem. When he grew old and began to make an accounting of his spiritual and physical life, it happened, as it often does, that his evil inclination whispered to him that he had actually never really enjoyed himself, for his entire life had always been one of honest and hard labor.

To be sure, he had wanted for nothing; he had many fields and vineyards, sheep and cattle, menservants and maidservants, and he was respected by all the people of his town. Every *Shabbos* he would attend the synagogue, listen to the wise men discussing Torah and take care that his wife and children had all that they needed. But his evil inclination would not leave him alone and kept on prodding him to enjoy life before going to his grave.

However, the good inclination of his personality also spoke to him, imploring him to banish such sinful thoughts, for he had passed all his life in honesty and in good faith and had been scrupulous in observing the commandments; yet now, when the day on which he would stand judgement before the Divine Throne was drawing near and he would have to account for all of his deeds he had done during his life in this world, he was liable to lose eternal life because of one frivolous act.

But the evil inclination proved stronger than the good, and the old man gave way to temptation. He went out and sinned. But even as he satisfied his physical pleasure, his soul from then on gave him no rest, and he felt remorse for what he had done. So he decided to go to Jerusalem to bring a *korban* to the *Bais Hamikdash* in order to purge himself of his transgressions.

This, however, did not prove an easy thing to do. He had to leave his town secretly, for if his neighbors saw him riding his donkey with a goat tied behind, the rabbi would hear about it, and all would guess that he had sinned and wished to atone for his sin by sacrifice. Then the respect his fellow citizens held for him would be diminished. So he left his house before dawn, asking the members of his family to tell anyone who asked about him that he had gone to Jerusalem to seek the advice of doctors.

The man had not considered the possibility that on the

way, as he passed through towns and villages, he would be
ridiculed by those people who saw an old man on a donkey
chasing a stubborn goat who always managed to free himself
from his tether. Exhausted from chasing the goat and from
the other burdens of the journey, the old man finally reached
Jerusalem.

In the course of his long and tiring journey he had had time
to think about what he had done and to understand that he
had acted foolishly and had been enticed by the whispering
of the evil inclination.

His heart began to afflict him so much that he broke out
crying with remorse for the deed he had done. His soul
reached such a state in which the Holy Blessed One forgives
anyone who has sinned and has repented wholeheartedly,
for he will surely not sin again.

And so the old man came to Jerusalem, left his donkey at
an inn and went up to the *Bais Hamikdash* to offer his
sacrifice. When he reached his destination, he reported to
the *Kohain* and asked him to make his offering for him. When
asked what sort of sacrifice he wished to make, he said
nothing. The *Kohain* pressured him and rebuked him, asking
how he could offer a sacrifice without saying what sort of a
sacrifice it was. The man had no choice but to tell his story to
the *Kohain*. He began his story in a trembling voice, and
when he finished, broken in spirit, he burst out crying once
again.

The *Kohain* who had heard the story called his fellow
Kohanim and told them everything that he had heard from
the old man. The *Kohanim* made merciless fun of the old
man and mockingly asked him how such an old goat as he
had let himself do something so foolish as to allow himself to
be enticed by his evil inclination and to sin so grievously so
close to his death.

These words made the old man's remorse even greater,
and the flow of tears from his eyes began anew. And as the
Kohain offered the sacrifice and spread its blood on the
Mizbayach as prescribed by the sacred law, the old man

collapsed and fell to the ground, the breath of life having left him.

The *rebbe* finished telling the story and added, "Only at that moment could it be said that the old man's sin had been forgiven."

While the *rebbe* had been telling this story, my grandfather had been watching the elderly *Chassid*. He saw that his excitement grew within him until he could no longer contain himself. Finally, to his utter astonishment, the old man fainted.

The *Chassidim* in the next room had heard the story and seen its effect on the old man. Eventually, they found out that the man ran a large country inn and farm estates and that his material situation was quite good. Moreover, he was married to a woman from a good home, although she gave him no sons. All considered him a religious man, hospitable and charitable.

When his wife passed away he began a relationship with his Jewish maidservant without marrying her according to Jewish law. In order to disguise his sin he took her to another town and introduced her as his daughter who needed to be immersed in the ritual bath before her forthcoming wedding. But pangs of conscience began to torment him over this deed. For this reason he had come to the *rebbe* and left the hundred-ruble deposit on the table thinking that this would make atonement for his sin.

The *rebbe*, graced as he was with prophetic insight, guessed the truth in his great wisdom. Thus he refused the deposit, but in order to lighten the man's unbearable heartbreak and console him he instructed him to return to the right path, keep the commandme nts and perform many acts of charity.

On the *Shabbos* following this incident, while preparing his table, the *rebbe* enjoined his followers to keep their hearts far from sinful thoughts, not to give in to their evil inclination, which can attack even elderly people who have observed the commandments all their lives. They must not forget, he warned them, that they were all members of a great and holy people and that it was their sacred obligation to preserve this holiness at all times.

The Correspondent of Krakow

Before leaving the *rebbe's* court at the end of the holidays, the *Chassidim* from Krakow who were Reb Shmelke Blitz's competitors got together and asked the *rebbe* for his advice and assistance. They described to him their difficult situation and asked him to influence Reb Shmelke to reveal to them who was helping him with his foreign correspondence, for in their opinion this was the reason his business had been so successful.

In his great wisdom, the *rebbe* guessed that this person must be none other than my grandfather Aharon Marcus and that thanks to him Reb Shmelke had succeeded in his competition with the others. Thus he invited both of them, Reb Shmelke and my grandfather, to his chamber, and when in the course of the conversation his assumption was confirmed, he explained to them that a true *Chassid* had to help not just one person but all Jews.

To be sure, Reb Shmelke was not happy with these words, but the will of the *rebbe* was regarded by him as sacred. Thus he asked for the *rebbe's* blessing for continued success in his business. He received the *rebbe's* blessing, and when he left the chamber with my grandfather he told the merchants from Krakow about what had been said during the conversation. My grandfather promised he would handle their correspondence as well. They all drank a toast, and everything was settled peacefully.

The entire group returned home to Krakow, with only my grandfather remaining a short time longer with the *rebbe*. He would gladly have stayed even longer at the *rebbe's* court, but this proved impossible. When it became known in Krakow that Reb Shmelke's "German" was fluent in several foreign languages, both orally and in writing, not only did the Jews rejoice, but they wondered why he had kept the fact from them for so long. They were glad that one of their own could intervene on their behalf with the authorities and could write requests for them without the help of the assimilated Jews or the Christians.

When my grandfather left the *rebbe's* court and received from him a farewell blessing, he also took with him the heartfelt advice that he ought to take a wife. When he returned to Krakow he became the correspondent for other merchants besides Reb Shmelke, and these merchants' financial positions improved greatly now that they were no longer dependent upon the Christian lawyers who charged them high fees for their correspondence. Moreover, my grandfather would take care of correspondence the same day; his style was concise and to the point and his handwriting clear and clean (there were no typewriters in those days).

My grandfather made do with a modest fee for what he did. He was a typical scholar; he did not know the value of money, and whatever he received he would in any case immediately distribute among the poor. When asked why he did not put

something aside for more difficult times, he would answer
that he could not behave otherwise, seeing around him such
poverty, families with hungry children suffering from undernourishment, sick people with no means to pay doctors or
buy medicines and old people with no bread.

Within a short time the rumor began to spread in Krakow
that young Aharon Marcus was fluent in more than ten
foreign languages. The rumor also reached the head of the
Jewish community. He was a proud, arrogant man who was
not well liked because of his haughty and repulsive manner.
He had attained his high position only on account of his
wealth and excellent knowledge of the Polish language. This
knowledge enabled him to deal directly with the authorities
without the aid of a translator and to intervene on behalf of
the Jewish population. Aside from this, he did not have any
formal education, and because he was in the business of
importing goods from Spain, Portugal and Italy, he, too, was
in need of the services of the Christian lawyers. The problem
was that the Christian lawyers themselves did not know the
languages of these countries, and they would have to
decipher his letters with the aid of a dictionary and translate
them into French or English, making many mistakes along
the way. This state of affairs often caused great anger.

At first, this man did not want to believe that my grandfather, this young *Chassid* from Germany, could know so
much. Nevertheless he decided to investigate, and sent his
servant to fetch my grandfather.

At the time, my grandfather was sitting in the house of
study poring over his Talmud and had no desire to separate
himself from the holy book. But the messenger pressured
him and did not leave him alone until he consented to go. The
others in the study house at the time also implored him to go,
as he was a foreign citizen and there was always a danger
that the authorities would catch him and deport him from
the country. If something like this happened, the intervention of the head of the Jewish community might be of help.
There was thus nothing to do but accompany the messenger.

My grandfather found the man sitting behind his desk examining some papers. He paid no attention at all to the person who entered his room and left him standing next to the door. My grandfather was a man who knew his own worth. Insulted by such behavior, he approached the rich man's desk and sat down on a chair without being asked to do so. Suddenly, he heard the man tell him sternly that he was not accustomed to having people sit before him without his permission. My grandfather replied that he thought he had heard an invitation to sit down, but if the chairman did not wish him to sit he could get up and leave at once.

The man looked at him with astonishment, but at last decided to extend him his hand. He said he had heard that my grandfather knew many foreign languages and asked if he could translate a letter written in Italian. My grandfather took the letter in hand, read it at once with no effort and within a few minutes penned an answer in the same language. At that moment, the man's wife entered the room and explained that she was most curious to meet the educated German about whom she had heard so much. She also remarked to her husband that he ought to pay him for his services. Her husband, to be sure, had not initially had it in mind to pay my grandfather for the letter, for which someone else would have demanded at least ten gulden. Rather, he had made do with a mumbled "Thank you." Only under the influence of his wife's comment did he put his hand into his pocket, fumble around in it, pull out a coin and give it to my grandfather.

My grandfather had a strong desire at the time to throw the coin back on the man's table, but he remembered the warning of his friends and responded with restraint to this insult. He took the coin and left.

From that time, my grandfather took care of the foreign correspondence of many of the wealthy Jews of Krakow and also wrote petitions to the authorities for the poor people of the town. While staying in Krakow he had mastered the Polish language and its grammar to such an extent that even people who knew it well were impressed.

All this while my grandfather continued to study the general sciences and literature, even though he devoted most of his time to Jewish learning.

A stroke of good fortune opened before him the doors of the library of the famous Jagiellonian University of Krakow. This is how it happened.

Once, while strolling along the splendid boulevards that surround the central part of the city, he was so involved in his thoughts that he ran into a man walking toward him. These boulevards, which had been planted in place of the ancient walls of the city, encircled the old quarter in a ring beginning at Wawel Hill with the royal castle and ending at the other side of the same hill. Not far from the palace the boulevards passed close to the Jewish quarter. In this segment, Jews of all ages and all walks of life could be found strolling or resting on the benches. Further along, the boulevards reached the area of the university where Jews were only infrequently seen.

Deep in his thoughts, my grandfather had not noticed that he had strayed far from the Jewish quarter and had approached the university area. This is where he ran into an unfamiliar man coming toward him. Of course, he immediately apologized to the man and asked his forgiveness. The man looked at my grandfather angrily, seeing before him a *Chassidic* Jew wearing traditional garb. But when he heard the fluent German my grandfather spoke, he was struck with amazement. He began to ask him all sorts of questions and presently struck up a conversation with him on questions of philosophy. My grandfather's responses and opinions made a strong impression on him.

It turned out that the man was one of the senior professors at the Jagiellonian University. He invited my grandfather to visit him in his home, placed his private library at his disposal and also obtained for him entrance to the library of the university. The professor's admiration for my grandfather reached such a level that he would invite him to the univer-

sity to take part in the philosophical disputations of the
students preparing for their masters examinations. My
grandfather would visit the home of the professor in the
evenings after spending the day studying Talmud. To his
Jewish friends he explained that his acquaintance with such
a person could be of use to the Jews in time of need.

After a while, my grandfather's visits to the professor
began to arouse dissatisfaction on the part of the professor's
wife. She was a converted Jew and desired as little contact as
possible with her former people. My grandfather, too, came
to the conclusion that it would be a good idea for him to limit
these visits, for he feared that his visits to the house of a
Christian would make him appear suspicious to his *Chassidic* friends. But the professor continued to correspond
with my grandfather about scientific and philosophical matters and frequently intervened with the authorities on the
Jews' behalf.

Many Jews were involved in petty trade, and because for
the most part they were not well-versed in all the various
laws and restrictions, not a day went by without a fine or
some other punishment for an infraction of an unfamiliar
law being laid upon some Jew. The violator would be summoned to report to the police station, where he would be
detained for many hours while his hungry wife and children
would worry what had become of him. The noble professor
heard from my grandfather about the tribulations of these
poor people, and before such matters were taken to court he
would intervene with the authorities at my grandfather's
request.

Had my grandfather made full use of his linguistic talents
and knowledge, he could have become wealthy translating
and writing letters. But he made do with whatever people
gave him voluntarily, and even this money he would distribute among the poor. He became known as an extremely noble
and generous man who had managed to overcome the natural feelings of abhorrence and revulsion and enter the homes
of the poor, visit the sick who lived in cold, filth and the most

squalid conditions, bathe their bodies, bandage their wounds, bring them food and do everything he could to lighten their burden of suffering.

I often think that if the Jewish people, persecuted and oppressed, managed after the Holocaust of the Nazi hell to create a splendid homeland of its own, it is thanks to the merit of honest and righteous people like my grandfather Rabbi Aharon Marcus.

Arrest and Release

Not only the great Rebbe of Radomsk but my
grandfather's best and closest friends as well
implored him to take a wife. He had many offers for a match,
but when he asked the counsel of the *rebbe*, the *rebbe*
expressed his opinion that my grandfather should marry a
woman from a good home and from a rabbinic family of at
least six generations. Finally the appropriate match was
found. Her name was Necha Lifschitz, and she became my
grandfather's faithful and worthy wife. Like her husband,
she too, performed many acts of goodness and assisted the
poor.

For many years they had no children. Perhaps Heaven had
decreed that before having children they should fill their
lives with deeds of goodness and righteousness. Only years

later did G-d bless the couple with five sons and two daughters.

My grandmother would assist young couples with tiny children; she would feed the babies and bathe them. My grandfather, who had grown up in Western Europe where bodily cleanliness was a matter of course, suffered greatly whenever he saw small children covered with dirt because they had not been bathed with soap.

The home of my grandparents was always open to the poor who would come from the surrounding towns to consult with the doctors in Krakow. Almost all of them had no relatives or acquaintances in Krakow who would put them up in their homes, and they were too poor to pay for a room even in a cheap hotel. Thus they would spend the night at my grandparents' home, where they would also receive a warm meal, encouragement and a wish for a speedy recovery. If they did not have enough money to pay for a doctor or for medicine, my grandparents would do everything they could to cover their expenses.

In the year 1866, shortly before his death, the Rebbe of Radomsk received my grandfather into his presence. At the time of his departure, the *rebbe* added that my grandfather must not give in to obstacles in life and that there were moments in a person's life when he would stand before great danger. In such moments he must remember that G-d was with him and would guard him against all evil.

This prophecy of the great rabbi was to come true quite quickly. In the same year, 1866, war broke out between Austria and Prussia. Krakow was at the time part of the Austro-Hungarian Empire. In this situation my grandfathers life was in danger for being a German spy. This is what happened:

Because my grandfather had taken a wife and established a family, he had to assure himself a steady source of income. He thus took on a job as an accountant for a large firm that dealt in building materials and had a factory for manufacturing bricks. It was located in the southern suburb of Podgorze.

This part of town was surrounded by military batteries and fortifications. These batteries and the hills around them served in normal times as a place where the local population would go for hikes and recreation. However, in wartime the civilian population was forbidden to set foot there.

One day, after business hours, my grandfather felt like resting and going out for some fresh air. He went for a walk, and while deeply in thought, he did not notice that he had walked onto one of the hills to which access had been forbidden. He took off his coat and absentmindedly began to dig in the ground with his walking stick. Not far away was a military lookout, and in a matter of moments, my grandfather found himself surrounded by soldiers. In his innocence, he thought that these were soldiers on maneuvers in the field and continued digging with his stick. Suddenly, though, when he saw about ten soldiers commanded by an officer closing in on him, he realized that something was amiss.

The soldiers bound his hands in chains, and the commanding officer charged him with digging in the ground in order to plant explosives, thus preventing the Austrian army from having access to the fortifications. In addition, he was accused of being a sophisticated German spy disguised as an Orthodox Jew.

My grandfather tried to explain himself and said that he had no idea what they were talking about. He was just a peaceful citizen who had gone for a walk. However, his fluent German merely made the officer more certain that he was dealing with a German spy. He struck my grandfather with his fist and informed him that as soon as his fellow officers arrived he would be shot as a Prussian spy. In the meantime, about forty more officers and troops arrived. One of them drew a pistol and pointed it straight at my grandfather's heart.

Then a miracle happened. Grandfather remembered what the *rebbe* had told him about G-d watching over him in time of trouble, and some voice from within him whispered that he would be saved and not die. The officers stepped to one side to discuss what to do, leaving the soldiers to continue kicking him and beating him with the butts of their rifles. When the officers had finished talking the matter over they decided to bring him to their commanding officer for interrogation, so that he might be forced to reveal his accomplices and expose the entire spy network to which he belonged. Thus he was saved for the time being.

My grandfather overheard his captors saying that they planned first to bring him to the police station to check his identity. This was a problem for he had never registered with the local police out of fear that the Polish authorities would deport him to Hamburg. But again a miracle happened. Grandfather was led on the road that passed alongside the brick factory where he worked. By chance, my grandfather's supervisor, who had remained late in his office that day, was leaving the factory at that very moment. When he saw his accountant beaten and bound in chains and being led away by soldiers, he was shocked. Fortunately, he knew one of the officers who was the liaison officer with the factory in matters of supplying building materials for army fortifications. After each visit the factory supervisor had always 'remembered' the liaison officer with a gift. Thus he approached the group and asked why his loyal and devoted accountant had been taken prisoner and what they wanted from him. He also mentioned to the liaison officer that once, when he had been away, his accountant had handled the deal and that the officer had praised the accountant highly for his great ingenuity and education.

While they were talking, they passed a tavern, and the factory supervisor bought drinks for the entire group. There, over a glass of liquor, the entire matter was settled. The supervisor pledged in writing that his accountant would report to the authorities whenever summoned. My grandfather was thus released temporarily, and the next morning he appeared together with the supervisor at military headquarters where both he and the supervisor were interrogated for quite a while. Finally, at the supervisor's request, he was allowed merely to pay a fine for violating emergency military regulations. My grandfather saw in this miraculous delivery yet another proof that the *rebbe*, whom he so admired, was blessed with the spirit of prophecy.

The rabbi of Krakow, Rabbi Shimon Sofer, also contributed to my grandfather's release. Despite the age difference between them, the rabbi appreciated my grandfather greatly and liked him. He saw parallels between him and his father, the Chasam Sofer, who had also been born in Germany and left his native city Frankfurt-am-Main, in order to wander eastward and settle among the Jews there. Rabbi Shimon Sofer was a most distinguished man in the eyes of the Austrian administration as well, and his intervention was most important.

The rabbi was well pleased with my grandfather's work for the offices of the Jewish community, which consisted of writing requests and inquiries to various government agencies on behalf of the poor.

Once, when one of the small communities nearby turned to Rabbi Sofer for a recommendation as to whom they might appoint as local rabbi, Rabbi Sofer recommended my grandfather. He also urged my grandfather to accept the appointment, for in his opinion he possessed all the necessary qualifications. My grandfather, however, turned down the offer, explaining that a small town did not need such a highly and comprehensively educated rabbi, whereas here, in a big city, he enjoyed a broad field of activity in which he would make use of his learning for the benefit of the community.

My grandfather would urge sick people from among the more common elements, who were prejudiced against doctors and who believed in all sorts of folk remedies, to consult medical specialists and not to depend upon their superstitions. He would also convince deeply religious people that the Torah actually obligated them not to rely on miracles but to make use of doctors.

In Krakow he was the person to whom everyone turned. He enjoyed the admiration of all segments of the population, religious and secular alike. Everyone respected him and listened to his advice. If someone else had tried to fight folk remedies and superstitions, the orthodox would have disowned him and banished him from town. But this could not happen to the 'German' *Chassid*, who knew and understood the language of the physicians and their prescriptions, who could explain a medical diagnosis to the patient and tell them of their chances to recover or, G-d forbid, to suffer should they decline to do as the doctor ordered.

Similarly, he would endeavor to help a sick person who could not afford to pay a doctor. He would find the necessary funds, so that the doctor would agree to treat him again should he be in need.

Rabbi Sofer helped my grandfather in this blessed labor, especially in cases where the needy person was ashamed to accept charity from someone he knew and needed to be helped through an anonymous donation. Rabbi Sofer was attracted to my grandfather's company and enjoyed being with him. He also was pleased that during the readings from the Torah in the synagogue my grandfather would correct the mistakes of a reader who was not strict in adhering to the written cantillation.

The Bishop's Manuscript

Once one of the notables of the community, a religious Jew, son of a Krakow family of many generations' standing, a man proud of his status, brought to my grandfather a manuscript written on and bound in parchment. Next to the Latin characters were mysterious and entirely incomprehensible marks and signs. The man promised my grandfather twenty gulden (forty gold francs) for deciphering these signs. He did not want to reveal his identity to my grandfather but said that he would return three days hence to take the manuscript back. He would do this even if my grandfather had not managed to decipher the strange writing by that time, and he emphasized that this was the longest he could wait and that there could be no extension. My grandfather glanced at the volume that lay directly before him and noticed that on its back were two stickers, apparently covering the books title. In discussion with the book's owner my grandfather learned that the book had been purchased from one of the antique book dealers for a large sum.

After the man had left my grandfather began to inspect the book. Quickly he discovered that the book contained words of praise and glorification of the Christian religion written both in rhymed verse and in prose, together with the author's assurance that he believed with all his soul and all his might in the truth of the holy Christian teaching. My grandfather began to observe those strange letters and signs that he had been asked to decipher. How great was his surprise when he saw that these were none other than Hebrew characters written in the Rashi script common among the Sephardic Jews. However, they had been written like Latin characters, from left to right rather than from right to left, as Hebrew is written. Nor were there any spaces between words or punctuation marks. Despite this my grandfather managed to decode it.

It turned out that the Hebrew text was diametrically opposed to that which had been written in Latin. In the Hebrew text the author poured out his suffering soul to G-d. He had been forced to lead a double life, to pretend to be a believing Christian while at the same time remaining a son of the Jewish people, faithful to the religion of his fathers. He asked forgiveness for this sin. The text also contained derisive remarks against the Christian religion and a description full of mockery of the monks among whom the author had been compelled to live.

My grandfather understood that he held a manuscript of one of the Marranos, those Spanish Jews who had been forced to convert to Christianity but who secretly continued to practice Judaism. This Jew had become a Catholic priest, but in the Hebrew text that he attached to his text he gave expression to the struggle in his soul. He had, however, written it in a fashion that could not be deciphered, so as not to put his life in danger.

From that point on, my grandfather's work went smoothly. He completed the job and closed the book, but at the last moment he gave a shudder. The stickers on the back of the book had fallen off, revealing the stamp they had previously hidden. It was possible to conclude that the book had been taken from one of the public or church libraries.

To be sure, my grandfather had not doubted that the man who had given him the book to be deciphered had indeed obtained it from an antique dealer, but when he saw the markings on it he began to suspect that the book had been stolen from a library. He was filled with fear. At first, he thought that the simplest thing to do would be to ignore the markings and return the book to its owner. But on second thought he realized that the theft of a manuscript from the fifteenth century would be discovered sooner or later and those guilty would be apprehended and placed on trial. Who could tell if he himself might not be accused of being an accomplice to the crime?

He also considered the possibility of turning to the police, but there was danger in this course as well, for he did not have the name or address of the man who had given him the book and thus might be suspected of collaboration with the criminal. Moreover, the fact that he could not provide identity papers for himself (since he resided in Krakow illegally without having registered his address with the police) prevented him from going to the police. Aside from this, his conscience would not allow him to be the cause of the arrest of the man who had promised to come to pick up the book three days hence. Even though in this case my grandfather was entirely innocent, he did not want to have any connection with the authorities, for in those days the Jews of Krakow tried to avoid all contact with the government because of the negative experience they had had in their relations with government officials.

Plagued by great emotional anguish, he decided to ask the advice of Rabbi Shimon Sofer, whom he served as honorary

secretary for many years. When he laid the matter before the
rabbi, he found himself tremendously impressed with the
rabbi's brilliant intelligence. Nevertheless, the rabbi could
not give him any advice. Although not a *Chassid*, he could
only suggest that my grandfather travel to one of the famous
Chassidic masters and consult with him.

My grandfather went to his *Chassidic* friends and without
revealimg the reason for his question asked them to which of
the masters he ought to go. They advised him to go to the
Rebbe of Sadeger, but on thinking it over they came to the
conclusion that since such a journey would take five days,
this was not the best suggestion.

In the end, it was decided that he should go to see Rabbi
Yosef Friedmann, who lived in Rymanow and was himself a
member of the Sadeger line, great in Torah and *Chassidic*
wisdom. He had been ordained a rabbi at an early age and
had acquired a reputation in the *Chassidic* world as someone possessed of the divine spirit.

My grandfather did not even have time to say goodbye to
his wife. He simply left her a message that he had to go away
on urgent business for three days and ran from the study
house straight to the railway station. His only request of his
wife was that should he not be able to return on time, she
should notify the owner of the manuscript that he had travelled to his friend in order to seek his assistance in deciphering the mysterious manuscript.

The next day he arrived in Rymanow and went directly to
the *rebbe's* house. Since he was not known there he literally
had to fight with the *rebbe's* assistant in order to be allowed
to see the *rebbe* immediately. The *rebbe*, who from his
chamber heard the voices, appeared in the doorway and
asked what was going on. My grandfather was enchanted by
the *rebbe's* noble appearance, the countenance that radiated spirituality, and when he showed the *rebbe* the
manuscript and explained to him the purpose of his visit, the
rebbe immediately invited him into his chamber.

The *rebbe* soon found out that the man standing before

him was a remarkable personality, a *Chassid* quite unlike the masses of *Chassidim* who came to him every day, and after conversing with my grandfather for over an hour, he instructed him in a clear voice and with determination to return home without fear, for the matter would end well. There was no danger that anyone would be arrested because of this manuscript.

My grandfather, who had already become quite convinced of the rightness of the *Chassidic* way, believed the promise of the Rebbe of Rymanow with no reservation and decided to remain in Rymanow an extra day in order to copy the deciphered Hebrew text in peace, so that when he returned to Krakow he could deliver it to the manuscript's owner.

This delay caused his wife, my grandmother, much nervousness and fear, for when the owner of the manuscript showed up at the house in order to take it back and heard from her that my grandfather had gone away and taken the manuscript with him, he threatened to call the police.

My grandfather returned to Krakow late at night. He found his wife beset with fear and great worry on account of what had happened during his absence. My grandmother had not managed to exchange more than a few words with my grandfather when suddenly there appeared before the house a splendid carriage pulled by four horses and attended by coachmen and footmen in livery. The door opened and revealed the honorable personage of the Bishop of Krakow. After him came another carriage, from which descended the Jew who had given my grandfather the manuscript to be deciphered. The man showed the bishop the way to my grandfather's humble apartment. A servant led the way in order to light the path before them.

My grandmother trembled all over in fear, but my grandfather was calm. He welcomed the bishop politely and expressed his surprise that the bishop had come to his humble apartment at such a late hour. It is remarkable how secure he felt in light of the promise of the Rebbe of Radomsk that he would come safely through all of the vicissitudes of life, and he was sure that this time everything would turn out well.

The bishop asked his servant and the Jew to leave the room. When he was alone with my grandfather he looked over the poor apartment and demanded in a firm voice the return of the manuscript. My grandfather answered him in perfect classical Latin that he had succeeded in deciphering the mysterious script, but he hesitated to reveal the truth about the contents of the writing. But the bishop, seeing that the deciphered text was written on the back of the parchment itself in Hebrew, instructed my grandfather to read him the Hebrew text.

My grandfather tried at first to make the things sound a bit nicer and to hide some of the blunter expressions, but he was not successful, as the bishop knew Hebrew himself. My grandfather's attempt to conceal the exact meaning of the text merely made the bishop extremely angry. My grandfather thus had no choice but to present the bishop with the unadorned truth. Nevertheless, my grandfather's words were so convincing and his Latin so perfect that the bishop became deeply involved in a conversation with him about the book's contents. He was amazed at the *Chassidic* Jew who could not only understand a Latin text but who could also discuss and interpret the text in the same language.

This conversation lasted a few hours. When it came time to part, the bishop gave my grandfather the sum of two hundred gulden. My grandfather refused to accept the money, to the complete disgruntlement of his wife, who had during the entire time served refreshments to the guests. This money would have been of great use to the family, for my grandmother would distribute even the family's modest income to the needy and the hungry.

My grandfather later explained his refusal by claiming that he did not want to derive benefit from the Church's money. He hoped his behavior would influence this high-ranking personality, who had access to the Pope, to instruct the clergy throughout Poland that in their sermons they should stress the great sin Christians were committing against Jews by oppressing them, by subjecting defenseless people to physical violence, by the unbearably heavy taxes they placed upon the stall owners and small merchants who carried the yoke of supporting their families from morning to night and could not manage to eke out even the minimum for subsistence. My grandfather looked upon this step as an act of sanctifying G-d's Name. And indeed, his refusal to accept the money made a deep impression on the bishop, who learned that Jews were not moneygrubbers. The bishop visited my grandfather's house several times after this in order to speak with him about intellectual matters.

Eventually the origins of this episode came to light. That Jew, who was not well-known in the community, served as the bishop's financial advisor, and the bishop made use of his talents in other areas as well. The manuscript in question had been sent to the bishop, who had gained fame in Church circles as a most learned man who commanded many languages. The bishop had been asked to decipher the mysterious writing, something that even the greatest linguists of Paris had not been able to accomplish. Since the bishop himself had been unable to decipher the text and feared lest his prestige suffer because of this, he turned to his Jewish advisor for help.

The Jew had heard of my grandfather and of his linguistic prowess and hoped that my grandfather would agree to do the job. But he himself had wanted to impress the bishop not only with his financial expertise but with his academic learning as well. Thus he had asked the bishop to give him the manuscript so that he could look it over and decipher it. The bishop told him he could work in the bishop's library, for he feared to let such a precious manuscript out of his reach. But the Jew, managed to convince the bishop to entrust the manuscript to him for a period not to exceed three days. The bishop also promised him two hundred gulden for his work. This sum was enough to pay rent on a three-room apartment for a year and a half.

Clearly, then, this was not a trivial sum at all. The Jew did not want to lose such a handsome amount of money, and besides this he wanted to increase his prestige in the bishop's eyes. This was the reason he turned to my grandfather. In order not to arouse suspicion, he covered the markings on the book with stickers and told the story about acquiring the book from an antique dealer. He promised to pay my grandfather twenty gulden for the work of deciphering.

Since the book had not been returned to the bishop at the appointed time, the bishop began to suspect that his advisor had either absconded with it or lost it. Thus he demanded that the book be returned immediately or else the advisor would be placed under arrest. The Jew, who saw that my grandfather was late returning from his journey and who feared moreover that he would lose his secure job with the bishop, thought to go to the police himself. But how could a Jew inform on another Jew to the police? It was simply unheard of, a violation of all accepted rules of morality, unless the most heinous crime were involved.

Thus there was no choice but to tell the bishop the whole truth and to explain to him that Aharon Marcus was the only one who was both a learned Jewish scholar and a man of general learning sufficient to decipher the mysterious writing. At that point, the bishop had decided to see with his own eyes if his advisor was telling the truth. He was also curious to meet such a Jew who lived in the same city as he, for this struck him as a novelty. This was the secret of that nocturnal adventure and visit to my grandfather's house.

Still, though, this was not the end of the matter. The Jewish advisor to the bishop summoned my grandfather to the rabbinical court of Rabbi Shimon Sofer, charging that because of his refusal to accept payment from the bishop he had caused him to lose one hundred and eighty gulden. He proposed to my grandfather to accept the money the bishop had offered, for the bishop was still willing to pay. My grandfather continued to refuse. Of course, my grandfather won the case.

When one thinks about the way my grandfather turned down a sum of money for which he would have to work months at his job to replace, one can appreciate how magnanimous was his spirit. He would not benefit from the monies of the Church, because the Church had ignited the fires of Jew-hatred in the people.

Forced into Exile

T he news of the bishop's visit to my grandfather's house spread like lightning throughout the city and became a subject of general conversation. For the Jews of Krakow this was an extraordinary sensation. It was simply impossible to imagine that the bishop himself would visit the home of a *Chassid* and argue with him for hours on end instead of ordering him to appear at his own residence. Such a thing had never before been recorded in the annals of the Krakow Jewish community. My grandmother could not handle all the curious people who kept asking her for details of the famous visit.

A while later, the bishop visited my grandfather's house again in order to thank him and at the same time to take the occasion to engage him in an extended discussion of Jewish religious philosophy and of such great Jewish thinkers as the Rambam (Maimonides), the Ralbag (Gersonides) and others. But following the bishop's third visit, in which he invited my grandfather to visit him at his residence, my grandfather came to the conclusion that it would be better not to keep up this contact. He decided, therefore, to leave town for a while, for dangerous rumors had been spreading throughout the city to the effect that my grandfather had actually succeeded in convincing the bishop to convert to Judaism.

Neighbors from the surrounding apartment houses claimed to have looked into my grandfather's apartment and to have seen how he taught the bishop to put on a *tallis* and *tefillin* and other such ridiculous things. If such rumors had reached the ears of devout Catholics—and such a thing was quite possible, since most of the Jewish households employed devout Christian servant girls—it could have set off a wave of anti-Jewish riots and bloodshed. My grandfather learned of these rumors in the house of study. He could deny them to his close acquaintances, who of course believed him, but it was beyond his capability to persuade an entire city thirsty for sensation.

This time, too, as always, he asked the advice of Rabbi Shimon Sofer. The rabbi advised him to leave town.

Now the problem was, where should he go? Several of his friends suggested that he ought to return to Hamburg, where his relatives and many of his friends lived. My grandfather rejected this suggestion, for during the years he had lived in Krakow among the *Chassidim* he had become accustomed to their way of life. He also feared that the conditions of prosperity in Hamburg, which stood to make life easier for his wife and children as well, would in the end present an internal obstacle to his eventual return to Krakow, and this was something he wanted to avoid.

Finally, he confided his concerns to his employer, who with a heavy heart consented to release his trusted and outstanding accountant. He also advised my grandfather that he should go live in the Polish village of Zgierz, where a relative of his lived who would undoubtedly, on his recommendation, give my grandfather a job. My grandfather accepted this advice gladly, because from Zgierz he could easily travel to see the *Chassidic* masters he so admired, the leaders of the Chabad, Czernobil, Kotzk and other *Chassidim.*

Rabbi Shimon Sofer instructed the bishop's advisor that during my grandfather's absence he should find an appropriate excuse to explain his non-appearance. The advisor was glad to take on this mission, for on account of the affair of the manuscript, his favor with the bishop had decreased, and now, with my grandfather gone, he would be rid of his competition; he would be able to resume his former position.

Thus circumstances forced my grandfather to take up the walking stick and move to a new and completely foreign abode. But fortified by his trust in G-d and by the memory of the blessing he had received from the sainted Rebbe of Radomsk that he would overcome all obstacles, he took leave of Rabbi Shimon Sofer and his friends and went with his wife to his new place of residence.

He had to go through quite a few difficult experiences on the way, including an illegal border crossing. Exhausted after wandering an entire night and frozen to the marrow of their bones, my grandfather and grandmother finally reached Zgierz. My grandfather's first steps in this place were directed toward the local rabbi; he brought with him a letter of introduction from Rabbi Shimon Sofer. The rabbi, who was delighted to receive a letter from the famous rabbi of Krakow, received my grandfather with the respect that befitted him and arranged for him a place to stay temporarily with one of the *Chassidim.* On the other hand, he expressed serious doubt over the possibility of finding work at the establishment of his former employer's relative, for this man, who was exceedingly wealthy, belonged to the assimilationist camp and looked with contempt upon the *Chassidim.*

Thus my grandparents found themselves in difficult straits, without a roof over their heads or a source of livelihood and with a meager fund of money that could last at most for a few days. My grandfather took one look at the apartment to which the rabbi brought him and saw with his own eyes the poverty in which the people lived. The only wealth was the young children, whom their father barely managed to support. Still, this poor *Chassid* had acquired a reputation as a generous host, in whose home anyone who came to town could find a place to stay.

After one night, however, my grandfather did not feel that he could take advantage of his host's kindness any longer, seeing in what conditions this impoverished but generous family lived. Thus he went to that wealthy man whom the rabbi had described as a hater of *Chassidim*. The man greeted my grandfather in the same haughty and contemptuous manner in which he was accustomed to greet *Chassidim* and made him wait a long while in the corridor until finally inquiring what it was he wanted. When he saw the letter of recommendation my grandfather was carrying he changed his tone somewhat, stating that although he was in need of someone to handle his French and English correspondence, his need for someone who could write in Russian was even more urgent. My grandfather promised to become sufficiently fluent in Russian to correspond in that language in a short time. When he said this, everyone within earshot began to laugh out loud. But after protracted negotiations the man finally agreed to take my grandfather into his employ in order to assess his qualifications. He set a salary of three rubles per week (about seven gold francs) and also promised to raise this salary should he be satisfied with my grandfather's work. This latter promise, however, was never kept.

My grandfather accepted the terms as offered, for he had no choice. He also hoped that in time he would be able to find something better. He himself came quickly to understand that without knowing the Russian language he would not be able to get very far, for all the negotiations with customers, suppliers and local officials were conducted in Russian. Exceptions to this rule were Orthodox Jews, who of course spoke Yiddish. In this part of Poland, which belonged to the Russian Empire, there was even less of an inclination toward the Polish language among the Jews than in Krakow.

Suffused as usual with a desire to broaden the scope of his knowledge and aware that without knowing the local language he would not go far, he immersed himself in the study of the Russian language, even though his new employer kept him busy between ten and twelve hours a day. He found a good book to teach him the language and within a few weeks he had mastered it fairly well. His co-workers were highly impressed. Prior to that time they had been compelled to send all their correspondence in those languages to Warsaw for translation. Sometimes it had been necessary to wait several long weeks for a reply, and this exacted a high price. Now, on account of my grandfather, all this correspondence could be taken care of quickly and without delays, and the business-building materials began to flourish.

The owner of the enterprise, who found out that not only could my grandfather now read letters in Russian but could answer them as well, expressed his appreciation to him. But in his great haughtiness and pride he did not raise his salary. My grandfather rented a modest apartment at three rubles per month, and with the nine remaining rubles from his monthly salary my grandmother tried to make ends meet until the month's end.

A Generous Spirit

I n Krakow my grandfather's absence was sorely felt, not only by Rabbi Sofer, whom my grandfather had served as secretary, but also by many of the merchants who required his services and who were now thrown back onto dependence upon the good graces of the Christian lawyers, as they had been before my grandfather's arrival. These lawyers, angry that the Jews had abandoned them for so long, now raised their fees exorbitantly and treated their clients to long delays and disrespect. Blitz and other merchants would thus send their letters to my grandfather in Zgierz, where he would try to translate them and return them as quickly as possible. This, too, took much time, but in this way my grandfather continued to maintain contact through the mail with his friends from Krakow.

The social conditions prevailing in Zgierz filled my grandfather's heart with sadness. Here the masses of Jews lived in squalor and destitution much worse than that of the Jews of Krakow. The worry and the struggle over a loaf of bread filled every hour and every day of their existence. Jews here lived in constant fear of what the next day would bring, under the unending threat of physical violence. The inflamed local population urged the authorities to take anti-Semitic actions. Regulations injurious to Jews were promulgated almost every day. Only the wealthy among the Jews were able to avoid these regulations by bribing government officials, but how many Jews could afford to do this? Thus their political situation was also extremely hard. In Krakow the representatives of the Austrian regime looked out for the Jews' well-being, whereas here the masses were given a free hand. Orthodox Jews were afraid to stray from the filthy alleys of their own quarters lest they be beaten bloody for no reason other than that they grew beards and *payos.*

The regulations and ordinances unfavorable to Jews were of an entirely political character. To be sure, it was possible to obtain relaxation of their enforcement for several days by bribing the oppressors, but immediately a new order would appear whose only purpose was to make the yoke on the Jews heavier and to drive them down. In light of the conditions that prevailed in Zgierz, the Jews of Krakow could be described as most fortunate and their status as that of completely free men.

Only a handful of the Orthodox Jews of Zgierz were counted among the wealthy or the middle class, while most of the relatively few wealthy Jews in the community were assimilated Jews who had managed to acquire a higher education despite persecution and the obstacles placed in the way of Jews. Some had educated themselves, mainly in the two official languages—Polish, which was used in dealings with the local population and the lower-level officials, and Russian, which gave them access to the town administration and to the district and provincial offices. With this language they could speak directly, without the aid of an interpreter, to the representative of the governor in his mother tongue, something that often helped more than bribery to avert a new decree.

The business and the life of all the Jews, Orthodox and assimilated alike, were centered in the narrow alleys of the town. In the streets that were inhabited by non-Jews, which were no less filthy, only non-religious Jews without beards and *payos* could walk freely, without fear of falling victim to an unprovoked beating.

Despite these difficult conditions, my grandfather held on in Zgierz for two years, during which time he acquired many friends among the Orthodox Jews and the assimilators alike. He was of great help in the management of the Jewish community, trying to restore domestic harmony to couples who had quarrelled—usually for material reasons, as the lack of sources of livelihood and the inability to keep small children fed engendered a high level of tension and nervousness. In such cases my grandfather would run all over trying to find some source of income for the quarrelling family. He would pressure his employer and other wealthy businessmen to employ more Jews, since most of them employed mainly Christians.

Here, as in Krakow, he was a concerned father to the oppressed poor who comforted the unfortunate and the downtrodden. Because of this everyone loved and admired him for his good heart and for his efforts. My noble grandmother was constantly occupied taking care of the sick and of undernourished children, just as she had been accustomed to do in Krakow.

Meanwhile, time went on, and my grandfather came to think that the matter of his connection with the bishop had been forgotten and he could return to Krakow. However, he was aware that when the local residents would find out that he planned to leave Zgierz, they would do everything to frustrate this plan. For this reason, he had no choice but to abandon most of his movable property in his apartment and to steal away on the pretext of traveling to Warsaw for medical reasons.

In order to make the illegal border crossing easier, my grandfather took the advice of his friends from Krakow, who recommended that he wait until after the holidays in order to join the throngs of *Chassidim* who would be returning home from their visit to the Rebbe of Radomsk. They would cross the border with the aid of an experienced guide, just as they had always done in the past. It was agreed that my grandfather and grandmother would wait for the *Chassidim* in one of the villages near the border. And indeed, at the appointed hour they took with them only two suitcases with their most important possessions and left Zgierz secretly. They managed to reach Krakow safely.

In Krakow they quickly learned that after they had left Zgierz the town found itself in a state of great confusion, especially the poor Jews for whose children my grandmother cared. When several days had gone by and they had not returned, the desperation of these poor people became great. My grandfather's employer was furious as well, for my grandfather had left without giving any advance notice. He simply sent a letter from Krakow that he would not be returning to his job. The employer's anger was understandable; he had lost an employee thanks to whom his business's income had trebled.

My grandfather was received in Krakow by his friends and acquaintances with extraordinary enthusiasm. His former employer gave him back his old job. He also resumed his former activities in the Jewish community as secretary to Rabbi Shimon Sofer, who gave him a free hand to act in communal affairs and to extend succor to those who turned to him. My grandfather's employer agreed that he could work whatever hours suited him, for he knew how anxious he was, as a true and honest *Chassid,* to make occasional visits to the courts of the *Chassidic* masters he so greatly admired. His employer recognized his honest character, his strict German precision and his unbounded sense of fairness. He often observed how my grandfather would remain in his office after normal working hours, sometimes for hours on end, in order to finish taking care of correspondence so that it could be dispatched on time.

Here in Krakow he felt good and could live for his ideals. From Krakow he could visit the Rebbe of Rymanow frequently, and his successor, the Rebbe of Rozin. He also became quite close to the Rebbe of Czortkow, Rabbi Dovid Moshe, although he always remained faithful to the sons and grandsons of the Rebbe of Rozin. These were among the descendants of Rabbi Dov Ber of Miedzyrzecz, the direct spiritual heir of the Baal Shem Tov, the founder of *Chassidus.*

As before, he would distribute his salary, which was never very high, to the poor, without any hint of disapproval from his wife, and every *Shabbos*, poor and sick guests, especially those who had come from the surrounding villages to consult doctors, would be invited to his home to dine at his table. Sometimes, my grandfather and grandmother would even leave their homes for the night and stay with acquaintances in order to give sick people from out of town who had nowhere to go a place where they could spend the night.

On this occasion, I would like to tell about something that happened to me a few years ago. One day, an elderly Jewish man from Bnei Brak, a suburb of Tel Aviv inhabited mainly by religious Jews, appeared at my home. He asked me if I was indeed the granddaughter of Rabbi Aharon Marcus, as he had been recently told. I invited him to sit down at the table and was privileged to hear from him a most touching story.

This elderly *chassid* told me that he was originally from Krakow and that he remembered Rabbi Aharon Marcus well. Aharon Marcus, he related, was at one time a clerk and account auditor in the Krakow branch of a leading Austrian bank. On account of their appreciation of his industriousness and his outstanding work, the bank managers freed him from the obligation of working on *Shabbos*. In those days, all writing was done with a quill pen and ink. On Fridays, before leaving the office, my grandfather would break the point of his quill pen, so that the clerk who took his place on Saturdays would not be able to write with it and thus would not profane the *Shabbos*. The supervisors of the bank put up with this trick of my grandfather's without calling him to task for it, for they knew that my grandfather was an exceptional personality and an extraordinarily talented mathematician.

What is more interesting than anything else is how he got this job in the first place. It happened that the bank had a serious problem, for its year-end ledger did not balance. Even though the chief accountants ran thorough checks several times they did not manage to find the source of the error. My grandfather was then well and widely known, and someone who knew him mentioned him to the bank directors who had arrived from Vienna. They summoned my grandfather and promised him a most substantial salary if he could uncover the error. They placed a separate room at his disposal, and he set to work with great industriousness.

It took only a few hours before my grandfather was able to announce triumphantly to the directors of the bank that he had found the source of the error and that all of the accounts balanced without any shortfall. The bank kept its promise and paid my grandfather a handsome fee for his services. My grandfather was delighted, for with this money he could assist the poor.

Instead of going home and making his wife happy with the good news, he made the rounds of the homes of the sick people for whom he cared and of poor families with many children for whom a slice of bread with butter and a glass of warm milk were considered luxuries. He went to visit old people who were hungry and bedridden because of the cold in their unheated rooms. To all, he distributed money and food he had purchased on the way. By the time he came home his hands were empty, and he had not a penny in his pocket. But my grandmother, who at the time was already the mother of several children and needed to practice the utmost frugality in managing her household, responded with only a sad smile when she learned that her husband had earned a large sum of money but had distributed all of it to the poor and the needy. My grandmother merely said, "You did a good thing, Aharon. It is a blessing from the Holy Blessed One when a person can feed the hungry and the sick. Thank G-d neither we nor our children are suffering from hunger." Neighbors and acquaintances who witnessed this scene, and who were moved to tears by it, spread the story throughout the city.

My eyes, too, filled with tears when the old man had finished telling this story about my grandfather. He was surprised that this detail of my grandfather's life had not been known to me until then, for even many years after the event the story had been told in the city. But I did not really know my grandfather and grandmother personally, for they died when I was just a little girl. It was from my parents' and others' stories that I learned what an extraordinary personality this man was.

The more I ponder the miracle of how I and my two children survived the awful Nazi hell, the more I believe that this happened on account of the merit of my near and distant forebears. My beloved daughter Nechama, who bears the name of my grandmother, and my dear son Yechezkel, named after his grandfather (his father's father), carry this noble heritage in their blood. They too perform many good deeds, and they do so with humility and without fanfare.

The Final Years

My grandfather was a happy man after he returned to Krakow. His wife gave birth to five sons and two daughters. His name became famous among Jews all over Poland. But unfortunately his peace of mind was once again disturbed, and he was again forced to take up his walking stick and wander afar.

One day, that same Jewish advisor of the bishop of Krakow came to the office of the Krakow rabbinate. He had been sent to find out my grandfather's address. The bishop wanted to renew contact with him, if only by letter. The Jew, who feared that the bishop would find out about my grandfather's return to Krakow, did not know what to do. Should he tell the bishop the truth? At first, they considered telling the bishop that Marcus's address was unknown. The Jew maintained, though, that if the bishop should find out that Marcus was in fact in town, he would lose his job. Besides, it would be hard to conceal the truth for long, for many in town knew that Marcus had returned. However, worst of all was the possibility that those same dangerous rumors would begin to circulate again among the Christian population about the Jew's influence on the bishop. In that case, the results were liable to be tragic.

Thus my grandfather was thrust once again into a difficult situation, and after extended consultations, all reached the conclusion that there was no choice except for my grandfather to leave town. This was a terrible blow to him. The decision to change the orderly and peaceful lifestyle to which he had become accustomed and to set off with his wife and children toward an unknown tomorrow was a difficult one.

Thus my grandfather, in order to prevent terrible riots against his fellow Jews, was forced to uproot himself from his residence and his community, from his friends and acquaintances, and go into exile. He was depressed that he had to leave everything—Krakow, the *Chassidic* community of which he had become a part, his job and, most of all, the poor and needy people whom he had aided and comforted.

His friends found him a job as a manager in a large concern that manufactured furniture and other wood items. The offices of this business were in Lwow, but the factory, forests and sawmill were located in the nearby small town of Wyniki. Many workers were employed by the factory, which prepared logs for various purposes. The logs were transported to their destination by train or by river raft. Sometimes, the products were sent abroad.

My grandfather was given a small country house with a yard and several fruit trees. A few times a week, he would go to Lwow, to the company offices, in order to take care of the accounts and the correspondence in various languages. His salary was high, fifteen gulden per month. In Wyniki, his job was mainly to supervise the work of the lumberjacks and other forest workers engaged over a wide area in cutting down trees, debarking them and loading them onto various vehicles for transport. This was not an easy job. He thus had to devote much energy to it.

He brought order not only to the company's accounts but also to the organization of the work itself. Among other things he discovered that every week a car loaded with logs would disappear. Being a strict worker and an honest man, he found out that the workers were stealing logs. Thus he introduced changes in the system of work and supervision in order to prevent such thefts. After checking and investigating the situation, he discovered that the thefts were continuing, and he warned the chief supervisor that he would be fired if the thefts did not stop. The man begged my grandfather to forgive him and to have mercy on him, his wife and their six children whom he had to support. He told him that other workers were in a similar situation, for their wages were low and were not sufficient to support a family. He offered to cut my grandfather in on the take. But this time he was faced with an altogether honest and unsullied man. My grandfather was furious at hearing this contemptible proposal. Nevertheless, he did not take disciplinary action against this supervisor. Instead, he decided to talk with the owners of the factory about raising their employees' wages.

I mention this detail about my grandfather's life because the reaction of the factory owner was astonishing. He had been convinced for some time that the workers were stealing logs, but he had calculated that raising their wages would cost him more than the value of the stolen materials. Thus he simply ignored the thefts. It took a long time before my grandfather was able to cajole his employers into raising their employees' wages.

After he had introduced order into the business and everything had begun working smoothly, he found more time to study the new scholarly books that came to him from Vienna. Similarly he continued to assist the merchants from Krakow in taking care of their foreign correspondence, and they were quite satisfied and thankful for this.

As a man of broad horizons who craved knowledge and education, he did not surrender to his fate, which had forced him to leave the big city and settle in a small town, far from the centers of Jewish culture and learning. He subscribed to the most famous and widely-circulated daily newspaper of the time, the Vienna *Neue Frei Presse.* This newspaper symbolized for him his connection with the world at large.

Now came time for him to realize one of his greatest wishes and to defend *Chassidim* from its opponents. Not only assimilated Jews opposed *Chassidim,* but also many Orthodox circles fought *Chassidim* savagely. Grandfather, the true *Chassid,* unrivaled in his generation in his mastery of *Chassidic* literature, in the writings of Chabad and Jewish mystical texts, attempted to prove the correctness of the *Chassidic* way.

In the German book *Der Chassidismus,* he wrote, among other things: "Modern philosophical doctrines, which have gained such wide currency, were known already in the investigative tradition of the prophets of Israel." In the words of the prophets and in Jewish mystical literature, he found many of the ideas just gaining currency in his time: "The intelligent and talent-blessed subconscious operates not only in the realm of the physical, the instinctual, under the influence of the reflexes and the processes of renewal; it operates also in the realm of man's spirit, of love, of feeling, of character, of artistic creation, of thought and of history, when the individual works in the service of great eternal goals without being conscious of this."

In addition to his book on *Chassidim* and the philosophy of Hartmann, he wrote an entire series of philosophical works, among them *Barsilai, Sprahce als Schrift der Psyche (Barzilai: Language as the Writing of the Soul),* a book about the *Kabbalah* and others.

When the First World War broke out my grandfather went back to Germany to live. The German defeats in the war caused him great sorrow. He followed the course of the war with great interest. It is indescribable how a Jew could be so attached to the German fatherland as my grandfather was. He admired German culture, the industriousness and punctuality of the German people, their loyalty and tolerance toward the Jews in contrast to the wild anti-Semitism of the Poles and the cultural backwardness and horrible social conditions in which the Jews of Poland were mired. In his most awful nightmares he could not have foreseen that these same German people he so admired for their culture, and to whom he felt himself bound with the deepest ties of his soul, would be capable of being swept up in such murderous madness and to annihilate six million people solely because they had been born Jews.

Grandfather died in Germany in 1916, during the First World War. His children, who continued to live in Germany, believed that the move from Poland to Germany hastened his demise. Were it not for this, they thought he might have lived many more years.

My grandfather's last request was to be buried in Krakow. His children carried out his wish. He left us the most precious legacy. He implanted in our hearts deep faith in G-d. May his soul rest in Paradise. May he stand before the Holy Throne of G-d and pray before the Master of the Universe for peace for the Jewish people and all the peoples of the earth.

BOOK TWO

Before the War

My Father's House

My father Yehuda Marcus of blessed memory, inherited from his illustrious father Rabbi Aharon Marcus all the highest qualities, and the heritage of Judaism my grandfather bequeathed to his sons and daughters was stamped upon the way of life of our entire house. My father was an impressive man with a fine face. From his father he inherited his extraordinary goodheartedness, a most important human quality. He was always ready to help other people, even though it was not always easy to do so.

He possessed an outstanding intelligence; his horizons were broad, and he was blessed with many talents, which he did not have a chance to develop because my grandfather, an Orthodox Jew, was opposed to his five sons studying in a university. He feared that there they would mix with young people not sufficiently Orthodox in their faith or even free-thinkers altogether and, under their influence, throw off their restraints and lose their faith.

Indeed, this dedication to faith which my grandfather passed on to his children bore fruit. Not only the sons but the daughters, my aunts, remained firmly Orthodox in their belief. All their lives they conscientiously observed the commandments of Judaism and led a religious way of life, until their death in the camp at Theresienstadt.

My father was a coal merchant. The coal would arrive in railroad cars from the mines in Upper Silesia, and my father would supply it to various establishments in Krakow. Still, the activity he enjoyed most was studying Jewish texts and learning languages, mainly English and French, which he picked up on his own with the help of the *Langenscheidt* series and other books. In study he found not only enjoyment but release.

My father's only son, a child of old age born after the five daughters, was my parents' pride and joy. He was a fine looking young man, and one of the most sought after matches in town. He was named Aharon, after my grandfather, and like his forebear he was blessed with talents above and beyond the usual. It was a great tragedy that he did not live long. The Nazis murdered him and burned his body in the furnace at Auschwitz.

My mother Rachel was the daughter of the highly respected Schnitzer family from the town of Oswiecim, the town whose name the Nazis changed to Auschwitz, infamous for the death camp they established there, which will forever serve as a symbol of the mass slaughter they perpetrated against the Jewish people. I do not remember my mother's parents; they died when I was still a small girl. They left four sons and four daughters. The eldest son David was a wealthy man; he owned a factory that produced shingles in the nearby town of Brzezinka. The Nazis joined this place to the Auschwitz camp and changed its name to Birkenau.

My mother's second brother Shmuel Schnitzer was her

favorite. He would come to visit us every Sunday. He was a scholar of deep faith. At every family gathering he would inspire a pleasant atmosphere and true happiness. I remember Uncle Shmuel well, especially the times when he tried with all his might to entertain the guests at the weddings of my two sisters Lydia and Frieda, as well as at my own wedding. He wrote comical verses in which he paid respects to the guests and danced in a circle with all the men with unequaled enthusiasm, as if he had married off his own children. All this was because he was very attached to my mother. He, his four sons and four daughters perished in the death camp together with their families. His wife Sarah, who was known to all by the affectionate nickname Surcie, managed to escape with two other daughters to the eastern districts of Poland, where they were arrested by the Soviet occupation authorities and deported to Siberia.

At that time, I was living in Tarnopol. They knew my address, so a few weeks later I received a letter from Russia without knowing from whom it was. When I opened it and read it, I saw black before my eyes. Its contents were shocking. My aunt and my two cousins were suffering terribly from hunger and cold. My cousin Leah wrote me that her mother could no longer leave her bed; she was bloated from starvation. My aunt begged her daughters to eat her ration as well, for they had to work at physical labor in the awful Siberian cold and were numb and exhausted. My aunt would repeat this demand constantly, stressing that it was more important that they remain alive because they were young while she had no more strength to go on living. Every additional little bit of bread would be useful to them. Indeed, there is only one love that is absolutely unconditional, and that is the love of a mother.

From people in Tarnopol whose relatives had been deported to Russia I found out that it was permitted to send small packages to the deportees and that the most important things to send were animal fat and honey. I knew no rest when I found out that my dear noble aunt Sarah, so modest and pious, was suffering from hunger. So I went out and bought some intestines of beef, cleaned them well, filled them with goose fat and honey, and sent them off. I shall never forget my bitter tears when I received an emotional letter from my aunt's daughters. They described the joy that my package had brought them. They had great hope that the food would help their mother recover her strength.

I sent two more packages and a letter, but from the answer I received I found out that one of the packages had been lost. Many of those who received packages from their relatives complained about the loss of deliveries and were terribly depressed on account of this. They did not know who was stealing the packages. My cousin requested in her letter that I send a little money as well, so that they could buy bread on the black market. I sent the money and also took a chance by sending some sweets for my dear aunt.

A short time later, I received a letter from which I learned that my aunt had died of hunger. Her stomach had become bloated, and she was buried somewhere out there in the Siberian taiga. A few months later, I received the bitter news of the death of her daughter, my cousin Bluma, who had fallen ill with typhus and had been buried next to her mother. May they rest in Paradise!

Only the elder sister Leah remained alive. She returned from Russia after the war and a short time later managed to emigrate to Palestine, where she married a widower who had lost his entire family during the Holocaust. She gave birth to a son, whom she named Shmuel, after her father, and a daughter, whom she named Sarah, after her mother. The war years weakened her greatly, and even though she loved life dearly and devoted her entire life to her husband and children, whom she loved to the depths of her soul, she passed away at a young age.

My mother's third brother Simmel perished together with his wife Erna, a beautiful and glamorous woman, and their three children. Only one daughter survived. After the war she settled in Belgium.

My mother's youngest brother Yitzchak served as president of the Jewish community in his town until the German invasion of Poland. His wife Gisela, their three children and their families perished together with him. Only one son was left. He too settled after the war in Belgium.

Let me now return to describing my father's house and the happy events in the life of our family. Our entire family was very musical. We were all blessed with pleasant voices, but more than everyone else G-d had blessed my sister with a magnificent voice.

Our house was known for its hospitality and for the warm familial atmosphere that prevailed in it. On *Shabbos* and holiday evenings, after meals, all our relatives would gather together at our house to sing *Shabbos* songs in a choir. But all of those *Shabbos* and holiday evenings were nothing compared with the joy that engulfed our household on *Purim*. In anticipation of the festive banquet, refreshments were prepared with royal largesse, cakes made from walnuts and almonds, all sorts of baked goods, fruits and, of course, drinks. As was the custom, relatives would send food packages to each other. In this way the house became filled with all sorts of good things to eat. We also sent generously stocked food packages to our relatives.

Toward evening the entire family would sit down to the festive *Purim* banquet. The banquet would last until the small hours of the night. During these hours many of our relatives and friends would join us. Some of them, especially the children, would be in costumes, and the happiness was great beyond measure. Jokes and stories about current affairs were told. More than anything else, we did a great deal of singing. All night long the door to our house remained open so that the poor and needy might enter, and we could fulfill the commandment of giving gifts to the destitute. We would invite them to our table and honor them with a drink and dessert.

Lydia, the eldest of my sisters, was a beautiful girl gifted with an exceptional sense of humor. She married a man with a noble soul and bore him a son and a daughter. My second sister Frieda married a lawyer, a very religious man. They had three children. Another sister Bronia was married after the war to a kindhearted man who had returned from Russia. She also had two children, a son and a daughter.

A Foretaste of Disaster

A number of years before the war, I experienced a series of events that caused me—and no doubt many other Jews as well—to sense personally a foretaste of what was about to transpire in our world only a few short years hence. Unfortunately the entire world was struck with blindness and looked upon these warnings passively and calmly.

My father had real estate in Berlin. When Hitler came to power my father entrusted the management of his property to a German attorney on the assumption that he would collect the rent from the tenants and transfer it to us in Krakow.

In 1934, my sister Lydia and I went to Berlin to take care of some business for my father. Lydia went to the attorney who was supposed to give her the collected rents for the previous few months. When she did not return after a long while, I called her on the phone and asked her if the man had given her the money. Suddenly, our conversation was cut off.

A few moments later, the telephone rang again, and someone I did not know told me to report the next day to the offices of the secret police, the Geheime Staatspolizei. At the time I had no idea to what a dangerous place I had been summoned. Only later did I learn that these were the offices of the notorious Gestapo.

When I appeared, a Nazi wearing a uniform with the symbol of the swastika showered me with an endless barrage of questions. Mainly, they were concerened why I had come with my sister to Berlin. I told the truth—that we had come to collect the rent from the tenants in my father's apartment houses that he owned in Berlin, because it was our principal source of income. The Nazi explained in a stern voice that this was a punishable offense, that Jews were not permitted to take money out of the country, even if it was their own money that they had rightfully earned. But since all the members of my family were German citizens and I was young and pretty, he would absolve me of punishment and would allow me and my sister to take along just as much money as we needed in order to make our return trip to Krakow.

Later on, it was explained to me that we had had good fortune in managing to escape from the clutches of the beast. My cousin, who lived in Berlin for many years, was unfortunately not so lucky as we had been. My mother's sister Chava had emigrated many years before, together with her husband and children, from Poland to Germany, because the Polish authorities placed upon them such a heavy tax burden that nothing remained for them on which to live. They established a factory in Berlin in which the family members were employed. In time, their business succeeded; they paid taxes according to law and acquired for themselves a reputation as owners of an established and honest business.

When Hitler came to power the entire family returned to Poland, except for the youngest son Mordechai who remained behind with a friend to liquidate the business. Mordechai was engaged to my sister Stella. Once everything had been done, he and his friends agreed on the phone to meet that evening at the "Zoo" train station (the famous station next to the Berlin Zoological Gardens) for the trip to Poland. As the two of them were about to board the train they were arrested by the Gestapo.

Mordechai's sister, who had learned from my parents that I had gone to Berlin asked me to inquire at the Polish Embassy in Berlin whether it would intervene on behalf of the two young prisoners who had been detained by the Gestapo. She begged me to do everything in my power to obtain the pair's release. She herself had already forgotten the Polish language altogether, so she asked me to intervene and explain to the ambassador that the matter concerned two innocent Polish citizens who had done nothing wrong at all.

In the meantime, I found out that Mordechai and his friend were about to be put on trial. I arrived at the courthouse in time to see the two prisoners brought into the courtroom. Mordechai was pale, his face white as limewash. I observed him scrupulously, and when our eyes met, I could see in his eyes a desperate prayer and a cry for help. I trembled as the judge screamed in a domineering voice, barking like a dog, "You Polish pig, you wanted to smuggle money?"

Was it a sin that after many years of hard and honest work he wanted to assure his parents a decent living in their old age?

When I came to the Polish Embassy, the first secretary of the embassy greeted me warmly, and I explained my problem to him. He informed me that the next day the ambassador was scheduled to have a meeting with Hitler, and he promised that he would intervene with the ambassador on my behalf.

In order to ascertain whether he had told the truth, I returned to the embassy at the appointed time, and with my own eyes, I saw how a few minutes later a car entered the Embassy compound, in which Hitler himself sat, together with two members of his entourage. I wanted to get close to the car and ask Hitler to free my sister's fiance, for their wedding date had already been set. Hitler glanced at me, but before I was able to open my mouth, he disappeared with his entourage behind the embassy door.

Again, the secretary promised and assured me that he would speak with the ambassador about taking action in my case, and he asked me to come back the next evening, after working hours, in order to obtain an answer.

When I showed up, the secretary explained to me that he had not had time to speak with the ambassador, but when he noticed how disappointed I was he was quick to comfort me. He promised me that he would try to do everything he could for me. He sounded very reassuring, but somehow, his words did not fill me with confidence. I left the embassy with a troubled spirit.

For a long time, I wondered whether he had really intervened on my behalf at all. Why would he? After all, the Poles had been anti-Semites for many years before Hitler came to power. Would they intervene with the Gestapo in defense of a Jew who was entirely innocent of any crime even if he was a Polish citizen?

My cousin and his friend were sentenced to seven years of hard and torturous labor. His sister, who visited him a year later in prison, found a man who had changed completely. He was sitting with criminals of the worst sort. When he spoke with her he used very vulgar and foul language, just like them, and his words aroused in her much fear and revulsion. He spent several more years in jail, until he was finally shot to death.

All along, my aunt believed that following his term in jail he would return to Poland and marry Stella, but she was still broken in body and spirit after his arrest. She was taken mortally ill, and sensing that her end was near, she made Stella promise that she would wait for him to return. Stella kept her promise; she waited for him and remained a lonely childless spinster for all her years.

A Suitable Marriage

It was through my sister Lydia that I finally met my
husband. My sister Lydia's husband had a relative
in Tarnopol, which is in East Galicia. He used to visit Krakow
often, where he would come to our house. On these visits he
used to hint from time to time that he had a good match for
me in Tarnopol, a member of the Taler family, with whom he
was on friendly terms. He urged me to meet the young man,
for he came from a respectable, wealthy and religious family.
Many matches had already been offered him, but he could
not yet decide among them, for he wanted only a pretty wife.
On the other hand, after each visit to us this friend of ours
would tell the young man in question about me, and this
aroused in him great curiosity and a desire to meet me.

I myself did not pay any attention to these stories. I loved life in the big city, whereas Tarnopol was located in East Galicia near the Russian border. Our friend wrote several times that the young man was prepared to come to us if we would only invite him. But my father decided to meet him first; only after forming a favorable impression of him would my father invite him to our home.

However, as fate would have it, my mother fell ill with nephritis, and the doctor recommended that she go to the resort of Truskawiec, known for its curative springs and mineral baths that were called *naftusia*, because they had a taste and smell resembling kerosene (*nafta* in Polish). These were of great value in curing all sorts of illnesses. So my mother went to Truskawiec, and while she was there she wrote my father that he should come with me for a visit.

Truskawiec is located halfway to Tarnopol. We decided, therefore, to take advantage of the opportunity and go to meet our friend's young acquaintance. The road to Tarnopol passes through Lwow, so my father arranged with this same relative of my brother-in-law that he would bring the young man to Lwow where we would meet him. We stayed in my cousin's home while she and her husband and children went off to a resort, leaving her apartment at our disposal. Since we travelled by night train and arrived in Lwow early in the morning, we ate a light meal in my cousin's apartment and thought to rest afterwards. But the relative showed up and announced that the candidate was waiting in a nearby coffee house. We determined that if the young man would meet with father's favor, my father would bring him to meet me. If not, we would go the same day to Mother in Truskawiec.

Since I was very tired following the overnight journey, I accompanied my father and the relative to the door, locked it after them and lay down to sleep. I slept so soundly that I did not hear the many rings at the door at all. My father rang endlessly, kicked at the door, pounded it with his fist, and when I did not answer, he was worried that I might not have turned off the gas bib after fixing breakfast and had been asphyxiated, Heaven forbid. Only a young person can fall asleep so soundly. But finally father's fierce kicking at the door awakened me, and wrapped in the robe in which I had lain down, I opened the door.

My father, happy that he had found me safe and sound, went inside with me, and in his characteristic good humor answered my question whether the young man met with his approval. He said that the young man had impressed him as an honest and fair person but that he was short. Still, in order not to disappoint him, since he had made a special trip to Lwow just to meet me, Father asked me to receive him graciously. He asked me to get dressed and added good-naturedly that I shouldn't lie down again, for soon he would return with the young man.

A short while later the doorbell rang again, and I opened it. A tall, distinguished-looking man stood before me and introduced himself as Moshe Taler. At that moment, some divine power whispered to me that I should attach myself to this man for my entire life.

A while later, my father and the relative came back, and we all spent several pleasant hours together. It was clear that the two of us were interested in one another, but when my father mentioned that the next day we would be going to Truskawiec, the young man pressured us to remain in Lwow so that we might be officially engaged. I suggested that it might make more sense if he would come a few days later to Truskawiec so that we could include Mother in this happy event. But our matchmaker also pressured me to agree to an engagement on the spot, in the presence of the young man's older brother, for the brothers were very close to one another. My father, who had formed an exceedingly fine impression of the young man, supported their request. So it was agreed, and the young man telephoned his brother to come at once. In the meantime, a suitable reception was prepared.

When the older brother Gustav and his wife arrived, I saw that he too was tall and distinguished-looking. I found out later that the two brothers ran a business together, but even beyond this they were as close to one another as Siamese twins; they were never separated.

Gustav's wife Hilda was a daughter of the Kremer family of Bolehcow. She held two degrees from the University of Prague. The couple had a baby a few months old. Indeed, Hilda impressed me as a fine and gracious woman, and I was pleased to have her as my sister-in-law. All in all, I had a feeling that I would fit in comfortably with my new family.

Thus we were officially engaged, and it was decided that he should come a few days later with his widowed mother to Truskawiec, so that the two mothers could get to know each other.

When my groom arrived with his mother in Truskawiec, I received from him a splendid ring with a diamond as an engagement gift. During the war, I hid this ring for a long time until I was forced to sell it cheaply in order to pay a Polish family for sheltering my son.

Both mothers were quite pleased with the choice their children had made. My fiance visited again several days later, this time bringing a box of candies such as I had never seen in all my life. It was very large, made of fine wood, and filled with the finest chocolates of all kinds. Such a box served afterwards for keeping silver and jewels, for it had a lock and a small key. I myself, however, did not taste any of the sweets in the box.

At the time, a relative of my mother's was in Truskawiec, also for therapeutic purposes. She was quite poor, and when she had fallen ill the doctors had sent her to Truskawiec to take the cure. She stayed there for ten days, and the stay cost her family its entire savings. Her husband wrote her that she should stay several more days in order to recover completely, because at home she would have to take care of the household and the children. But he did not know that it was not worry for her family but monetary constraints that had caused her to cut short her stay at the resort. I did not say anything to anyone, but I took the box of candies to the nearby town of Stryj and sold it at the largest candy shop in town. The owners of the shop looked at me with astonishment, but I explained to them that I had lost my purse and did not have any money with which to buy a train ticket home. I had no idea how much the box was worth, so I left it to them to set its price.

I brought the money I received to our relative. She did not know where the money had come from and did not want to accept it from me. I had to plead with her for quite a while and finally told her that she should pay me back when she was able. With this money she would be able to stay another week at the spa; and I was happy to have been able to help her. I would have felt guilty had I eaten the candies with no cares at a time when her pale face testified to her great weakness and need. The warm blessings she showered upon me caused me great excitement.

I had to tell Mother the truth about what I had done with the box. She wondered why I had not come to her. I explained to her that I was well-off and happy in any case, whereas our relative's situation was quite bad, and I would have felt myself a hypocrite if I had not done as I did. Mother's eyes filled with tears. The warm blessings of both women, the relative and my mother, perhaps contributed later to the fact that I and my two children survived the war.

A short while later, we were married and moved to Tarnopol to live. Moshe's father, who had passed away a year before our marriage, had left his two sons a thriving business, and they had developed and expanded it. Nonetheless, all of us felt that this success was not enough to guarantee our continued existence in Poland. We often spoke of the rising anti-Semitism in the country and dreamed of liquidating the business and emigrating to Palestine. Haifa, a port city, seemed to offer the best chances for developing a business, so my husband bought a three-story building, with three shops on the ground floor, in the city's commercial center on Haneviim Street.

When my husband first came to Haifa he found that it was not easy to find a suitable building for sale, for this was the time of heavy immigration from Germany, whose Jewish inhabitants were leaving *en masse* for fear of the Nazi regime. Since most of them were people of means, they bought houses, lots and other properties in Haifa. Even though the selection was small, my husband managed to find this building, which was old, to be sure, but built well. The rooms in it were spacious, and from its balconies there was a marvelous view of Mount Carmel on one side and the ocean on the other. My husband bought the building from a family of Russian Jews who had been in Palestine for many years. When he returned to Poland my husband told me that he had great trepidations about purchasing the building, for he feared that I would not like it, but I received the news with great joy.

In spite of all this, though, it was very difficult to make the decision immediately to liquidate the business in Poland. The store my husband ran together with his brother, a sort of small-scale department store, had acquired a reputation among its customers. It employed several salespeople, a cashier, a warehouseman and an accountant. Unlike smaller stores, the prices in this store were fixed, the service courteous and the selection of merchandise varied. Most of the customers were from families of military men who served in the garrison at Tarnopol, the provincial capital, and civil servants. In addition, many customers came from the nearby villages; they would buy clothes, and the peasant women would buy big colored scarves, a costume that was quite popular with these women.

There was one thing that I especially liked. Because we were strict about observing *Shabbos*, we had to close the store early on Friday evenings. In wintertime it began to get dark around three or four o'clock in the afternoon. As a result it was necessary to begin closing up outside while continuing to take care of the customers who were still in the shop. From our regular customers, army officers and their wives, I often heard that we were losing much money by closing at such an early hour. But they did not understand that *Shabbos* was the most beautiful gift from G-d there could be. With what joy and excitement I would light the *Shabbos* candles, bless them with the greatest devotion and pray to G-d to bless me with fine and pious children! My father would always repeat in my ear, "When lighting *Shabbos* and *Yom Tov* candles you can ask G-d to give you good children."

My father was an extraordinary man. He was well educated, a lover of the beauties of nature and generous. I remember one incident that stirred me greatly. A match was made for the daughter of friends of the family, extremely Orthodox people, with a young man equally religious. The young people met on two occasions, and the daughter looked forward to further meetings in the hope that they would become engaged quickly. But the young man did not show his face any more. A while passed, until one day the young woman showed up at Father's house and pleaded for him to appear to the Rebbe of Husiatyn to persuade the young man to declare his engagement to her. She knew that the young man and his parents were followers of the Rebbe of Husiatyn and would certainly accede to the *rebbe's* request.

Thus one day my father turned up, to our great surprise and delight, at our house in Tarnopol, extremely tired, worn out from the long journey to the *rebbe* and back. He explained to us that he could not refuse the tear-filled entreaties of this young girl. My father, a man with a heart of gold, decided to go to the *rebbe*, the one person who could help in this delicate situation and influence the boy's parents and their son to agree to the match. The *rebbe*, may his righteous memory be a blessing, summoned all the parties, including my father, and among them it was decided that the young people should become engaged and should marry within a short time. The *rebbe* believed that the match would be a successful one and blessed them with all his heart. My father radiated happiness, as if his own daughter had been involved.

He also brought us the happy tidings that the *rebbe* had

blessed us, and with G-d's help we would have children. I shall never forget my father's words, "Remember, when you are pregnant, surround yourself with the beautiful things of nature, with flowers, with pictures; try to spend time in the company of good people. All of this has an influence upon the formation of the character of the children who are about to be born."

A Lecture on Purity

After our marriage we lived temporarily in a nice rented apartment while our permanent home was under construction. It was to consist of six spacious apartments in addition to the ground floor. There would be an apartment for my mother-in-law and her maid, one apartment for us and one for my husband's brother Gustav, his wife Hilda and their beautiful son whom I loved. Sadly, not a single member of that family survived. All three of them perished along with the martyred millions.

The fact that I had come to Tarnopol from a big city, that I was well-dressed and wore fashionable hats I had obtained in Berlin, aroused great curiosity, because I kept all the commandments of Jewish law strictly.

Rabbi Babad, the rabbi of Tarnopol, was a highly respected

personality. Because of his illness he spent a great deal of time in Switzerland recovering. A short time after I arrived in Tarnopol, Rabbi Babad was scheduled to return to the city, and the members of his congregation hung large placards around his house welcoming him home. Several weeks following his return, his wife came to visit me and asked me in her husband's name to pay him a visit, for he wished to speak with me. I did not know the rabbi personally, and I was surprised at this invitation and curious to know its purpose. My husband and my mother-in-law felt that the rabbi's invitation was a great honor for me.

Of course, I was quick to accept the invitation, and I appeared at the rabbi's house. The rabbi's face, pale from the illness he had just been through, expressed extraordinary spirituality. But the rabbi's request perplexed me. The rabbi told me that many families, even some from respected Jewish homes, did not strictly observe the laws of family purity. For this reason he was asking me, as if I were his own daughter, to help him. From reliable sources he had learned that even though I was a wealthy woman with a secular education who aroused much interest among the inhabitants of the city, I was extremely strict about this matter. Therefore, he was asking me to give a lecture in the municipal auditorium about the importance of Jewish family law. Should I accept, a date would be set for the lecture, and it would be announced in all the synagogues. The mayor himself was putting the auditorium at our disposal for a lecture on a Sunday, since no other public activities would be taking place that day.

I had no idea how to go about carrying out this task. I asked the honorable rabbi to release me from this duty. I explained that there were women who had been in town longer than I, who were older and more experienced, who were themselves well-educated and from religious families, who would not be embarrassed to appear in public as I was. But the rabbi touched the most sensitive of my heartstrings by telling me that in return for performing this good deed I would receive G-d's blessing and would be blessed with off-spring who would be a blessing for the Jewish people. Besides, I was the granddaughter of a great man and a great *Chassid*, Rabbi Aharon Marcus, of blessed memory, and this obliged me to accede to his request. Thus I gave my consent to the lecture, but I asked for sufficient time to be able to prepare properly.

When I returned home, the first thing I did was call my parents in Krakow on the telephone. I told them that I was embarrassed to appear in public talking about this subject and that I had no idea what sort of explanations I ought to give in order to persuade modern women. My father was glad that I had taken the task upon myself and calmed me with his assurance that he would send me in the mail a book by Rabbi Shamshon Rafael Hirsch that dealt extensively with these laws. My father's promise gave me encouragement, and when I received the book, I set to work immediately. My husband procured a typewriter for me and gave me every encouragement in my work. Thus I spent many hours over the book searching for convincing arguments in the writings of this famous Jewish scholar.

The lecture took place on a summer morning. When I walked into the auditorium I could not believe my eyes. The hall was filled to capacity, mainly with younger women.

At first, I was afraid that the young modern women would be critical of the things I had to say, but suddenly, it was as if some divine spirit descended upon me. I felt calm, began to speak, gained confidence and delivered a fluent lecture.

When I finished my lecture, I was literally besieged by young well-dressed women expressing how impressed they were that I had managed so delicately and convincingly to deal with such a sensitive topic.

I shall not forget the moment when an older woman with a kind face pushed her way up to me and gave me a hug and kiss with tears in her eyes. "G-d bless the mother who gave birth to such a daughter," she said over and over again. Her words moved me to tears.

I had never expected such a great success. Word of the lecture reached the nearby towns as well. I received a fine letter from the rabbi of Podwolezyska expressing his great admiration for my activity. He asked if I would repeat my lecture in his town. I acceded to his request. I travelled to Podwolezyska and there too, to my great satisfaction, I made a great impression on the audience. My happiness was even greater when a short while later the wife of the rabbi of Podwolezyska appeared at my house, thanked me in the rabbi's name and told me that in the wake of my lecture many families had begun to fulfill the sacred commandment.

Here I must mention one deeply-felt experience from those days which I often relived in my mind during the most tragic moments of the war.

As I have already mentioned we built our own house in Tarnopol. Before laying the cornerstone I went with my husband to the Rebbe of Husiatyn to ask his blessing. At that time, he was staying with his relative, the Rebbe of Mesebesoh, who lived in Tarnopol. My entire family was among the followers of the Rebbe of Husiatyn. The *rebbe* took one of the gold coins that my husband had given him and placed it in an envelope together with his blessing. The *rebbe* knew how much I wanted to have children. Thus he gave me the envelope and instructed me to place it under the foundation of the house during the celebration of the laying of the cornerstone. I did so.

We invited the men who worked on the building to take part in this celebration. We gave them generous refreshments, with drinks and all sorts of cakes.

The face of the *rebbe*, full of spirituality, is engraved in my memory, the face of a holy man who looked at me with his boundlessly good hearted eyes as if he were my natural father.

"From you, my dear daughter, the granddaughter of Aharon Marcus, will come forth great children," he said out loud.

My whole body trembled with excitement.

Not long thereafter I gave birth to two children. My daughter Nechama was named after my grandmother, the wife of my grandfather Rabbi Aharon Marcus. My son Yechezkel, born shortly after her, was named after my husband's father.

When the tragic fear-filled days of the war came, when death stalked us at every step and turn, I remembered the blessing of the great rabbi, and deep in my heart I prayed, "Please, great and merciful G-d, cause us to remain alive, that I may be worthy of your bountiful grace and that I may be able to bring up my children in the spirit of reverence for You!"

BOOK

THREE

My Shattered World

The Russians in Tarnopol

On September 17, 1939, in accordance with the Ribbentrop-Molotov Agreement, which had been signed but a few days before the outbreak of the war, the Red Army crossed the Polish-Soviet border and occupied Poland's eastern provinces. Thus, Eastern Galicia, including Tarnopol the city where we lived, was conquered.

Because the house in which we lived was new and located in a fashionable part of the city it was soon confiscated by the occupation authorities who used it to house a Russian couple and their daughter. The family took our large living room and the adjoining room for themselves, leaving us with two bedrooms. We shared the kitchen and bath.

It is difficult to imagine a more poorly matched couple than this one. The wife, Yevdotia Tarasova, was older than her husband, and her face was covered with smallpox scars. Her husband was named Sasha Oryol, but she had not taken his last name. The daughter Valya, a pretty blonde girl of eighteen, was Tarasova's alone.

Sasha Oryol was a good-looking man with a kind face. I couldn't understand what had brought him to marry such a woman. It took a while before I was able to guess the reason. Yevdotia was active in the Communist Party, a high-ranking commissar, and because of her position she enjoyed benefits that allowed her to live relatively well. Evidently, Sasha had sold out to her in order to partake of the advantages she commanded. Of course, there may have been other reasons of which I was not aware.

Right after our new housemates were presented to us, they made it known that they had reliable information that we belonged to the class of capitalist parasites, the enemies of communism. Several days later, Yevdotia advised me to send my husband to sleep somewhere else, because the police were searching the area for capitalists to be deported to the Russian interior. Of course, she said, she could arrange for our entire family to be thrown out of our house right away, but because we had two small children she had decided to let us remain for the winter. In the spring, however, we would have to leave Tarnopol, the provincial capital, and resettle in an outlying town. She let it be known that we ought to thank her for such leniency, as people like us deserved to be shipped off to Siberia.

I was young and inexperienced. In my innocence, I thought that communism sought the equality of all classes of the population. In this I saw a noble ideal. But reality opened my eyes. The exalted slogans were nothing more than empty propaganda. The reality was entirely different.

It did not take long before I found out how serious the situation was. Sasha warned me that there was about to be a raid in which men would be rounded up for deportation. He told me to make sure that my husband and his brother did not sleep in our house. They took his advice and went into hiding. That night, as I lay awake in bed, I heard the rumble of trucks mixed with frightening screams. By morning, everyone knew that in the dead of night people had been roused from their beds and loaded onto waiting trucks, which were to carry them off to parts unknown.

Later, Tarasova advised me to transfer all my husband's clothes, along with my sewing machine and other valuable items, to her room. It seems that houses were about to be searched and such items expropriated. Among other things, I gave her my silver *shabbos* candlesticks, whose glitter as they reflected the white tablecloth and delicacies bedecking the festive table had always given me a special feeling of holiness. I felt a great stab in my heart as she hid them in the large living room cabinet that she had made her own, promising to return them in good time.

As time passed, I noticed that Sasha Oryol would go off somewhere at night and return in the morning loaded down with expensive foods. One morning, when I went into the kitchen to prepare breakfast for my family, I saw him butchering a pig on my kitchen table. On the porch were some slaughtered chickens and a basket full of eggs. I wondered where he got such things, which at the time were very hard to come by.

Because Sasha Oryol liked our family very much, and especially the children, I felt confident enough to ask him where he had gotten these things. He told me that he and his comrades from the Party were conducting nighttime searches in the homes of the wealthy peasants—the *kulaks*, he called them—who had grown fat on the backs of the working class. I said nothing to him. I did not want to take the chance that he would detect what I really thought of his loathsome ideology.

What bothered me most was when Tarasova would put a healthy slab of pork into a pot in my kitchen, cook it with onions and other spices to make a dish the Russians called *zharkoye* (something like our *cholent*, from the Russian word for hot) and invite friends over to dine with them. I would have to wait until she finished everything before I could go into the kitchen, for as an observant Jew I did not wish to cook together with her. After she left the kitchen, the maid and I would scrub the table, the range and all the utensils she used with soap and hot water, so that I could prepare meals for my family.

When their guests would assemble for the evening, Yevdotia would ask me to lend her the tea cups, for after a meal rich in fat they were accustomed to drinking vodka from large mugs.

Since my husband and his brother often spent the night with relatives, and I would stay home alone with my two children, Yevdotia and Oryol would invite me to come sit at the table with them. They knew that I would not taste any of the food they prepared, but they urged me to drink a toast with them. I was shocked when I saw the way they drank, how they gulped down vodka in large mugs as if they were drinking cold water or tea. The guests were very courteous to me, but only with great difficulty was I able to persuade them to pour me no more than half a shot glass of vodka. And even after such a small amount, I needed to eat some bread, for the drink was very strong.

Valya, Yevdotia's young daughter, was enchanted with my little girl. She would take her into the dimly lit living room, set her down on her knees, put a little flag into her hand and repeat with her over and over the slogan of the Communist youth organization, *Bud gatov* (be prepared). The little girl would have to answer loudly and clearly *Vsyegda gatov* (always prepared). The little one repeated the words with difficulty, but Valya did not give up until she finally managed to teach the girl to pronounce them perfectly. It was no wonder that Valya was so insistent about this, since she was head of the local branch of Komsomol, the Communist youth organization. From that point on, she put pressure on me to bring my daughter to the parties that they held in the house at night.

I mention this because they were courteous not only to me,

but they really loved my little daughter. They would set her down upon their knees, lift her up and do anything to get a smile out of her, since she did not understand their language. I saw that they were basically good people, and I used to find rationalizations for them in my heart, out of understanding that their hostile attitude toward the *bourgeoisie*, the confiscations of property, the deportations to a land of suffering and all the other persecutions were dictated from above, and failure to carry out these orders was liable to bring them a similar fate. Moreover, there was another fact that explained their behavior. The merciless dictatorship in Russia had not done them any good; their standard of living was so low and miserable that they could not withstand the temptation to taste a little from the finer things in life whenever they chanced upon them.

Once, a high-ranking army officer in uniform who had just arrived from Smolensk, was invited to one of their parties. He understood some Polish, and it was easier for me to converse with him. He pressured me to eat their *zharkoye* with them. With great difficulty I managed to explain to him that I was a vegetarian, besides which I wasn't hungry, for I generally ate earlier together with my family. I served the guests delicious cookies and cake that my mother-in-law had prepared. My mother-in-law was anxious and worried about her sons and thought it a good idea to keep on good terms with our new flatmates.

I looked at them in astonishment when I saw them draining several large glasses of vodka and not getting the least bit drunk. Nevertheless, I noticed that Sasha's face had become as pale as that of a corpse. He kept on drinking with his friends, even though the color of his face showed that he could not hold down any more. There was something I could not quite put my finger on that made me have much pity on him.

It did not take long to find out just what it was that provoked my sympathy. Once Tarasova came back from her office in an extremely foul and angry mood. I was alone in my bedroom when I heard her talking quietly to her husband. Her voice began to rise and get louder and louder, and she blurted out in great anger words that I did not fully understand. Suddenly I gave a start, for I heard her shouting at the top of her voice, "You're not Sasha! You're not Sasha at all! You're a Jew! *Zhid!* Izak! *Zhid!*" Her words were as full of venom as her scarred face was ugly.

There are evidently certain inner hidden threads that bind one Jew to another, some blood connection. I felt that Sasha's behavior toward me had been different from that of his wife, in spite of everything. He made no secret of his clear affection for my two children, and even for me and for my husband.

I decided to take advantage of this opportunity, and a few days later I asked him quietly if he would cut up and prepare the meats he brought home in his own room or in the living room. I promised to put a special table in the room for this purpose. Moreover, I asked that he not make any problems if once a week I brought the old *shochet* to the basement in order to slaughter our chickens for *Shabbos* and for the week according to Jewish religious law. The poor old *shochet* was deathly afraid that he would be arrested and deported to Siberia if someone would inform the authorities what he was doing secretly in our basement. All of us knew that kosher slaughtering was strictly forbidden under the communist regime.

I looked into Sasha-Izak's face and asked him with an innocent expression if he had ever heard that Jews were forbidden to eat the flesh of animals such as pigs. I added that he had certainly noticed that we were religious Jews. The answer he gave me made me laugh. He looked me straight in the eye and blurted out in a juicy Yiddish, *"Mach dir a tsimes fun dein kosher'n esn."* (You can go stew in your own kosher food.) But in spite of the mocking expression in his words, his goodhearted smile remained on his face. He advised me that the *shochet* should do his work secretly, without leaving a trace after him, even a single drop of blood, and he promised me that nothing would happen to him. My mother-in-law, brother-in-law and his family breathed easier.

Tarasova and Her Mother

How was it possible to believe the inflated propaganda of this regime, which promised equal rights to all the national minorities under its rule? How was it possible to believe in the enormous achievements of which it boasted, when at the conclusion of the second decade of dictatorship the people was still mired in horrible poverty and destitution?

These thoughts plagued me after an incident that took place one night when my husband and brother-in-law were sleeping elsewhere. Horrible cries and screams reached me from the living room. I woke up suddenly at the sound of the screams, which were getting louder and louder. I knew that Sasha had gone out with Valya on one of their night raids. I rose from bed and went into the living room.

Tarasova was lying on the couch wrapped in a wrinkled dress, writhing in pain. The color of her face had changed completely. It was dark red, and she pointed to her stomach, which was hurting. Quickly, I awakened my young housekeeper, who was fast asleep, and asked her to go call our family doctor immediately. I went into my room and took down a jar of cologne and one of my nightgowns. In those minutes I was no longer a capitalist, an enemy of communism in her eyes, but a human being, a woman like her, who saw it as her duty to help her fellow human being and to ease the pain and suffering. She was covered with sweat, and I wiped her face and body with cotton dipped in cologne. The smell of the cologne and the feeling that she was wearing a new and pretty nightgown helped calm her down a little. I sat next to her, for she was alone, and we waited for the doctor.

As I was wiping her body, I wondered to myself that I no longer looked upon her as an enemy, as one who had rudely and inconsiderately invaded my house, caused my entire family to suffer and thrown us into fear that at any moment I might be in danger or that my husband, the father of my small children, might be wrested from me and packed off to some penal colony deep in the Russian interior where I would never be able to see him again. I could not grasp how it could be that a woman with a high-ranking position, a commissar of the Communist Party, could be lacking such a basic item as a nightgown. Only later did we, the inhabitants of the occupied territories, discover that in the communist paradise clothing items could not be had, food was for the most part severely rationed and people would stand for hours on end in long lines in front of the various stores, in bone-chilling cold, in order to receive a portion of bread, milk or other essential items.

The wait for the doctor lasted a long time, for he had not wanted to open the door when my housekeeper had knocked. Only when she called from outside that she had come on behalf of our family and that the matter was urgent did he agree to come.

The doctor checked the patient thoroughly. The diagnosis was an extrauterine pregnancy. He ordered her transferred to the hospital for an emergency operation. I paid him for the nighttime house call and did not leave the woman until dawn when her husband and daughter came home. They decided to take her by the next train to the hospital in Kiev. Before they departed, they told me that during her absence Yevdotia's mother would arrive, and they asked me to give her a small bundle that they had prepared for her.

And indeed, a few days later an old woman turned up at my house. She was extremely tall and thin and dressed in clothes that showed that she had come from a village. Even though I had by that time begun studying Russian and could with difficulty carry on the simplest conversation in that language, I was not able to understand even a single word the old woman had to say. Hilda, my sister-in-law, spoke Russian better than I did and served as interpreter for me.

When I brought the old woman into the living room, she began to look around with great curiosity. She stroked the couch and chairs with her hand, as if she was seeing such things for the first time in her life.

I gave her the bundle her daughter had left for her, without having any idea of what was inside. When she opened it I was astounded and could not believe my eyes. It contained some old, dried-out slices of bread. I did not know what she would do with the bread. I brought her two fresh slices of bread with butter and a cup of tea with milk and sugar. But she hid the fresh bread in the cupboard, took out a few slices of the dry bread, dipped them in the tea and ate with a gusto that befitted the tastiest delicacy.

Later, she removed an object from the cardboard box that she had brought with her. When I looked at it closely I saw that it was an icon of a Christian saint. My sister-in-law asked her about it and later explained to me that the woman had to keep the icon hidden from her daughter; otherwise, her daughter would throw it into the trash. The old woman could still remember the time when the Tsar had ruled Russia, when religious worship had not been forbidden and prayer in church was common among the population.

One night, I woke up to the sound of noises that reached me from the old woman's room. Because I was alone I opened the door to the living room quietly. It was dark, but through the windows that were not covered the light of the moon filtered through. I was taken aback when I saw the tall, thin figure of the old woman wrapped in a robe of rough cloth down to her ankles. She did not notice my presence, and I observed her walking back and forth across the room, stroking every object, the couch and the velvet chairs. She looked like a ghost. I went in and turned on the light. I asked her why she was not asleep, but I did not understand her answer. The next morning, Hilda explained to me that the old woman remembered furniture like ours from the time of the Tsar.

The old woman's presence in the house tied me down and caused me great discomfort. While I would be preparing our meals, she would not leave the kitchen for a moment. She seemed to have descended from another planet. It was as if she had never seen a tablecloth upon a table or a china plate or forks, or that she had never tasted such dishes as I prepared. It was completely clear that I would not be able to swallow even a single morsel without inviting her to eat with us.

My husband was a most noble man, and even though at the time it was extremely difficult to obtain foodstuffs, he would say time and again that hunger was a disease that struck all, and every human being was obligated to come to the aid of the poor and the hungry without regard for race or ethnic origin.

She would stand in the kitchen and breathe in the luxurious smells of the foods cooking on the stovetop, her Adam's apple bobbing up and down as she swallowed her saliva. It was clear that she was suffering from undernourishment; that was why she was so thin. My heart went out to her.

Tarasova returned from Kiev with her husband and daughter. She greeted me with the utmost warmth, for I had

saved her life when I summoned the doctor in time. I heard
her tell her friends that I was like a mother to her. Nevertheless, it was impossible to say of her that she behaved toward
her own mother like a living daughter. The very next day
after her arrival, she sent her mother back to her village on
the pretext that she would disturb her and would not feel
comfortable in her home. Since even Valya had a room all to
herself, there was certainly room for one more person, but
evidently they wanted to get rid of her. The old woman took
leave of me warmly, and her emotion was genuine.

The Stolen Linens

S asha had no compunction about wearing my husband's suits and even his winter coat. We said nothing to him about this. But the thing that angered me most of all was that Tarasova did not return any of the valuables she had taken to her room, ostensibly for safekeeping. Nevertheless, she continued to introduce me to her guests, who would play with my children, lift them up high, set them down on their knees and invite me to drink a toast with them over a glass of vodka. When I observed these people up close, I came to know them as sentimental, good-hearted creatures.

But one day something happened that changed my opinion of them for the worse. For many weeks, I had been putting off laundering the many dirty linens that I had collected, if only out of fear that Tarasova would see them. I knew how Tarasova's eyes bulged when she saw the pajamas and robes I had received from my parents together with my dowry. From the expression in her eyes I could tell that good sense obligated me to do the laundry only when she was not at home. But when following her return from Kiev she was full of nothing but praises for me and promised that she would never forget the good deed I had done for her, I became less cautious. When she told me on one occasion that she was going to hold an important conference with a delegation of party members from Moscow, I understood that she would be occupied outside of the home until late at night. So I decided to take advantage of this opportunity to wash my linens.

Today, tablecloths, napkins and other table linens are actually made from synthetic materials that are easily laundered. But in those days it was necessary to soak the laundry in hot water which had been boiled for a long time and afterward to wash the linens well by hand. My tablecloths were embroidered, as were our handkerchiefs, with the initial of our family name, and they were meant to serve their owners for many years. Trying to speed up the process of laundering as much as possible, I decided to wash my own undergarments and those of the children myself, while my housekeeper took care of my husband's things and the bedsheets.

Suddenly, Tarasova came storming into the kitchen like an ill wind. I expected her to rush into her room, but instead she stood beside the laundry tub as if riveted to the ground, looking on as my housekeeper wrung the linens. She watched like a wild carnivore, and I could not shake the feeling of bitterness that enveloped me. I pitched in feverishly in the rinsing and wringing, and afterwards, helped my housekeeper hang everything to dry in the two attics, mine and my sister-in-law's. When I had done this I breathed a sigh of relief.

The attics were spacious and well-ventilated, and since

during the two days following laundry day the weather had been extremely fair, I asked the housekeeper to go up to the attics to see if the linens had already dried so that we could take them down from the line. To this day I shall never forget how I shook with fright when the housekeeper came back and informed me that someone had stolen all of our linens. She too was quite shaken. I immediately ran upstairs to the attic and saw with my own eyes that both rooms had been emptied; not a single item remained in either of them.

It is difficult to describe how great was my sorrow over this theft. I knew how much love Mother had put into preparing my dowry and all of the items for her daughters toward their marriages, how many blessings for a life of happiness she had included along with the tablecloths and handkerchiefs as she was embroidering them with her own hand, how many prayers she had offered to G-d that He might permit us to enjoy the fruits of her labor for many years to come.

I had no doubt at all that Tarasova was the one who had stolen all of the linens and hidden them somewhere. My husband and my mother-in-law, who saw how unhappy I was, advised me to be very careful in talking to Tarasova, for she had it in her power to expel all of us from the house at any time she wished.

Nevertheless, I plucked up my courage, and trying to keep calm, I told her that someone had stolen all of the linens she so admired. I had no idea, I said, who could have done such a thing. I asked her how I might recover even a part of what had been stolen. I regretted having said this last sentence, for I saw how her gaze froze at my words. I felt a twinge of pain deep inside my heart. I understood the hint that I was better off keeping silent, for if I did not, then we, the hated *bourgeoisie*, would pay dearly.

For a few days, I walked around like someone who had swallowed poison. Today, many years later, after the entire terrible tragedy of our people, after the murder of six million of our brothers by the German Nazis, this whole experience looks like a trivial matter. But at the time, I was young and inexperienced, and this injustice hurt me very much.

A few days later, we were visited by the officer from Smolensk I have mentioned before, the one who had been so nice to me and my children. This time he went out with Oryol on a night raid. Apparently, he spent the night in the living room together with the couple, for in the morning he came into the kitchen where I was preparing breakfast for my children. He greeted me kindly and asked me for some shoe polish and a brush. I told him that someone had stolen all of my linens while they had been hanging out to dry in the attic, and I asked him if he thought I should go to the police about this.

Quickly, I learned that I had made a very big mistake. I should never have asked such a question. He looked me straight in the eye and warned me in a dry voice that if I did such a thing I could be certain that all of us would be packed off to Siberia with the polar bears.

My whole body began shaking. Apparently, he reported the content of our conversation to Tarasova, for I could sense in her behavior toward me that I had made a mistake by not keeping quiet and refraining from telling anyone about the theft. The lack of any feeling on her part, the lack of a sense of justice and, most of all, her hypocritical promises that she would never forget how good I had been to her hurt me very much. She had not even left me a handful of items from among my linens as a keepsake from my parents. Now that she had all of our valuables in her hands, she had no choice but to get rid of us, so that she could present her daughter with a portion of the beautiful luxuries and enjoy my precious linens. Sasha, who in spite of everything still had the heart of a Jew beating inside him, took me aside one day and advised me that we ought to look for a new place to live, somewhere in the country. If we did not do this, he said, we might be forced to leave our house empty-handed altogether.

So my husband and his brother travelled to the small town of Brzezany, where several of our acquaintances, merchants from Tarnopol, were already living. They had been urging him to move there with the whole family, because the living conditions there were relatively comfortable. We prepared to leave our house with deep sorrow, feeling that we had been done a great injustice.

My husband and his brother returned from Brzezany, where after much running around they managed to rent a room on the ground floor with a separate kitchen in a hut in the courtyard of the building. We were also to be permitted to cook in our room, in which there was a coal-burning stove for heating. The landlords, a devout Catholic family that manufactured sausages and various meat products, were coincidentally named Moskwa, even though they were not devotees of the regime and the authorities that were based in that city. So we moved into their house and began a new life in altogether different conditions from those to which we had been accustomed previously.

The Early Days in Brzezany

I n Brzezany, we opened a new chapter in oour lives. We had to get used to new and unexpected living conditions. In the single-story home that belonged to the Moskwa family we were given a large room with a corner in which to cook. We also had access to a kitchen, but in order to get there, it was necessary to pass through the yard. In the kitchen, too, there was room for two iron-frame beds, a small closet and a chest for sheets, blankets and pillowcases. In the yard there was a well from which we would draw water for cooking and washing. There were also several other structures in the yard in which the members of the Moskwa family would manufacture various meat products. Until the outbreak of war, they used to sell their products in a store that was located in the central square of town. When the Russian army captured the town they had been forced to liquidate the store, but they continued to manufacture their products and sell them from their home.

The Moskwa family had two daughters. The elder, not terribly young, had just recently been married. The younger daughter, Wladzia, was a high school student. She came to like my children very much. The landlady's sister Mrs. Zie-linska was a widow and lived with her fifteen-year-old son on the hill near the church. She was a regular church goer. She liked to listen to the fascinating sermons of the young priest who was in charge of the local church.

Only a few days after we had begun living in the new place, a Jewish couple with two teenage sons arrived in Brzezany. They were refugees from Western Poland, which was occupied by the Nazis. They had left behind them a bakery and house and had arrived with only a minimum of belongings, whatever they had been able to pack up and carry along with them. On the way, they had taken in a young Jewish orphan, the son of their neighbors whom the Germans had murdered. This boy had been left to wander about like an abandoned dog.

When they arrived in town they spent an entire day looking for a roof to place over their heads, but they were unsuccessful. Finally, they came into our yard, and when I saw how exhausted they were, physically and emotionally, I let them have the kitchen in the yard, with the landlord's permission, until they could find a permanent place to reside. The orphan, whose name was Yitzchak, was shivering from cold, for his coat was too short for him. My heart went out to him.

As I think back to those days, I find it interesting that all the time we had been living in Tarnopol under one roof with the Russians, none of our many friends and acquaintances had come to visit us. They had simply been afraid to do so. But here in Brzezany all sorts of acquaintances would come over often. These were well-known merchants from Tarnopol who had settled in Brzezany when the Red Army had conquered the area. Among them was Tamar, my old and dear friend from the Gur-Aryeh family of Skala on the River Zbrucz, who had married a lawyer from Tarnopol. After she had given birth to her son, the two of us used to take our children for walks together. Her parents were wealthy estate owners. Following her father's death, her mother had gone to live with her daughter in Tarnopol, and after they were expelled by the occupation authorities they had moved to Brzezany.

Among other visitors to our home was Zalman, a veteran resident of the town who lived near the Moskwa family. He had been our agent and found us our present apartment with the Moskwa family. Because he was a bachelor and lived alone, he would spend many hours with us and play with our children. Here he could warm his frozen bones, for we did not skimp on heating, whereas he used to sit at home in the cold for want of money to heat his room. Despite his suffering and want, he was a proud man, for whenever I would serve my family lunch he would suddenly disappear on some excuse or another. My husband would go looking for him and bring him back against his will. It was not difficult to guess that he was just as hungry as we were.

When the Russians had conquered Tarnopol and nationalized our business, we had managed to save a portion of the merchandise. My mother-in-law had hidden it, and thanks to this we were able to use it in order to exchange it for food items that the peasants would bring to Brzezany from the surrounding countryside. The mother of the family living in the kitchen in the yard helped us make these exchanges. Her name was Rivka-Breina.

I remember Rivka-Breina until this very day, for she would finish every conversation with me with a blessing.

"Remember, my dear woman," she would say to me, "that I, Rivka-Breina, will make sure in my prayers to the Holy Blessed One that you shall never know hunger and that He will keep you from all harm."

She was a woman of medium height, thin and extremely lithe. She worried for the four men in her family as the best mother would. She would go to the market in the morning when the peasant women would be bringing in bread, potatoes, butter and cheese, and she would buy these products in exchange for items of clothing and linens. Since she was so grateful to us for the shelter we had offered her and her family, she would bring the peasant women with their merchandise home to us, so that I too could exchange various belongings for food. She would bargain with them and make sure that they did not cheat me, for it was impossible to obtain for any price the clothing I offered.

Rivka-Breina and her family were especially fortunate that the landlords allowed them to stay where they were for a long time. This was on account of the boy Yitzchak, the orphan, who was extremely industrious. He would chop wood for heating and for the landlords' meat processing plant that was located in the yard. He would also bring their water for them, and he was happy when once in a while they would give him something to eat. It was difficult to obtain enough bread, and here he had a chance to overcome his hunger.

Thanks to Rivka-Breina's efforts and ingenuity we did not want for a thing, and there was not a single *Shabbos* on which our table was not decked with sufficient chicken for the entire family, and even for an unexpected guest like the famous dwarf from Tarnopol.

The Russians had expelled not only the wealthy merchants and *bourgeoisie* from the city, but also the handicapped and deformed people, including the famous dwarf, the likes of whom I have never seen in my life. He had a perfectly normal head and a long beard, but his body was so small that he used to wear clothes meant for a boy six or eight years old. He was quite a sensible person who spoke to the point, but he often cursed the merchants of Tarnopol for not inviting him to their homes to spend *Shabbos* with them. Our family was the only one that offered him hospitality. For this reason, he would come every *Shabbos*.

My husband displayed great tolerance toward him, seating

him on a regular chair, upon which he was incapable of seating himself without assistance, thus making it possible for him to partake of the meal with us. And even though he was so small, he would eat like any other man with a normal appetite.

The landlady and her daughters used to peek into our rooms on *Shabbos*, and they could not praise my husband enough for taking food off his own plate and giving it to the dwarf, who would finish eating before anyone else at the table. The landlady, who was a devout Catholic, wished us that G-d should reward us for the kindness and patience we displayed towards the dwarf of Tarnopol.

One day, I had an accident; I fell and broke my right arm. I had to travel with my husband to Lwow to Professor Gruca, the famous specialist, who reset my arm. For several weeks, my arm was in a cast and I could not do any work with it. Thus there was no choice but to employ a housekeeper. The girl that we hired for this job was about twenty years old, healthy, with a round face and ruddy complexion, and her black hair was done up in braids. She was known as Pepa, and she herself was a Jewish refugee from the German occupation zone of Poland.

The shortage of food was so great, that we would hull and grind the wheat that we obtained through barter and brew it into a substitute for coffee, which was unobtainable altogether. From the wheat grounds that were left over I used to bake flat rolls, just as others used to do. I would add a little bit of black flour and a pinch of soda, mix it with water and bake the mixture on top of the cast iron stove.

Pepa, who was always ready to eat, was extremely envious of my two extra guests who would join us for meals, Yitzchak and the dwarf. She couldn't stand the sight of me pouring the coffee substitute I had prepared into the mugs together with some warm milk and serving it, along with rolls spread with jam, to these two poor souls, and also to Zalman if he was at home at the time.

When she saw that on *Shabbos* I would serve the dwarf a

portion of meat equal to the ones I gave the other members of the family, she could not restrain herself. She would yell at me that since I had to support both my two children and her, it was only fair that I should send the dwarf to eat in other people's homes. After all, I didn't owe him a thing. Each time this happened I would scold her once again and tell her that she should be ashamed of speaking this way. To be sure, she was young and healthy and possessed a healthy appetite, but he, too, even though fate had dealt him a difficult blow, felt hunger just as she did.

At that point, something happened that would have made me dismiss her happily had I not needed her assistance, and had she herself not been alone and without family in a strange place.

Once, when I went into the kitchen in the yard in order to look for a small pillow in the linen chest, I came upon a small bundle. At first, I thought that it belonged to Rivka-Breina who had left it there. I opened it, curious to know what was inside. To my utter amazement, I found dozens of slices of dry bread.

Pepa, who coincidentally turned up in the kitchen at that very moment, admitted that she was the one who had been hoarding the bread, for she felt that she had to stock up on supplies that would last her for a long time. After all, she said, it was wartime, and the day might come when there would be nothing to eat at all. So she used to steal slices from our bread, out of fear that I would give it to my guests, who were a thorn in her side. Poor Pepa simply was not capable of understanding that a superior force directs all of our lives and that a person's fate is not something he controls himself. A person who is born egotistical and thinks only of his own good is someone to shake one's head at in sadness, for he does not know the feeling of satisfaction that comes when a person helps his fellow man. Indeed, Pepa was eventually punished severely for her stinginess of eye. But of that I shall have more to say later.

Once, my friend Tamar's mother came to me and requested

that I buy from her a large beautiful silver *Chanukah menorah* which contained a music box that played a famous tune. The music it played was so clear and lovely that it was a real pleasure to listen to it. We, her friends, could not, of course, agree to her offer, for it was clear that the *menorah* had special sentimental value for its owner. So my husband loaned her a sum of money without setting a time for its return, and he requested that she take back the *menorah*. However, a while later, the woman came back and again offered the *menorah* for sale, claiming that others had offered her a ridiculously low price. Both she and her daughter would be extremely happy if this precious item would remain in our possession. Reluctantly, my husband accepted it.

Under German Occupation

Sadly, the *menorah* remained with us only for a short time. In 1941, the Germans turned on their erstwhile Russian allies and conquered the area in which we lived. The first order they promulgated was one stipulating that all Jews had to turn over immediately, under pain of death, all valuable items in their possession, such as gold, silver, jewelry, men's and women's furs, fur hats, mufflers and other such items.

This order did not augur well for the Jews, and they were seized with fear. They obeyed, however, for the most important thing was to stay alive. We, too, turned over our valuables, but with one exception—the fur coat my husband had bought himself for our wedding. The story behind the coat is not a particularly pleasant one.

One of our former customers in Tarnopol had been the wife of the chairman of the City Council. Along with other Polish officials, her husband had fled the country at the outbreak of the war, crossing into Romania, but his wife had been delayed in Brzezany and was forced to remain there. Now she became a frequent visitor in our home. She was a vivacious woman who used to dance at every party. As a member of high society she did not wish to appear every time wearing the same clothes, so she would buy all sorts of accessories in order to vary her attire. These high society ladies used to shop at my husband's store with pleasure, for it had a reputation as a respectable business, and the prices there were fixed and fair.

When she saw the panic the German order aroused among the Jews in the village and how they rushed to bring their furs to the collection point, she proposed to my husband that she go to the local priest and ask him if he would hold my husband's fur coat, which was an especially fine one, for safekeeping until the end of the war. My husband agreed, for he knew her family. So he took down his fine and expensive fur coat and brought it to the home of the priest for safekeeping. We hoped that one day the fur coat would be returned to us.

Meanwhile, the Russian army was fleeing in panic before the German advance, leaving chaos behind. The news of what was going on in Western Poland, in the German occupation zone, had not yet reached us. We had become accustomed to the horrible conditions of life under the yoke of the Russian occupation. Fortunately, we were among people who were concerned for each other's welfare. We were glad that even in these difficult times we were able to help those who needed it.

We had already witnessed how the Germans had taken over our village. One day, our landlords had called us to their spacious kitchen to watch from their kitchen window what was happening right on the street next to the house. Before our eyes we saw how German soldiers armed with machine guns were advancing on Soviet troops only a few steps away, shouting, "Hurrah! Hurrah!" Bullets were flying in every direction, and youngsters were falling like flies. Some of the bullets struck cavalry soldiers and their horses, who let out blood-chilling screams.

For the first time, I saw war between two great powers up close. We looked upon what was happening in the streets of our town with horror and revulsion, and we came to see how little value our enemies placed upon human life. When I thought about how much care and toil every mother puts into raising her children to the point where they can stand on their own, and how great is the destruction and devastation that war brings, I felt that it would take spiritual strength that I could not imagine in order not to break down altogether.

Suddenly, planes began circling overhead, and every few moments, we heard the horrifying thunder of explosions. Our landlady's brother, who had arrived after us, reported that Ukrainian villagers had taken up positions atop the Jewish houses and were pointing them out as targets for the bombers. Houses were left in flaming and smoking rubble. Our landlord's house was filled with bullet holes; after the battle it looked almost like a fishnet. I had to take my children into the hall in order to escape the flying shards of glass from the broken windows.

Just then, the house took a direct hit from a German bomb. The shock was so great that it blew the roof off our house, and we were left exposed under the open sky. I was certain I was about to die, and I screamed aloud the *Shema Yisrael* prayer that Jews recite in their final moments.

At that moment, a German soldier, armed with a machine gun, barged in. He looked at me and the children.

"Who was that shouting?" he asked.

I did not reply.

He told me gently not to stand where I was standing, to go inside. Then he went away.

The next few days were filled with terror. Ukrainians with

whips in their hands rousted the Jews from their homes and put them to work clearing the rubble that was choking the streets and making it impossible for traffic, even pedestrian traffic, to pass. The stones and bricks were loaded onto wheelbarrows and dumped in the courtyards of the apartment houses in town.

Among those impressed for labor was Yitzchak the orphan. I knew he had not eaten, and when I saw him pushing a heavy wheelbarrow filled with bricks and stones, I called to him and gave him a good-sized piece of bread with butter. Suddenly, a Ukrainian burst into the house madly waving a whip, which he intended to bring down upon Yitzchak. I could not restrain myself. I grabbed his hand and shouted, "How can you beat a poor orphan?"

The landlady, Mrs. Moskwa, who saw what was happening, called out to me, "Saints in Heaven, shut up!"

The Ukrainian threatened me with the whip, looked me straight in the eye and left. Yitzchak went after him to work. The Ukrainian didn't bother him anymore.

I broke down crying, shouting the passage from the *Pesach seder*, "Pour out Your wrath upon the nations who did not know You!"

The landlady later told both my husband and her family how lucky I had been to get away from that Ukrainian. But that was only the beginning. From then on each day brought with it a new shock.

One day, a unit of twelve German Wehrmacht soldiers appeared in our yard. I was standing with the children next to the well, drawing water. The soldiers asked in German if they could wash up at the well and rest on the grass outside our window. I translated the request for our landlady, and naturally, she agreed. After they had washed up, two of them took out a couple of white rolls and pieces of candy and gave them to my children. For my children, this was a great treat, for they had not tasted such delicacies in a long while. The soldiers were happy that they had found someone who spoke their language, and they showed me pictures of their wives and children. One of them told me that the local Ukrainians were about to make a house-to-house search for Jews who might be hiding.

I went back into the house where I found my husband sitting in our room with three business acquaintances from Tarnopol, who used to spend hours each day at our home. Through the window of our room I could see the soldiers sitting on the grass. They were tired, it seemed, from the endless marching of the military campaign. The soldiers lay down on the grass, covered themselves with blankets and quickly fell asleep.

About an hour later, I heard loud voices coming from the yard, and I went to investigate. Three tall, stout Ukrainians armed with clubs were asking our landlord where the "*Yids*" were hiding. Our landlord did not answer. I was scared to death. I went inside and told my husband and our visitors to climb out the window onto the grass and lie next to the soldiers who had given the rolls to our children. My husband did so immediately, but the others hesitated until it was too late. The Ukrainians barged into the room, beat them with their clubs, dragged them outside and loaded them onto a waiting truck. My landlord tried to comfort me, explaining that many people were impressed this way into clearing the rubble that was left after the bombing.

After the Ukrainians left, I went outside and told my husband the coast was clear. None of the soldiers had felt him lie down among them, so tired were they from the hardships of war.

From then on we had no peace. We knew that the blind hatred of the Ukrainian anti-Semites who were doing the Germans' bidding would not let us rest. They would continue to make periodic searches of houses, for some Poles were informing on others in whose houses Jews had rented rooms.

It was our good fortune that our landlords sympathized with us, perhaps because we, like they, were deeply religious people, and they appreciated the way we behaved. They and their daughter would frequently invite our children over and give them freshly baked cakes. Yitzchak would cut firewood and draw water for them in exchange for food. They could see how worried and downtrodden we felt, for we could never be certain that one day the Ukrainian thugs would not come and drag my husband off to parts unknown. Our landlady advised us that in case the Ukrainians did come searching my husband could hide in the attic; they would take away the ladder so as not to draw attention to it. They also kept the door to the hallway locked, so that we would not be taken by surprise.

Tamar came to visit me with her husband and her mother to see if we had made it through the recent events and to ask our advice about what to do in the future. Tamar's husband was, to be sure, a talented and renowned lawyer, but in the face of such brutal and violent force he was as helpless as all of us.

The Roundups Begin

O ne saddening event followed on the heels of another, and it was not long before a most tragic incident took place. In the marketplaces and in the central square of the town, on the walls of the schools and synagogues, there appeared announcements concerning the duty of Jewish men between the ages of fourteen and sixty-five to report with their identity cards at the appointed time to the assembly point in the main square. The oppressors had chosen to carry out their crime on the holiest day of the Hebrew calendar—*Yom Kippur*, the Day of Atonement, when Jews pray and pass the entire day in hope of receiving G-d's forgiveness. A heavy atmosphere of mourning descended upon all the Jews. The notice had said that anyone who did not report was subject to the death penalty.

Unfortunately, we knew that these criminals enjoyed not only the cooperation of the Ukrainians but also of many anti-Semitic Poles, who looked forward to getting rich at the expense of the unfortunate Jews. Tamar came running to me again with her entire family to ask what we had decided to do.

My husband had decided to report, but I, in opposition to what he thought, believed that if the Germans had chosen to carry out their scheme on this day and not another, then only G-d knew what their real purpose was. Under no circumstances would I let him report. I recommended to Tamar's husband that he hide together with my husband in the attic, but he adamantly refused. He was of the opinion that being taken off for forced labor was less of a danger than the one in which he placed himself if he were to be found hiding. In that case, he would be shot immediately. Thus, he went and reported together with hundreds of other Jews. Neither he nor any of the others ever came back.

My husband, shocked and pale with fright, took the *Yom Kippur machzor* with him and climbed up into his hiding place in the attic. He intended to pray with all his heart and soul and to ask the Master of the Universe to have mercy on His people.

That day no searches at all were carried out in the houses, and my husband came down from his hiding place in the attic towards evening. All of us sat down to eat the meal marking the breaking of the *Yom Kippur* fast. If after such experiences a person could go on living, then he must be a creation of G-d's hands, the strongest of all creatures.

What punishment from heaven did the German people deserve if they could destroy honest, weak, defenseless human beings without pity? Father in Heaven, Shield of the Poor, have mercy upon us; Helper of the Destitute, save us! You have witnessed Your people being trodden down into the dust. You who chose us from among all peoples, do not allow others to destroy us. Even though You have put us through many difficult trials, You promised that You would never abandon Your people!

That evening, following the conclusion of *Yom Kippur*, Mrs. Zielinska, our landlady's sister, came to us. She was shocked to the very depths of her soul because of what had happened to her. The Ukrainians had been whispering among themselves that all the Jews would be murdered. She had not been able to believe what she had heard about the Jews being led into the forest on the outskirts of town for forced labor. She decided to go find out for herself if it was true.

She hid at a distance behind some trees and saw large groups of Jews digging deep pits covering a wide area. It was explained to them that these pits were being dug for military purposes. The Jews worked and sweated on their holiest day. Then an order was given for all of them to jump into the pit that they had just finished digging with their own hands. The soldiers, armed with machine guns, began to shower a hail of bullets upon them. The Jews fell like flies. Many of them were only wounded, but the remaining Jews who had not yet been shot were ordered to cover their fellow-Jews with dirt, so that they would be buried alive. Those who were not shot on the first round were led to another place, where a similar fate awaited them.

The woman swore to us on everything that she held holy as a believing Catholic that when the Germans left the place a while later she saw tha ground above these graves moving, undoubtedly because many of those who had been shot had not been killed instantly. Those criminals, the greatest in the world, saved bullets by letting these poor people die slowly in excruciating agony.

Tamar cried bitterly over the death of her husband. She was now left alone with her widowed mother and her young son. Others from among those we knew had been saved because they had decided to remain home praying and fasting on the holy day without regard for what would happen to them.

Even though several weeks went by after that awful day,

we could not shake the oppressive feeling in our hearts. What had happened was worse than any of the atrocities of the Middle Ages.

How terrible is the life of a person who has no security, for such catastrophes used to befall us suddenly and without warning. They would surprise us in a completely unexpected fashion.

One day, I went to visit Mrs. Zielinska, in order to ask her advice about where to hide in case of danger. She lived in a little house on the hill. Not far from her house I met the priest, who was going for a walk on this cold clear winter day. From a distance, I noticed that he was wearing a long coat that reached his ankles. As I came closer and greeted him, I saw that he was wrapped in the fur coat that belonged to my dear husband, which I had turned over to him for safekeeping. The priest was of medium height, whereas my husband was tall. Therefore, the fur coat was too big for him, but it kept him nice and warm just the same. The priest apologized to me and told me that only because of the bitter cold had he taken the liberty of wearing the fur coat. I assured him that I had nothing against him, since in any case we had been prepared to hand it over to the Germans along with all of our other valuables.

I told Mrs. Zielinska about this meeting with the priest, and she counseled me that in the event that a roundup of Jews would be carried out again, I ought to rush to the church to hide. This was the safest place; up to then, the authorities had never searched there at all. She also told me that news had been arriving from the western areas of Poland that the Germans were deporting thousands of Jews to concentration camps and that nothing was known of their fate. Hundreds of Jews who had escaped from there were looking in our immediate vicinity for shelter. Her forthright words to the effect that she believed with all her heart the Germans would be punished for the crimes they were committing did not comfort me.

One day, two young Jewish refugees from Western Poland

came to the Moskwa house. They had heard that the family was in the meat processing business. Since they had worked in this business before the war, they offered to help the family in return for a place to live. These young people had managed to escape from the Nazis, who had conducted a Jew-hunt in their town. Mr. and Mrs. Moskwa put them up in one of the huts in the courtyard. They were glad to have their assistance, for they could not handle their business alone. The two Jews turned out to be hard workers who knew the business thoroughly.

During this time, I gave thanks for each day that passed without incident or shock. As I lay in bed at night I would pray to G-d to watch over us in the times to come. During the day, I sometimes used to invite the two young people to our room for hot coffee and a slice of bread and butter.

Several weeks went by peacefully, but then, on a cold morning, Mrs. Zielinska, like a beneficient angel, knocked on my window and told me to wake my children and take them to the church. The Germans and Ukrainians were rousting all Jews—men, women and children—from their houses. She suggested that my husband hide in the attic and promised that when the danger had passed she would come to the church to let me know. I woke Pepa and asked her to help me dress the children in their warm coats and told her that she could come to the church and hide with us. Each moment seemed like an eternity to me. Pepa, however, stated that she preferred to hide somewhere else, for our young son might cry and give her away.

My poor husband looked on with an aching heart as I dragged the frightened children with me, after taking them out of their warm beds without a chance to dress them in anything more than their coats. He would have been happy to accompany us, but that was too dangerous. A woman alone with children did not arouse excessive attention.

We ran quickly to the church, which was already open despite the early morning hour. I ran so hard I was out of breath. When I got to the church, I sat with the children in a corner. The cold pierced down to our bones. The children were shaking all over, and they pressed close to me to warm themselves a bit.

Slowly people began arriving for the morning prayer. Afterwards, the priest came, and instinctively I bowed my head so that he would not see me. But suddenly he came up to me and asked me in a whisper to leave the church with my children, because he was responsible for the place. A sharp pain stabbed at my heart. Since I had nothing to lose, I asked him why he did not pretend not to see me. After all, anyone could walk into a church and pray. He did not have to recognize all of the worshippers or know them personally. I asked him, in his capacity as a spiritual leader who in his sermons called upon everyone to love his fellow man, not to forget that we too were creatures of G-d. This argument apparently made an impression on him, for he walked away from me and began the prayer service.

The children shivered as if in a fever, but they remained completely silent. It seems that a child's intuition does not fail him; both children sensed in what a bad situation we were, and they remained silent. Every minute was like an eternity.

The worshippers began to disperse slowly, and then again, like a good angel, came Mrs. Zielinska with a bottle full of a warm beverage for the children. She whispered that we could go home, for the danger had passed.

With all my heart I blessed this good woman, and even though after the war I did not manage to find out anything about what happened to her, I prayed for her that she would have every good thing in life.

As time went on we came to realize that after every round-up the Germans conducted there would follow a period in which the roundups were not repeated.

My husband greeted us with tears, and the landlord came into our room to tell us a sad piece of news. He had no idea where the two young Jews had hidden, nor did he know where Pepa had gone. Thus he was quite shocked when he saw that the Germans, who had been directed to the right place by the Ukrainians, carried out a detailed search in the storeroom and in the barn, in which the barrels and other assorted items were stored. They dragged Pepa out frightened, and with her the two young people, loaded them onto a truck and left.

The landlord maintained that he could see clearly that G-d wanted to save our lives. Therefore, he agreed that in the event of renewed danger we could hide in the deep pit under the kitchen. It would be necessary to widen it now so that there would be enough room in it for all of us. My husband accepted their proposal eagerly and with a feeling of relief. But I, influenced by some hidden feeling, said that I did not want to be buried alive. My husband worked with the sweat of his brow to fix the place up. He padded the floor of the pit with blankets and asked me to go down with him for just a few minutes in order to see if there was enough air to breathe. He did not succeed in convincing me, however, to do so.

At this time, Mrs. Zielinska advised me to travel with the children to Lwow, to her sister, Mrs. Juzeczynska, who was willing to put us up for a short while in exchange for a hefty payment, for she had heard only good things about us. Her two daughters were high school students. Her elderly husband did not work, and the money that we would pay her in return for providing us with shelter would come in quite handy. Moreover, it would also be easier for my husband to hide when he was alone.

The truth is that everything depends on fate. Poor Pepa who loved life so much and was so careful, who hoarded bread for weeks so that she would not have to suffer from hunger, vanished in the wink of an eye, just like millions of our brothers and sisters. May all of these tortured martyrs rest in Paradise.

Toward morning, Yitzchak showed up. He was exhausted, worn out and hungry. He had managed to hide from his pursuers in an old barn outside of town. I cried for joy and happiness as if he had been my own son.

Heaven had mercy on us. To be sure, I had written several times to Krakow, to my sister Lydia who was hiding on the Aryan side with the help of false identity papers, but only now did I receive an answer. She informed me that she was trying to obtain false Aryan papers for all of us so that we could pretend to be members of the Aryan race, just as she did.

Another set of circumstances also came to our aid. An announcement was posted in town to the effect that Jews who could pay a large ransom would be permitted to work legally for the German district officer. We paid the ransom, and my husband was given a job as a gardener. He was happy that this physical labor would free him from the worry of what the next day would bring. Moreover, he was not alone. Several of our acquaintances worked with him in the same place.

Danger in Lwow

With a letter from Mrs. Zielinska in my hand, I arrived with my children in the home of her sister in Lwow. Mrs. Juzeczynska, a heavy woman in the prime of life who was married to a Ukrainian fifteen years older than her, together with her two daughters Stefa and Janka agreed to the terms we offered. Their income, which was not sufficient to feed the family and pay tuition for the two girls, stood to grow considerably. Nevertheless, they were well aware of the dangers involved in giving shelter to Jews.

My unimpeachable Aryan appearance gave me no small advantage. Still, however, I had to teach my children the rudiments of Catholic ritual and send them to church. As a religious Jew this caused me great pain.

The winter of 1942 was unbearably hard, and we had to struggle constantly against the cold. The children would sit bundled in their coats shivering. I asked the landlady to leave the kitchen door open so that we could at least get some of the heat from the stove, but she refused. Her elderly husband, she claimed, could not tolerate the stream of cold air that came into the kitchen with the door open. She did tell me, though, where I could buy coal, for good money, as long as I was willing to carry it home myself. This I did, where upon Mrs. Juzeczynska deigned to light the stove in my room. Now my children could finally take off their coats.

The feeling of relief that came with the heat did not last long. I soon found out that while I would be out buying bread and milk for my children the landlady would open the door to my room and use the fire in my stove to heat the entire house. Because of this I needed to keep my absences from home to a minimum. I thus made a deal with Stefa by which, in exchange for payment, she would buy bread for me on her way home from school. This however, did not prove a satisfactory arrangement, for Stefa, an unscrupulous and gluttonous girl, would eat the crust on the way, leaving me with only the sticky, tasteless middle. She would also dip her fingers into the packages of butter that my husband, who had remained in Brzezany, would send us from time to time. Nevertheless, no matter how angry I was at her, I never spoke to her about this. Instead, I thanked G-d for the goodness He had shown me and my two small children.

It was not always easy to do this. As a pious Jew my heart was filled with sorrow as I watched my children being turned into Catholics before my eyes. The family would teach them to repeat prayers and would take them to church, and I could do nothing about it. The landlady was a devout Catholic who honestly believed that by returning my children to the Church she would redeem her own soul. Yet for all her piety she had forgotten to teach her daughters the precept, "You shall love your neighbor as yourself."

My health was slowly deteriorating. I had not been eating

properly, saving what little we had for my children. I was in bad spirits as well in consequence of the noxious spiritual nourishment the two daughters regularly forced down my throat. Upon returning home from school, they would make sure to tell me how Jews were being dragged out of their hiding places and shot without mercy. One day Stefa barged into the house in high spirits, summoned me to the kitchen and in front of her parents began to tell me how the Gestapo had just discovered six Jews masquerading as Aryans and had hanged them on the main street. I froze and turned white as a sheet. Stefa's sister Janka begged her to spare the gory details.

To my surprise the old man, Mr. Juzeczynski, whom I had in itially feared the most, turned out to be the most human of the lot. Seeing how depressed I became he would order his daughters to change the subject whenever they brought up Jews. Of course, he too was conscious of the monetary benefit to be derived from our presence, as we shared with his family all our money and foodstuffs, which were worth their weight in gold.

In such a forsaken atmosphere several months went by. But it seems that even the value of gold is limited.

One morning, out of the blue, Juzeczynski ordered us to leave. The neighbors, he said, suspected him of hiding Jews. His announcement left me thunderstruck. Where was I to go in this strange city where death stalked the Jew at every turn? Lwow was filled with *Volksdeutsche* (people who claimed to be of German descent) as well as with Poles and Ukrainians, among whom there were those who willingly joined in the murder of Jews. With no identity documents of any kind, and with a circumcised son and small daughter, I was not about to go wandering about the city streets. Still, my landlords demanded that I leave and advised me not to show my face in the neighborhood. So I packed my two suitcases full of all the movable possessions I had left and asked them if they would be willing to keep them for me for a few days until I found a new place to live.

I was consumed by anxiety. I took my children with me and went out in search of a place to take refuge. First, I tried to work through the advertisements of rooms for rent, but everywhere I went I was asked to show my identity papers. I could understand the reason for such caution. All over the city warnings had been posted against giving shelter to Jews. Violators, it was stated, would pay with their lives. On the other hand, anyone turning over a Jew to the Gestapo was promised a reward of, if I remember correctly, ten thousand zlotys. Thus wherever I went I was besieged with a shower of questions about where I was from and whither I was bound.

We were hungry, and my children were about to collapse from exhaustion. In desperation, I turned to the owner of one of the advertised apartments and begged her to let us rest for a while. The children were crying for food. The woman took a long look at my children's faces and took pity on us; she allowed us to pay for a light meal. After eating, my children went over to the sofa and immediately fell asleep. I closed my eyes, too, and prayed silently to G-d that He would lead me on the right path and not tear my children from me.

I knew that my uncle, my mother's brother Yitzchak Schnitzer, lived in Lwow on Bernstein Street. My uncle had been the head of the Jewish community in the town of Oswiecim, the town whose name the Germans changed to Auschwitz. I knew as well that he had managed through his wealth and connections to obtain an American passport. Reluctantly, I decided to look for him and to call upon his advice and resourcefulness, even though I was well aware that any approach to the Jewish quarter was like stepping into the lion's mouth. Still, I could not see any alternative. Knowing that I was risking my life, I boarded a streetcar headed for the area where my uncle lived.

When we arrived in the general vicinity, I went up to a newsstand to ask directions to Bernstein Street. Nearby I noticed a man looking us up and down. He came over and offered to take us to our destination. We had only gone a few steps when the man ordered us to step into the entrance of a nearby building. There he showed us a badge identifying him as a member of the Gestapo and demanded our identity papers. He asked exactly where we were going. I knew that I could not tell him that I was looking for my uncle, so I tried to explain that I was searching for friends I had known before the war began but who might have moved elsewhere. His response was unequivocal. He announced that he suspected us of being Jews and ordered us to accompany him to the nearby Gestapo station.

While he was doing this, my little boy caught hold of my coat and whispered, "Mommy, why don't we go home?" His pulling at my coat reminded me that I had sewn into the lining some American gold dollars that my husband had given me before we left Brzezany. I also had several hundred Polish zlotys. I was already deathly white, for I knew that at the Gestapo station they would see that my son had been circumcised, after which our fate would be sealed. Evidently, the Gestapo officer sensed this, for he asked me why I had turned so pale. I told him that my children were on the verge of collapse and immediately pulled out my Polish money, begging him to let us go. The man hesitated.

"Let's suppose for a moment that your suspicions are correct," I said. "You are a man of middle age. I would guess that you too have a family with children. You also no doubt believe in the Creator of the Universe who had commanded each of us to love his fellow man."

"Then my suspicions were correct; you are Jews," he replied. "The children are very beautiful." His eyes rested upon them.

I quickly whispered a prayer. "G-d, who aids the poor and supports the unfortunate, save me and my children in this hour of trouble; I swear before You, G-d of my fathers, that shall I remain alive after the war my children will fear G-d and love mankind. They will be civilized people who keep far from sin." And G-d answered my prayer.

The man dropped the money into his pocket. Evidently he had taken pity upon us. "You had better get out of here," he said. "Wandering around in this place is crazy. Death lurks here at every turn."

He opened the gate and let us go.

With quick steps, we turned toward the streetcar stop. Despite what had happened I was still pursued by fear. I was afraid that the man would still be spying on us from the last car in the tram, so I got off with the children at the next stop. We pushed our way into the gate of an apartment house, and I dragged the children after me up the stairs to the top floor. My heart was beating so hard it actually hurt. I peered down over the railing of the banister in order to make sure that the man had not surreptitiously slipped in after us through the gate. The children too were tense and nervous and demanded in no uncertain terms that I take them to a place where they could stay.

I calmed down a bit. I left the concourse of the building with my children, and with our strength completely exhausted we retraced our steps to our former landlords. Again I had to beg them to give us an extension for a day or two until I could find shelter for myself and my children.

The next day, I left the children in the home of the Juzeczynski family and went out by myself to search for another place to live. I wandered around for a long time until I came to one of the more prestigious areas in the city. Suddenly, my eye spotted a small announcement on the gate of one of the apartment houses: "Room for rent." The owner of the apartment, a young, good-looking woman, agreed to rent the room to me and the children. This time I said that I had come to Lwow in order to consult with doctors and to take care of some personal matters. I agreed without hesitation to the high rent she demanded, and that same day I brought my children to their new shelter.

The landlady took an instant liking to the children. She behaved warmly toward them, and I prayed in my heart that we would find rest for a while. My children were polite and quiet. The survival instinct apparently was at work.

We found ourselves in a new atmosphere. The young

woman began to reveal to me details of her life in the past. She was a divorcee without children. Her room was next to mine, and through the walls I could hear a male voice singing accompanied by the sounds of a guitar.

Several days passed. One evening, when it was very quiet in the house, I listened to the words of the song. To my amazement, I could make out German lyrics. The landlady had command of this language as well. Her suitor used to visit her almost every evening. His very presence beclouded my tranquility. Even though I was 'content' with the shelter we had found in this house, this cultured woman was apparently one of the minority of Poles of German descent known as *Volkdeutsche.*

One day my landlady told me that her friend was curious to know who lived in the next room. At that moment, a red warning light went on in my head. The time had come to move on, I told myself. Once again, I tied a peasant's kerchief, which enhanced my aryan appearance, over my head and went wandering for hours on end.

Several days went by until I found a room in the basement in the home of a Mrs. Domaniewska in the Kriparkow quarter, near the insane asylum that the Germans had converted into a military hospital.

Once again, we moved ourselves into new living quarters. The landlords were a middle-aged couple with grown children. This time also, I explained that our stay would be brief. I paid two weeks' rent in advance, and again I lived in the hope that some miracle would happen that would allow us to put down our stakes for an extended period, without needless suspicion and inquiries.

The furnishings in the room were spartan, the windows small and narrow. But the fact that we had found shelter lessened my sorrow a bit. The daily worry did not get any smaller. Every time I went out to go shopping I was putting myself in danger. Wandering about the streets was liable to put me in suspicion of being a Jew. The children, who would remain at home alone, were liable inevitably to run into questions about where they came from and to be inter-rogated about who their father was and what he did for a living.

In Desperate Straits

S everal weeks passed. The winter had come, and Christmas was on its way. Mrs. Domaniewska's curiosity became piqued over the fact that I was not going home for the holiday. Apparently, I had aroused the suspicion of my new benefactor. I made no preparations at all for the holiday; I arranged no surprises for the children; I did not buy a Christmas tree; I did not stockpile foodstuffs for a holiday feast; and most of all, I received no letters from my husband. All of these things made Mrs. Domaniewska suspicious.

Christmas eve came. The events of that night are engraved in my memory and will not leave me until my dying day. My daughter had not been feeling well for several days. On the morning before Christmas eve, her temperature became feverish and she was seized with an attack of nausea and vomiting. The girl was not able to swallow a thing.

In our basement there were two old beds, but only one down blanket and one woolen blanket were at our disposal, and the cold was fierce. The little room was heated slightly. During the morning hours, while I used to cook lunch on the stovetop, the heat from the burners would fill the room with warmth. In any event, I used to put the two children to sleep together in one bed and cover them with a single blanket. But this time I took the little girl, who was shivering from the high fever, to my own bed, and I clasped her close to me. I was so immersed in worry that I didn't even feel the cold on my exposed back. The girl breathed heavily.

Suddenly the girl's lips began to mumble verses from a Christian prayer she knew from the time we lived in the Juzeczynski house.

I shuddered. All of my bones shook, and my heart was about to burst apart. In the dim light of the tiny oil lamp, I could make out the burning face of my little girl and her jumping fiery eyes. I was in terrible straits, but I did not have the courage to summon the landlady in the middle of the night. In sadness, I tried to give my daughter first aid as best I could. I wrapped her feverish head in cold compresses, and my lips murmured a prayer. I repeated from memory the passages from *Tehillim* that I knew by heart, and I cried to my G-d to help me.

This night of horrors seemed endless. When dawn broke I could see red spots all over the little one's body. There was no one I could consult. The landlady and the members of her family were waiting anxiously for us to leave. To them we were like a bone stuck in their throat. We were supposed to have vacated the room before Christmas, yet here we were still occupying the premises.

Since there was no choice, I acted on my own. I spoon-fed my daughter with lukewarm water. She calmed down some and fell into a deep sleep, while I continued to pray silently for her recovery.

Toward evening, her condition took another frightening turn for the worse. I had no thermometer, but I felt that the girl was burning up and that her temperature was rising. The color of her face looked like that of a beet, and the spots were getting redder as well. Helplessly, I stood by the little one's sick bed. The door opened and Mrs. Domaniewska entered, carrying borscht, strudel and biscuits—a holiday gift.

This time, the riddle was finally solved. It was clear that we were pretending to be Christians and that we were in fact nothing more than persecuted Jews. The scene laid out before her with no husband, no Christmas tree, no holiday feast, left no room for doubt that we were a Jewish family being hounded by cruel fate from place to place.

Mrs. Domaniewska had pity on us; her eyes showed that much. Her gaze was fixed upon the feverish little girl covered with red spots. But when I asked her to call a doctor, she refused for a clear reason. If a doctor came, he would order the girl hospitalized. At the hospital we would be asked to show our Aryan papers. Since we did not appear in the local population registry, we could not be regarded as legal residents of the city. We would thus bring a catastrophe on ourselves and upon her family as well. In the end, she revealed to me that her son-in-law was making her life bitter over the fact that she had given shelter in her house to such suspicious characters.

Dear G-d! How many times have I envied the domestic dog, lying in his doghouse with his dish of food ready and waiting? The dog was allowed to breathe by law, and no one would chase him to the ends of the earth.

Immersed in my troubles, I was persuaded that Mrs. Domaniewska was right in what she said and that there was nothing she could do for us. I was left alone, with no medical help, with two children and with only a sincere prayer in my heart to the G-d of my fathers, who alone was still able to save me.

Another sad day went by, and a second night of horror descended upon me. The singing of my benefactors and their family cut through the silence of the night. They were sitting down to eat at the traditional holiday table, singing beside their Christmas tree, decorated with candles and all sorts of ribbons and ornaments.

My daughter breathed heavily, and I, helpless, could do nothing except murmur *Tehillim* and plead, "My G-d, my G-d, turn Your countenance toward me and bless me, for I am alone and poor. Redeem, O G-d, Your people Israel from all its sorrows; lend Your ear and hear the silent cry of a suffering Jewish mother." Thus, wrapped in my sorrows, I awaited salvation.

At dawn, my daughter opened her eyes.

"Mother, I'm thirsty," she whispered. "Please give me something to drink."

Her fever had gone down, and the spots on her body had become lighter. Her condition improved by the hour. The landlady showed interest in her state of health, and I told her about the gradual improvement. She felt relieved, for she had feared for the child's life just as I had. However, a few days later she once again raised the issue, gently but firmly, of our leaving.

I managed to gain some more time in consideration of my child's health, which continued to get better. I obtained an extension to send a letter to my sister Bronia, who was living in Krakow. I begged her to do all she could in order to get me out of Lwow.

My sister was my last hope. She was living on Aryan papers that had been given to her by a Polish widow. I wrote to her in accordance with the maxim, "Cast your bread upon the waters," without knowing how and when it would arrive. I listed Mrs. Domaniewska's address for the reply, but without waiting for the answer to come I packed my bags and left with my children again for the unknown.

I hesitated to turn either to the right or to the left. Where would I find my salvation? In one hand I held the heavy suitcase that contained everything we owned, and in the other hand, my children, who held each other's hands.

It was frightfully cold, and the snow was coming down so fast and strong that our suitcase and coats and even our eyelashes were soon covered with white. The children tried to keep pace with me, but every few steps, they had to stop to catch their breath, for the cold pierced to the marrow of our bones.

We were standing in a large field on the outskirts of town, in a suburb known as Kulparkow. We walked in the direction of the German military hospital, hoping that there we could at least wait out the storm. But about two or three hundred yards from the building my daughter simply could go no more. Exhausted, she collapsed on the snow-covered ground.

I feared for what would become of us. It was twilight, and I had to find shelter before nightfall. The sight of a woman laden with suitcases, wandering around with two children, would surely arouse suspicion. Somehow, though, both she and my son understood how precarious our situation was. My little boy looked at me with a gaze filled with love, sorrow and endless exhaustion. He clung close to me. But when he saw the worry on my face, he went up to his sister and whispered in her ear, "We'll just rest here a little bit, okay? Then we'll go on."

And my daughter, only a year older than my son, worn out from the sickness from which she had just recovered, gathered together all her strength and replied, "I'm ready. Let's go!"

Opposite us was a row of houses. None of them displayed a sign indicating a room to rent, but I summoned my courage and, leaving the children standing with the suitcase, knocked on all the doors one by one, asking if perhaps anyone knew of an available room for even a few days. Most of the doors were immediately slammed in my face. I feared for my children, left alone in the field with the suitcases.

In the meantime, night had fallen. The children begged me to take them to the nearby field where they could sit and rest on the snow-covered rocks, and I began to sense that there was nothing else to do. So we retraced our steps and made our way to the field. I stretched out on the ground. My son laid his head upon my lap and fell asleep, and my daughter's beautiful eyes looked into mine with sorrow and pain. I took her head between my hands, in order to hide the tears that were pouring down my cheeks.

Again, all I could do was pray to G-d, who upholds the falling and the downcast. "G-d of my salvation, hasten to my assistance. Your holy books have taught me that You are the G-d of the universe. May G-d redeem the souls of those who serve Him, and may those who trust in Him know no guilt. Even the path of those forthright of heart who believe in You with all their might is not always strewn with roses, but their salvation is at hand nonetheless."

I lay there in the wild field, abandoned, between heaven and earth, hugging my two exhausted children, constantly fearing discovery by the Gestapo or by local Poles or Ukrainians. The snow was coming down without cessation; our coats and hats and eyelashes had become covered with white flakes. Silently, I prayed for G-d's mercy. We were waiting for a miracle. And a miracle happened.

Suddenly, through the darkness of the night, I could make out two men in uniform walking slowly toward us. They stopped to look at the queer sight of this pitiful trio. They were speaking a language I did not understand but which I guessed was probably Italian. From their gestures I could tell that they were talking about the children. I called to them in English to no avail, then in French, which they understood. This language was to be the bridge of communication between us.

It seems they were unaware of what was happening to the Jews of Poland, for they could not figure out why a woman with two small children would be lying in a field on such a cold, snowy winter's night. I tried to explain that I had brought my children to town from a nearby village in order to seek medical care for them. In the meantime, the children had become too tired to go on any further. But how, they asked, had I set out from the village without first arranging for lodgings? Without hesitating, I told them that I had planned to stay with my acquaintances, Mr. and Mrs. Domaniewska, but when I saw how crowded their house was I felt I could not impose upon them.

I don't know how I thought up such a story, but it was evidently convincing. Their response was beyond anything that could be expected in those days of madness. The two Italians, who, it seems, were stationed at the military hospital, offered to take us back to the Domaniewska house; they were sure that when Mr. and Mrs. Domaniewska heard what had happened to us they would not refuse to take us in. One of them carried my son, the other my daughter and the suitcase, and I directed them back to the house.

The family was seated around the dinner table when we arrived. Seeing us in the company of two Italian soldiers, allies of the German occupiers, did something to change their attitude towards us; they invited us to join them and sit down to a hot dinner. The fact that soldiers in uniform of the allies of the Germans had brought us back to their house, carrying the exhausted children in their arms, reassured them.

The Italians apologized that they had to go, but they promised to return soon with food for all of us. And indeed, half an hour later, they came back with a car loaded with the finest foods and drinks of every kind. Such delicacies were simply not available to civilians at that time, and the whole household was immediately bathed in a festive atmosphere. I shall never forget the taste of that bread and the wonderful Italian jam they served with it.

My gratitude to the two Italians knew no bounds. When I had left Brzezany I had taken the bracelet my husband had given me on our first anniversary. Now I took it from my suitcase and offered it to them. They were taken aback at the offer and implored me not to part with such a valuable possession. But I was determined that they should have it. They had been like angels of deliverance sent from heaven; in the chance meeting with them I perceived a sign from G-d that our salvation was at hand.

Reluctantly, they took the gift, and I thought I heard one of them say to the other that they should return the present's value. They showed us pictures of their families and explained that their children were about the same age as mine. They also promised to make sure that we did not lack food. It seemed to me that they were bothered by taking the gift. I thought I heard the one who put the bracelet into his pocket say to his companion that they would return its value in money.

Seeing that we might bring them material benefit, and having filled their bellies with bread, sausage and the finest wine, the members of the Domaniewska household, and especially the son-in-law , pronounced themselves willing to have us stay with them until we could find another place to live. They also offered to look after the children while I searched for a new room, in order to spare them the cold and hardship. In the face of such events, even the most confirmed non-believer cannot deny that the hand of G-d directs our lives. Here, without a doubt, Heaven had intervened and helped us.

Only a few more days passed, and good news arrived from Krakow; Bronia wrote that she was on her way to bring us to live with her. Finally, after so long a separation, I would see my dear mother again! I also learned from her letter that Mother was living on Aryan papers, but our father had passed away .

For all my sorrow at my father's death, I hardly had a chance to mourn. The life and death struggles of daily existence, the fear of discovery that shadowed me at every step, left little room in my heart for grief. Only at night was I able to find release for my pain and shed tears for my father, who at least had died a natural death and been spared the tortures of the Nazi jackboots. Not that he had been spared entirely. I later learned that he had died of a broken heart over my brother, his only son, who had been brutally murdered at

Auschwitz. At my father's funeral there had been no one to say *Kaddish*.

I could not bear the wait for Bronia. Would she save us from the hell of Lwow? My heart sang a song of praise to G-d.

Bronia's Story

Bronia had not written when exactly she would be arriving to take us to Krakow. I feared lest she show up while I was out of the house shopping for our daily necessities and would not find me at home. Fortunately, Mrs. Domaniewska helped me out with this problem. She was so happy that we would soon be leaving that she agreed to do the shopping for me. I was grateful to her for her willingness to do this. The fact that I did not have to leave the house and endanger myself during our final days in Lwow, running the risk that someone might spot me and trap me, gave me a feeling of relief.

Since the landlords had asked me to save on light, I used to put the children to bed at nightfall. I too went to bed early, because it was cold in our room.

As I would lie in bed at night, with eyes open, unable to sleep, I would ponder our fate, the fate of the persecuted and tortured Jewish people, and I would wonder if we were really such a sinful and criminal people that we deserved to be sentenced to such a severe punishment from Heaven. Still, I took comfort from the knowledge that just as in every generation, so too in our own, the hour of salvation was near, and just as the Holy Blessed One had brought the ten plagues upon Egypt and redeemed us from that land, so too this time would the G-d of Israel bring destruction to the evil Hitler and save His people from the clutches of the Nazi beast.

Several days of anxious expectation went by. One day Mrs. Domaniewska brought my sister Bronia into my room. It is difficult to describe our happiness. Once the two of us were left alone, Bronia told me that she had not been able to set a definite date for her arrival because she had had to wait for a suitable opportunity to travel to Lwow in the company of a German acquaintance of her girlfriend. The friend, with whom Bronia had once attended school, had converted to Christianity before the war, but in her heart she had remained faithful to her people, and her conscience plagued her over what she had done. For this reason she did everything she could to help my sister. She warned Bronia that at railway stations, and especially at the station in Lwow, Polish and Ukrainian detectives and informers, as well as ethnic German local residents, the *Volksdeutsche*, would lie in wait for their Jewish victims. Thus she introduced Bronia to this German acquaintance who was about to travel to Lwow on business and asked him to take Bronia with him.

During the train trip, Bronia had told him in broken German—even though in actuality she could speak German well—that she was employed in Krakow by the Meinel firm, which imported coffee, and that she was going to Lwow on behalf of the company. On her way back to Krakow she wanted to take her friend and her two children with her. Her friend wanted very much to see her family.

The Germans, unlike the Poles, were not able to tell a Jew

from a Pole by sight if the Jew did not have distinctly Jewish
facial features. In contrast, the Poles used to look with extra-
careful attention in trains and in railway stations at every
face. Every worried movement or facial expression would
immediately arouse in them suspicion about the ethnic
origin of their bearer. These Poles, and Ukrainians as well,
used to hand thousands of innocent souls over to the Gestapo in return for a generous bounty that was awarded for
these heinous criminal acts.

Bronia had noticed during the trip that the conductor and
others among those making the journey were passing from
car to car looking at the faces of the passengers. The fact that
she was sitting beside a German in uniform gave her some
relaxation. When she saw how a railroad clerk asked one of
the passengers for his identity papers she began to engage
her German travelling companion in animated conversation,
and she continued in this fashion until she arrived in Lwow.

The German was quite pleased at making this new
acquaintance, for my sister was young, intelligent and
charming. For her part she pretended that she was fond of
him. They arranged between them that three days later, on
Sunday, he would come to Mrs. Domaniewska's house in his
army car to pick her up, along with her friend and her
friend's children, and take them to the train station. They
would return to Krakow with the night train.

When the train reached the station in Lwow, the German
took Bronia's packages and together they walked down the
long platform. On the way, Bronia noticed certain men who
were walking up and down the platform following the passengers with their eyes. Despite the enormous fear she felt in
her heart, she smiled at her German travelling companion
and managed to get out of the station without incident.
Before they parted, the German promised her again that he
would take her, together with her friend and her friend's
children, to the train station on the appointed day, and he
also gave her his telephone number in case she needed it.
When she got into the taxi in order to come to me, he smiled

and waved goodbye. As fate would have it, that moment was to turn out to be of major importance for our survival.

Boundless joy and happiness filled my heart when Bronia appeared in our basement room in the home of the Domaniewski family in Kulparkow. What a wonderful moment, what happiness it was to see this precious soul, my younger sister, after so many tragic events.

Bronia told me that my pale and sad appearance was liable to arouse suspicion. Something had to be done to improve it. So she went to the marketplace to buy a red fox choker that would enhance my Aryan appearance. The landlady directed her to the appropriate stall in the marketplace, and after some time, Bronia returned holding a fox fur, which at the time was quite fashionable.

Bronia had brought with her the forged Aryan papers which we were to use. They had false names, and they cost a lot of money. From now on my name would be Anna Kwiatkowska, my daughter's Danuta Kwiatkowska and my son's Jan Kwiatkowski.

With great excitement, I listened to Bronia's story about everything that had happened to her on the way. Her presence brought me great delight. The children, who had not seen their father for so long and missed the company of children their own age, could sense how serious the situation was. Their relationship with Bronia was interesting. It is unbelievable how strong the ties of blood are. From the first moment they became attached to her and loved her. Their aunt immediately became close to them, and she would kiss them, enchanted by their beauty.

"With such gorgeous children, you have no reason to be sorry," she told me. "With G-d's help, we shall make it through the war."

That afternoon all of us ate together in a pleasant family spirit for the first time in many months. However, when I began to ask my sister about the family and what had happened to them, she asked me to wait until evening, after the children were asleep. She had serious reasons for this request. And indeed, that night we sat up for hours by the light of a small lamp, and I listened to what she had to tell.

At one point, she gave me a most emotional hug, and I understood that bad tidings were awaiting me this time. It was difficult for her, she said, to tell me the truth, but I had to know before I saw Mother. The news she brought struck me like thunder from heaven. My only dear brother was dead. Since Mother had not been told that he had been murdered, I needed to know the whole truth to avoid asking Mother superfluous questions. So I listened as Bronia related a shocking horror story.

My brother Aharon had been blessed with the gifts of a genius, just like his grandfather Aharon Marcus, after whom he had been named. At age twenty-two, he completed the course of studies in the law school of the university. In addition he was quite a handsome lad, tall, with flowing light-colored hair, regular features and blue eyes. His facial appearance was completely Aryan.

Even before the enclosure of the Jews of Krakow in ghettos and their deportation to the labor camp at Plaszow had begun, the Nazi murderers had imposed upon the Jewish community leadership the task of regulating the distribution of food to the Jewish population. All matters and inquiries of the authorities by members of the community had to be delivered through the offices of the community leadership.

Because my exceptional brother knew the German language perfectly he was appointed to the post of liaison man between the community and the occupation authorities. Aharon would arrange transit permits for people who wanted to rejoin members of their family who were living somewhere else. He would write all sorts of requests on behalf of the members of the community and would also intervene personally in order to help them arrange their affairs. Nevertheless, he had to be careful and act precisely in accordance with the instructions, without deviating from them even the slightest bit, for any deviation or minor infraction of the German orders was liable to bring imprisonment by the Gestapo upon him and upon those on whose behalf he worked. Still, he performed his task meticulously and with full responsibility.

The bureaucrats of the German administration treated him with sympathy; several times they had remarked how sorry they were that he was a Jew. On the other side, hundreds of Jews blessed him for his goodheartedness and his good deeds. Thanks to him they would be able to receive an increased food ration for their sick children. My father used to carry bread with his own hands to lonely and hungry people in order to save them from death by starvation.

For many months my brother had toiled in this fashion in the offices of the Jewish community. Doctor Landau, who served for many years as head of the Krakow Jewish community, and young Rabbi Kornitzer as well, the son of the rabbi of Krakow who had died before the outbreak of the war, loved him as if he were their own son. They were indeed blessed with a dedicated and industrious worker.

Then came the terrible day. A letter came to my parents' house addressed to my brother Aharon. The letter stated that he was to report to the head of the Gestapo in order to clarify a particular matter. An atmosphere of mourning descended upon the house. My parents pleaded with him not to obey, to run away and hide somewhere. Their hearts foretold the worst; they could sense the danger in store for him. But my dear brother, who was so beloved and admired by his parents and by the entire family, explained to them that it was his duty to report, for if he did not the entire family would be arrested. He could not allow that to happen.

Aharon went and never came back. Only later did my sister Lydia find out indirectly that he had been imprisoned, first at the prison on Montelupich Street in Krakow, then in the concentration and death camp at Auschwitz. Lydia told our dear mother, who had been broken in body and spirit after Aharon left, that Aharon had been sent for forced labor abroad. For a long time thereafter, Mother lay in the hospital with a heart ailment.

But that was not the end of our misfortunes. Father, who sat for hours on end pouring over the holy books in an effort to find in them some small comfort for his grief that did not leave him either by day or by night, received a letter in the mail one day, together with a small package. In the letter there was a notice from the Gestapo that all of the leaders of the Jewish community and community employees had died in Auschwitz and their bodies had been burned in the crematorium. As an exceptional gesture, Aharon's ashes were being sent to his parents, so that they could bury them. Father did not suffer such tortures much longer. From this blow he was not able to recover. A short while later, he died of a heart attack.

Mother had returned home from the hospital and found neither husband nor son. Lydia took upon herself the duty of taking care of Mother and making sure that she stayed alive. She used to forge Aharon's handwriting and bring Mother letters from him in which he reported, as it were, that he was living in a camp in Germany, that his condition was good and that immediately after the war he would return home. Until that time he would try from time to time to pass along news about how he was getting along.

Lydia used to produce for Mother in regular fashion every few weeks such letters from Aharon, until she herself fell victim to the Nazi murderers. My dear sister Lydia, too, died the death of a tortured martyr, but for her noble deeds, for her great love for our mother, her soul ascended to heaven with the souls of all of the other tortured martyrs who died to sanctify the name of the holy G-d. I am indebted to her that Mother was privileged to remain alive after the war, full of hope and faith that her dear son would return. Thanks to her I was able to see my dear mother again, and because of my mother's prayers and words of encouragement my own spirit did not break even during the moments of greatest despair.

Father's funeral turned into a mass demonstration by the Jews of Krakow. Hundreds of Jews accompanied him to the cemetery where his father and others had also been buried and where the box containing the ashes of his son had been interred. The Jews of Krakow cried over the death of this honored man, who had been so devoted to them and had performed so much good on their behalf.

Shocked to the depths of my soul, I listened to Bronia's story. She gave me a kiss and made me swear that I would get over my deep sorrow. I must not break now; I must be strong, for my children's sake. The very fact that I would soon see Mother ought to cheer me and strengthen my spirit. After all, it was a real miracle, the hand of fate, that she had been accompanied by that German, who had promised to take us with him to the train station.

The three days passed, and Sunday came, when we were supposed to leave. I went to great efforts so that Bronia would see me calm, but the truth is that my whole body was trembling from worry. I took leave of my landlords, wishing them all the best in my heart. They also emotionally wished me a safe journey.

The German showed up exactly at the appointed hour. My sister introduced me as her friend, and we climbed into his army car. Bronia sat next to him, while I sat in the back seat with the children. It was dark inside the car. Before starting the motor the German illuminated our faces with a flash- light. Even though everyone said that my face looked unquestionably Aryan, my features regular, my eyes blue and my hair light-colored, I always thought that the worry hid- den in our eyes might reveal our Jewish origin. So I pre- tended that I was cold and buried my face in the fur, for in truth I was nervous and restless.

The car started off, and in a little while we reached the train station. The German took leave of us and we turned toward the platform in order to board the train. Bronia carried our suitcases while I and the children trudged behind her.

Suddenly, I felt the blood freezing in my veins. I could clearly hear one of the porters saying to another, "That young woman looks to me like a Jew." But his friend responded that he shouldn't talk nonesense, for he remembered how the girl had arrived three days earlier in the company of a German. Evidently, she was his fiance, for the manner in which they had talked and laughed could only be of an engaged couple. My heart was pounding at a ridiculous pace. We boarded the car, and even though the two porters were not following us any longer, I was shaking from fear lest someone stop us while I was with my circumcised son.

In those days, the railroads did not run on time; usually there were delays in departure. So it was no wonder that every passing moment seemed to me like an eternity. Every passenger who walked by and looked into the compartment made my heart beat faster. My sister Bronia did not notice the panic that shone from my eyes because of the poor lighting in the compartment. The children fell into a deep sleep, and I prayed silently and with closed eyes that G-d would allow me to reach my destination and see my mother.

The trip lasted all night. When we left the compartment in the morning I had already calmed down. The city that I knew from childhood and the long-awaited meeting with my mother gave me a feeling of security. To be sure, the fears that I could run into one of my Polish friends with whom I had gone to school, or that our presence in Mother's house, where we were slated to spend our first night, might endanger her, continued to gnaw away at me. But I tried to overcome them and to banish them from my mind.

Reunion in Krakow

Words cannot describe my great happiness and the thrill that went through me when my mother embraced me and clasped me to her bosom. Mother's presence brought deep tranquility to me and to the children as well. The children were overflowing with happiness. An atmosphere of joyfulness and freedom and new feelings of grandmotherly love enveloped them and calmed their spirits. I shall never forget the first meal in Mother's house, which she prepared with care. All of us sat around the table and ate together. It was like a dream.

After a sleepless night of travel, I was completely exhausted. My mother offered me her bed. I lay down and turned my face toward the wall so that Mother would not see the stream of tears flowing unchecked from my eyes. An unknown joy flooded me, and waves of love beat inside me; once again, I was feeling a mother's love. Tired but free of tension, I recalled some verses from the poem of the Polish poet Adam Asnyk that I had always liked to recite for Mother:

Always remember Mother
Her love knows no bounds
So banish all doubt
Pure of heart
Believe in the beauty of the soul
And in everlasting love.

Suddenly I felt myself freed of the burden of responsibility for the lives of my children and even of my own life. Mother! She would keep us from all harm. With her present nothing evil could befall us. She would always protect us. Her prayers would surely be answered. And again I whispered to myself, "Always remember Mother," and a deep, peaceful sleep fell upon me.

When I woke up Bronia had already left. She had gone out to arrange for a room for us in the home of the widow of Professor Bujak, a noble woman who had given shelter to Bronia's friend for several weeks without payment. When we showed up at Mrs. Bujak's home the next day and were received with warmth and kindness, I still felt worried and tense, in spite of everything. She wondered out loud how she would manage to hide our presence, especially that of the two children, from the prying eyes of her neighbors. And indeed, what we feared eventually came to pass. One morning, Mrs. Bujak came into our room white with panic and whispered to me that two Gestapo men were in the attic looking for Bronia's friend. She helped me dress the children quickly, and like thieves in the night, we slipped out toward Mother's house.

A pleasant surprise awaited us there in the person of my eldest sister Lydia. Since childhood, Lydia had always been marked by a healthy sense of humor and an exceptional intelligence. Her pretty head had been adorned by two long light-colored braids until she had become engaged to be married at an early age to Yisrael Rand, the son of a fine family from Bolechow in Galicia. Her husband was a Jewish scholar who also had an excellent secular education. After he became engaged to Lydia he used to correspond with her frequently, mainly in verse and rhyme. He had lost his mother at an early age, and perhaps it was for that reason that he felt so close to our family and displayed such love for our mother. Mother treated him as if he were her own son and lavished affection upon him. After they were married, Lydia and Yisrael lived close by our house, and my parents used to invite them over often, not only on *Shabbos* and *Yom Tov* but on weekdays as well.

My parents appreciated their son-in-law Yisrael for his honesty, his politeness, and his well-groomed, cheerful appearance. He used to repeat a saying, "A scholar with a grease stain on his clothes deserves to be put to death." In his opinion every person should always be careful to appear neat and clean. I remember well how we, the younger sisters, used to giggle and even break out in laughter when our brother-in-law Yisrael brushed his teeth with great care after every meal. But his teeth were always white and healthy.

The war separated us. From the time it began in 1939 I had not seen my brother-in-law nor his children, Aharon and Kitty. The unexpected meeting with Lydia caused me great excitement. I wanted to hear from her and to find out all that had happened to them. I learned that during the first deportation of Jews from Krakow, Lydia, her husband and their children had managed to make their way to Tarnow. My father's brother Yisrael Marcus and his family, and my mother's sister Miriam Engelberg and her family, were already living at that time in the Tarnow ghetto, which was still open to new residents.

Eventually, my brother-in-law was impressed for labor service in the village of Rzaska near Tarnow. In the order, the day and time for him to report had been indicated. Uncle

Yisrael had advised him not to report for labor. Lydia's husband had not listened to this advice and had obeyed the order. Since then, all contact with him had been cut off, and he had disappeared without a trace. Lydia did not know what had happened to him.

At the time this happened, my mother had been living with my sister Frieda and her husband and children in the village of Slomniki near Krakow with a Polish family named Michalski.

Frieda's husband, Pinchas Lubinski, was the son of a wealthy family from Lodz. He was an extremely religious man, a lawyer by profession, and his mother descended from a long line of famous rabbis. My sister and her husband lived in a spacious apartment with seven rooms and employed maids and servants and even a boy who opened the door for clients. My brother-in-law's office was closed on Saturdays and Jewish holidays, and he also took care that his appearances in court would be scheduled for weekdays only. All of this went on, of course, during normal times, before the war. Now, as I have said, they were crowded together with Mother in a tiny apartment.

The head of the Jewish council—the *Judenrat*—in Slomniki was a Jew by the name of Bialobroda. His job was to manage the registry of Jews living in the village. At his disposal stood the men of the Jewish civil guard, a sort of Jewish police whose task was to carry out the instructions of the German commander. They wore armbands with the initials "O.D." (*Ordnungsdienst*, or Order Service). They also used to compile lists of Jews who were fit for labor as they saw it, and they would transmit these lists to the local German commander. It is clear that people with a conscience avoided joining the Jewish police, for they did not want to collaborate with the Germans and to decide which of their Jewish brothers would live or die. Bialobroda, who had the utmost respect for my brother-in-law, gave him an O.D. armband to wear on his sleeve, but when he asked him actually to join the police and not merely wear the armband for his own protection,

Pinchas Lubinski was taken aback and refused to obey his order. Bialobroda tried to convince him that this was the only way for him to save himself and his family, but my brother-in-law would not listen to him.

Out of fear, Pinchas and his family escaped to Krakow, hoping to find shelter and a hiding place for each family member separately. His thinking was that if, Heaven forbid, one of them should be discovered, the others would at least survive. It was decided that for the time being Bronia should stay behind in Slomniki with Mother.

However, a short time later, a cleaning out action was conducted there. My mother was standing next to the window when she saw a large group of Jews—men, women and children—being led away by the Nazis. Displaying great resourcefulness, Mother lay down immediately in bed and covered herself with a blanket, while Bronia hid under the bed. As it turned out, they were lucky. The Germans entered the room, opened the closet doors, searched through the closets and finally decided that the apartment was empty. "Evidently," they remarked, "they managed to escape from here."

After that, Bronia and Mother also moved, on Lydia's advice, to Krakow. Mother found temporary shelter in a home for the elderly without relatives. The director of the institution took Mother in without checking up on her identity, but she stressed that Mother would have to leave within a matter of a few days. My sisters managed to procure Aryan papers for themselves and began feverishly searching for a place to live. Through an advertisement in the newspaper, Lydia found a place for her fourteen-year-old daughter to work as a housekeeper for a German family. She herself and her son wandered about from place to place, spending each night somewhere else.

My sister Frieda found a job as caretaker in a German government office. She was also put in charge of the incoming and outgoing mail. The job included a room on the ground floor in which to live. Her happiness was boundless when her employer, an educated German, allowed her to bring her son and daughter to live with her. In the evenings, when the director and staff would leave the premises, Frieda would breathe easier. Every night her eldest son joined them after spending the daylight hours wandering all over the city. Sometimes, he would spend the days with Bronia. Every morning, before work began, the boy would slip away secretly.

Still, most of Frieda's worries were for her husband, who wandered endlessly from place to place. He was consumed by fear and pursued by terror. Because of his noble appearance he believed that the simple people who rented him tiny rooms in their primitive apartments looked with suspicion upon the fact that he sat at home all day. Even the very fact that he would live in such poor conditions stood to arouse suspicion. My poor brother-in-law envied the Jews who had been taken to the concentration camp at Plaszow, outside of town. At least they could go to work every morning in organized groups, returning to the camp at night. Their hard labor bent their bodies and made them sleep soundly at night, whereas he, consumed by fright, was turning into a bundle of nerves in his loneliness. Every time he would meet his wife or Lydia he would declare that his nerves were at an end and that he would volunteer for the labor brigade that was incarcerated in the camp.

And he was as good as his word. One day, he came upon a group of Jews who were coming back to the camp from work. In the detail he noticed his cousin Shachne Rabi. He fell surreptitiously into the ranks and sneaked into the camp. Now he could breathe easier; he preferred a small crust of stale bread and a portion of watery soup to playing hide-and-seek in an atmosphere of constant terror in which every bit of Polish rabble could inform on him and hand him over to the Gestapo.

Whenever Lydia or his wife would sneak food packages into the camp for him he would reproach them for taking the chance of getting caught. Jews living on Aryan papers knew

well that if one of them were caught, he would be forced by
cruel torture to reveal the whereabouts of his relatives and
immediate family. Unfortunately, it happened more than
once that those who were caught were so exhausted and
weak that they could not withstand the torture and pressure
exerted on them, so that they exposed whole families, all of
whom were executed together. My brother-in-law, like many
thousands of other Jews, believed that if they did the jobs
they were told to do they would remain alive. He felt comfortable as a Jew among Jews, together with his brothers in
misfortune, and he took comfort in the fact that he could
share their fate.

His wife Frieda continued to do her job to the satisfaction
of her supervisors, and her life went on in a routine fashion.

In the meantime, Mother had been forced to leave the
shelter for old folks without relatives. The director of the
institution noticed two young women coming and going all
the time bringing her food—kosher, by the way—and concluded logically that this old woman was not without relatives at all and that therefore it was only proper to expel her
from the establishment.

Frieda, who loved Mother without bound, decided to do
something. She set up a screen in her room; behind it she put
a small bed, so that Mother could stay with her. Frieda's
children, who sensed the danger, used to walk on their tip-
toes; they would get close to their grandmother, enjoying the
warmth she radiated toward them during their mother's
absences.

Were it not for her worry over her husband, Frieda's happiness would have been complete. She knew that our cousin
Shachne Rabi worked in a factory, so she decided to use him
to pass on to her husband a sum of money so that he could
buy bread.

One day, she approached the gates of the factory at the
hour that the workers used to return to the camp, so that she
could drop a package containing a few bills into Shachne
Rabi's hand. This factory, which before the war belonged to a

Jew named Bauminger, manufactured all sorts of nails, screw and hooks. The Germans had confiscated the factory for military purposes.

Frieda observed the prisoners lined up in long columns and noticed that only a single German guard was responsible for them and was gathering them together. As a result, it was not difficult to find a suitable moment to place a bundle wrapped in paper in Shachne Rabi's hand. It was all so smooth and simple. But at the moment she approached the gates of the factory, a young Ukrainian, evidently a guard, came up to her.

"Whom are you looking for among these Jews?" he asked her in Polish. "You must be a Jew, too!"

Despite the fright that overtook her, Frieda did not lose her composure and answered that he was mistaken. She wanted to leave, but he took hold of her arm and led her to the German who was rounding up the workers. All her arguments and explanations were to no avail; she could not convince him that it was simply a coincidence that she had been passing by the place. He shoved her into the line of prisoners.

There was nothing left for her to do but to pray for a miracle: "Master of the Universe, I beseech You, if not for me, then for my suffering mother and my tiny children, help us." What would happen to Mother and the children if she did not return? At that moment, she caught the sorrowful glance of our cousin. He knew from her husband that she was hiding the children and her mother, but there was nothing he could do to help.

When she was walking through the gates of the factory, a German came up to her and asked what she was doing walking around there. Our sister Lydia had taught her that in a time of danger the thing to do was to pretend that she did not understand the German language. This was because most of the Jews understood German, on account of its similarity to Yiddish. The Jews of Krakow in particular knew German very well, because this area had once been part of the Austro-Hungarian Empire.

When the German repeated his question and Frieda did not respond, pretending not to understand what he had said, he summoned a young Jewish woman from among the inmates of the camp to translate for him. She looked at Frieda with pity and asked her in Polish why she had been brought there. Frieda explained that she had gone out to buy milk for her children, and as she had walked past the factory, a Ukrainian had stopped her suddenly on suspicion that she was a Jew.

"He's always drunk, you know," said the German in his language. "Go home to your children and keep your distance from the Jews."

Was this not a miracle from heaven? It was nothing less than G-d answering her prayer. By virtue of her mother and children, my sister Frieda had been saved. She returned home at the appointed hour, but she did not tell Mother anything about what had happened to her, so as not to cause her anguish.

Frieda, Mother and the children continued living in the government offices for several more weeks. One day, Frieda was summoned to her supervisor, who informed her, to her great surprise, that she was eligible to receive a small apartment on Karmelicka Street. He understood, so he said, that it was not easy for her to manage with two children in one tiny room.

And was this too not a miracle from G-d?

Dr. Krantz, Frieda's supervisor at her place of work, treated her as a dedicated and industrious employee who had known better days and only because of the war had been forced to take this job in order to support herself and her two small children. In this fashion, Frieda managed to move into an apartment house on Karmelicka Street that had been confiscated by the Germans.

I heard all of these things from Lydia upon my return to Krakow. I understood that not only I and my children had tasted the cup of bitterness. My family and my relatives had all been through the torments of hell. This news beclouded the happiness of my return to the family and my reunion with Mother.

Searching for Shelter

Bitter reality and the ongoing demands of day-to-day life kept me from sinking into despair. Quickly, I recovered and decided to venture forth in search of a place to live. The two-room apartment in which my mother lived together with Frieda was not large enough for me and my two children as well. The superintendent of the apartment building, who lived on the ground floor, used to keep an eye on everyone who entered or went out. She knew that my mother's apartment was meant for Frieda and her two youngest children. For Jozef, the oldest son, the apartment was out of bounds. My sisters Bronia and Lydia scoured the city to find a place for seven-year-old Jozek, as he was called. The boy's appearance was "good," meaning that he had Aryan features and did not arouse suspicion of his Jewish origin. He was also an extremely bright boy.

Hitler used to emphasize time and time again in his speeches the superior qualities of the German race, the noble Nordic master race distinguished by its blue eyes and light-colored hair. This mad tyrant lived an illusion, not realizing that thousands of Jews, including members of our own family, possessed these very genetic traits.

Jozek was a beautiful boy. He looked just like his sister Danusia, who was a year younger than him, and like his younger brother Aharon, known as Adasz. Thanks to his Aryan features my sisters managed to arrange for Jozek to live with a Polish family. But this idyllic situation did not last long. The boy could not stand up to the interrogations to which he was subjected, in spite of the coaching he had received about how to respond to certain questions. This innocent little boy simply did not realize the tremendous danger and used to beg his mother to allow him to stay in her house, together with the rest of the family.

He thus had to wander from place to place. Bronia once found a place for him in the home of an elderly retired teacher. The woman was a devout Catholic and dragged the boy with her to church. The woman did not cease to heap praises upon the boy before Bronia when she would come to visit him, and she declared that she was prepared to keep him with her in her home indefinitely. From time to time, the boy would discover a chance to come home to visit his mother and grandmother.

One day, the boy came home and told Mother that one time, when he had gone to church with the old lady, the priest had come up to him, patted his head and invited him to participate in the mass as an altar boy. He deserved a prize, said the priest, because he was such a gifted and polite boy. Jozek was not eager to accept this flattering offer. Mother urged him to accept the priest's invitation and explained to him that in order to save a life it was permissible to do virtually anything. Under such circumstances, taking part in a service in the Catholic church would not be counted against him as a sin. Because the priest liked him, Mother said, he would be able to survive there for a long time and would free his mother from the constant worry for his life.

It seemed that his grandmother had succeeded in convincing him, and the boy returned to the home of the old teacher. However, a few days later, as the hour of the service approached, he ran away to his grandmother's house. He cried demonstratively and begged them to find him a different hiding place. Thus the search for a shelter for the boy began once again.

I, too, as I have already mentioned, needed to find a place to live for myself and my children at once. So I left the children with Mother and went out on a searching expedition. I walked over the streets and byways of the city on the lookout for a room to rent. I could have found a place for myself were it not for the children, for most places for rent stipulated that no children were allowed. Tired and discouraged, I found myself suddenly standing in front of a small hotel that rented rooms with breakfast included. This hotel did not object to renting a room to a woman with children, but it was willing to take us for one week only. Still, this was the best arrangement I could find. With spirits elevated I returned to Mother. I made a meal for all of us, and after we had eaten we left for our new residence. We were given a room on the ground floor. It was late, so I made the beds and put the children to sleep. They fell asleep right away. The next morning, I was to pay one week's rent in advance.

However, that particular night I was unable to fall asleep. I tossed and turned in bed from side to side, but my weary body could not find relaxation. I simply could not be calm. I began to mumble to myself the words of the *Shema Yisrael* prayer.

Suddenly, in the black of the night, a rude voice came splitting through the entrance to the hotel, "Open up! German police! This is a night inspection!"

My heart began to pound like a hammer. I was taken aback, but I did not lose my composure. I awakened the children and told them to be absolutely silent. I helped them get dressed quickly. Earlier, I had noticed that there was a side entrance leading straight from our room to the courtyard. As the owner of the hotel was going to the front door to open it for the Germans knocking upon it, I opened the side door and dragged my children after me. We were in luck. Outside there was not a soul in sight. The street was completely empty.

I did not know where to turn. I breathed a sigh of relief. We had escaped from this building, where we had been in mortal danger. In one of the nearby alleys I could see an open cellar door with steps leading down into a basement that was used for storing all sorts of odds and ends. The place looked to me like a suitable place to seek refuge until dawn, when we could continue on our way. A hidden force was pulling me back to Mother's house, but I could not barge in on her at night, lest I frighten her.

When I reached home that morning and saw Mother, I did not find my sister Frieda, as she had already left for work. Mother was a bit taken aback and asked why I had come at such an early hour. Somehow, I managed to avoid telling her what had happened that night. I wanted to spare her undue excitement and worry. So I suggested that I make breakfast for everyone. Only later, when my sister Lydia came by, did I tell what had happened to me.

Lydia was furious that I had not consulted with her before moving into the hotel. From her I found out something I had not known before, that the Germans kept their eyes on small hotels and frequently raided them at night for identity checks on guests, hoping to catch Jews. Every night, thorough searches were conducted in all sorts of inns and hostelries, and hardly a night passed in which poor victims were not caught.

So Lydia, too, joined in the search and helped us look for a place to live. At the time it was necessary to find shelter for Lydia's son Adasz. I realized that it was impossible to stay in Mother's apartment during the day, for the superintendent of the building followed our movements and even cross-examined Bronia about the woman with two children who came by to visit Mother so often. If my sister had only known how I longed just to be in Mother's presence under any circumstances or conditions and how great was her calming influence upon me! But this one wish I could not have. To my sorrow it remained merely a wish.

Every morning, I used to prepare a bundle with slices of buttered bread and some fruit, and I would go out with the children to Dietlowska Boulevard, which passed through the center of town. Along the boulevard there were long benches for the comfort of the passersby, mostly mothers or governesses with children. I tied my hair up in a kerchief, after the fashion of the peasants, in order to look like one of the nannies so as not to stand out in the crowd. This way I would rest for a few hours while the children would find an outlet in movement and play.

For the afternoon hours I had found another solution. I would go with the children into the Reduta movie theater on Lubicz Street, next to the train station. The theater used to show films all day, nonstop. I would take the children into the dark theater. There I would sit them down and feed them, and they would soon fall asleep. In this way, I felt a certain relief, although the tension did not vanish entirely. The usher, who would accompany entering viewers to their seats, managed to frighten me, for as he would pass by me he would shine the light from his flashlight. My heart beat with fear that he meant to arrest us. Moreover, the fear crept into my heart that the usher had caught on that for the price of a single ticket I used to spend long hours in the theater. Thus from time to time, while the usher was busy opening the doors, we would quickly move to another place, changing our seats from one side of the theater to another.

BOOK

FOUR

In the Lion's Den

My First German Employer

O ur exhausting trips back and forth to the movie theater finally came to an end. One day, my sister Lydia appeared like a redeeming angel holding a newspaper with an advertisement that read: "A German seeks a housekeeper who cooks well; there is a maid for rough jobs and cleaning."

Lydia applied at the listed address at the appointed hour in order to check whether the place and job were indeed suitable for me. When she returned she gave me her news. She had presented me to the employer as the wife of a Polish officer who had been taken prisoner or fallen in battle. She also indicated that I was fluent in German and was quite familiar with all aspects of household management. She praised my honesty and dependability and added that I had been left with a small girl from whom I would not be able to part. The employer expressed his interest in interviewing me and in setting with me the conditions of my employment and my salary.

That very day I showed up at his home on Pilsudski Street, a street whose name had been changed a few years prior to the outbreak of the war to Wolska Street, after the great leader of independent Poland, Marshal Jozef Pilsudski. This was one of the most prestigious streets of Krakow. My new employer's house had belonged before the war to a wealthy Jewish industrialist.

Sep Wirth—that was my employer's name—opened the door himself and led me into an elegantly furnished living room. I sat down on a velvet chair, and he looked me over carefully and with keen interest. He was impressed with my command of the German language, and this proved to be the decisive factor in my favor. He agreed to take me on together with my daughter. When he asked what monthly salary I required, I replied that since this was my first such job and I was not yet well-versed in matters of salary, I would not make excessive demands, particularly as I would be receiving room and board for my daughter as well as for myself. Expressing satisfaction with what I had said, the gentleman asked me to report for work three days hence, on the first day of the coming month.

I learned that three days on the calendar do not always go by so quickly. With my own eyes I saw how three days can sometimes be an eternity, as long as the exile of the Jewish people. Happy that I had gotten the job, I went to see Mother, who had prayed for my success.

At Mother's house, I found Lydia downcast and worried. While she had been walking on the street, she whispered to me, she had run into Julia, the daughter of the woman who took care of the building in which we had lived with our parents for many years before the war began. Julia was a very ugly girl, with blond hair and a repulsive personality. Her voice was nasal and grating, and in addition to this she was also an anti-Semite.

Lydia feared that Julia had recognized her and had even tried to follow her home. Lydia had thus taken a circuitous route to Mother's house, but her mood was sad. Lydia whispered all of this to me so that Mother would not hear, and she advised me not to spend even a single night more at Mother's house. If Julia had in fact followed her home, she said, she might turn all of us over to the Gestapo for a large financial reward.

That same night, Lydia took my two children out of Mother's house and put them up in her own apartment, while I found temporary shelter, for a single night only, with Mrs. Bujak, after promising her that I would be gone the next morning.

I did not shut my eyes all that night, and in the middle of the night I hit upon an idea. I had been instructed to show up for work the next Monday morning. Why, though, could I not come early, on Sunday evening, assuming that Sep Wirth would be spending the weekend away from home? In this way I would take care of the problem of finding a place to spend that night, and at the same time, I would be able to size up the maid.

I told Lydia about my idea, and she encouraged me to do just as I had thought. In the meantime, my son would be staying with Lydia and so I took my daughter with me, and together we carefully climbed the back stairs to my employer's apartment.

I knocked on the kitchen door. At first, there was no answer, but when I knocked more vigorously, I heard steps, and a voice asked in Polish, "Who is it?" I answered that it was I, the new housekeeper, and the door was opened.

Before me stood a young girl, about eighteen years old, plump and innocent-looking. I took one look at her dark, pretty eyes, and a shudder passed over my body. They were the eyes of a Jew, sad and inquisitive. Eyes like that used to give us away, even if all other physical features aroused no suspicion. Even when we looked completely Aryan, we could not manage to maintain a calm look in our eyes. Our eyes gave us away.

The Polish Jewish poet Julian Tuwim was able once to describe those eyes:

Eyes radiating fear
Reflecting the heritage of generations
Children without a homeland
Scattered throughout the world
Wanderers, a bundle of nerves.

This great poet was born a Jew, and even though he viewed himself a Pole in every respect, he did not convert to Catholicism and was conscious of the tragedy of our people, persecuted from generation to generation.

The maid told me innocently that the master of the house made it a custom to return home late on Sunday night. The next morning he would have breakfast and go out again, not to return until lunch time. I breathed easier, and a weight was lifted from my heart.

So the two of us sat calmly next to the big kitchen table. I made up a story, a lie, of course. I said, exercising my imagination to the fullest, that I had just now come to town with my daughter from our village, and that there was no point in returning home for a single night when I would merely have to come back to town early the next morning. So I asked her to open up one of the bedrooms on the second floor for me, and I promised that the next morning I would leave and come back to report at the appointed hour.

The girl agreed without hesitation. She gave both of us something warm to drink, and I took out the sandwiches I had brought with me. Afterwards, I put my daughter to bed, and she immediately fell fast asleep.

We began to talk. Tusia—that was the girl's name—sat and told me about our common employer. Her Polish was not all that good, and I could make out a Yiddish accent. Fortunately for her, the Germans were not sensitive to this, for they generally did not speak Polish. From her I found out that she came from a small town in Poland and that she had a sister a year younger than she who also worked as a maid and governess in the home of a German family. Tusia confessed to me that she was frightened of the boss. She did not understand his German very well, since he was an Austrian from the Tyrol. The two of them were often left alone together. Even though up until then he had always treated her fairly, she had made it a practice, for the sake of caution, to lock the door to her room at night.

Tusia could sense that I posed no danger to her, and with tears in her eyes, she confessed to me that she was a Jew. A warm feeling toward this poor girl flooded my heart. I was seized with a strong desire to hug and kiss her. She had become close to me, and I felt in my heart that from then on I would pray to G-d to keep her from all harm.

I did not reveal to her that we were sisters and that we shared a common G-d. I refrained from doing so out of fear that Tusia would not be able to restrain herself and would give away my secret to the woman who took care of the building and her husband, with whom she had become friendly. The caretakers were very inquisitive people and frequently questioned her about the way the German Nazi treated her. Tusia did not even consider the possibility that these people might develop doubts as to her origin, but I supposed that those Poles had already noticed her foreign accent and had guessed who she really was. I rebuked her for having revealed to me the secret of her Jewishness without knowing who I was.

Early the next day, I began my job. In the apartment there was a pantry filled to the brim with all sorts of things to eat. I set the table in the dining room carefully, prepared lunch and waited on tenterhooks for my employer to return back home.

The zero hour approached. And indeed, the front door opened wide, and the master of the house arrived. When he saw the set table in the dining room with all the silverware and platters nicely laid out, he hurried into the kitchen to welcome me and asked to see my daughter. He looked into the girl's face, saw her blue eyes and blond hair, and I could see the great delight on his face. Lunch proved quite tasty to him, and I was privileged to receive an explicit expression of thanks from him for it.

I was given a fine room for myself and for my daughter. There was nothing left for me to do but to give thanks to G-d for his abundant mercy.

My presence in the house was a comfort to both Tusia and myself. In the course of time, I told her, of course, that I was a Jew, and not only that, but that I was religious and observed all of the commandments of Judaism.

After several days had gone by, my employer called me and suggested that I take my meals together with him. I thanked him but politely declined, explaining that during meals I preferred to sit together with my daughter, so that I could feed her. Naturally, I refrained from demonstrating my deep hatred of his people, who had been so cruel to mine simply because we were Jews, even though we had done nothing to him or his people.

In any event, I forced myself to do my job properly and to manage the household to my employer's satisfaction, so as not to lose the shelter I had come by with such great difficulty. Every now and then, I wondered whether my employer could imagine that before the war I too had been a lady, that I lived in a spacious house and had employed two maids, that I had been married to a young and handsome man who showered me and our children with love and pampering. I cannot deny that Sep treated me as his equal, and my work did indeed please him. He even complimented me often and appreciated all my efforts. But I could not accept his generous offer to join him at the same table, for I had to hide from him that I would not touch even the smallest morsel of food that I prepared for him. I made do with bread, butter, cheese and eggs. Even such items were regarded at the time as luxuries, and they were not commonly available. I refrained from eating prepared foods, mainly for reasons of the Jewish dietary laws, but another consideration was my identification with my fellow Jews who were suffering and dying from hunger.

I Am Called Frau Anna

One day, Sep Wirth returned home in a happy
mood and informed me that he had invited a few
high-ranking guests to the house. He asked if I could prepare
an appropriate spread. All sorts of cold cuts, cheeses,
smoked fish and other delicatessen items had been ordered
from Hawelka, the famous delicatessen in the center of the
main square of Krakow. My job would be to prepare salads,
cakes and cookies. But the host had also promised his guests
an Austrian dish known as *nockerl*, with which I was not
familiar and had no idea how to prepare. So Sep went into
the kitchen with me, rolled up his shirtsleeves, broke apart a
few eggs, added a little flour and mixed the batter into a thin
paste. He rolled this dough out with a rolling pin, cut it into
thin strips and boiled the strips in salt water. Then he

removed the cooked dough from the water and poured a sauce over it.

The example was instructive, and soon I had gained the "wisdom" of how to make *nockerl*. On the appointed day, I made the *nockerl* myself. I tried to put my best foot forward, for in the conditions of those days I could not have dreamed of a better and safer refuge.

The party had been set for Sunday. On that day, during the afternoon hours, while I was still in the midst of all the preparations, I suddenly heard a knock at the back door. I opened it and beheld Lydia's daughter, whom we called Kalusia, standing before me. Kalusia—now Kitty—was beautiful and charming. She worked as a housemaid for a German family. Her behavior and her exquisite manners astounded and excited her employers. At the time, she was a young girl, about sixteen years old, but she was able to fulfill all of her employer's demands. She did the shopping and took care of deliveries. Her employers valued her and treated her with extreme warmth. Every now and then, they would invite her to dine with them at their own table, and they would compliment her incessantly to the effect that were she not a Pole—and thus a member of a hostile people—they would want to see her marry their only son. The son was serving in the army and had almost certainly taken part in the killing of Jews.

When Kitty came to me on the day of the party she immediately sized up the situation, put on an apron, picked up a knife and began helping me with peeling the fruits and vegetables, decorating cakes and arranging the platters, activities that take up a great deal of time. When she had finished helping she got up to leave, and I gave her a warm hug. What a beautiful, wonderful creature she was!

My employer was also quite tense that day. He rang up and asked if I could manage to prepare the table by myself. Perhaps I would require his assistance? I reassured him and told him that he could show up a little while before the party and see for himself that everything was ready.

I shall not be exaggerating if I say that the table was a most splendid one. Expensive china place settings and antique silverware next to crystal goblets and vases filled with flowers—all these came together to form an almost fairy tale-like picture by the light of the glistening chandeliers. Platters filled with delicacies had been brought over from the Hawelka delicatessen, as had the finest beverages, which were served over ice.

Sep was standing in the doorway as I finished setting the table. I shall never forget how amazed and astounded he was. He stood transfixed, not taking his eye off the splendid table for even a second.

"Frau Anna," he said. "I guess that you come from a most elegant family. In any event, I have never seen such a fine table."

This Tyrolean German, the son of poor parents, as he himself had once admitted, had stolen a very large amount of Jewish property. Only "thanks" to Hitler had he come to enjoy a plenty of which he had never dreamed. I was shocked when I saw his closets. He had filled them with the finest clothing. In the camp at Plaszow, the finest Jewish tailors had been put to work without compensation. They would sit and sew suits from the best cloth, which had been stolen from Jewish warehouses. Sep was a supplier to the military. He himself did not wear a uniform but went around in top-quality jackets instead.

I was also shocked to see how many shoes he had collected—brown ones, black ones, white ones, sport shoes and riding boots. All of them were laid out row upon row, like soldiers lined up for inspection, all shined and polished. Tusia was the one who was responsible for this department and who took care to see that the shoes were always neatly arranged and shined.

The long-awaited moment arrived, and the guests came in one by one. All together there were some eight to ten people at the party, some of them high-ranking officers accompanied by their wives.

I wore a modest dress and brushed my hair carefully, and Sep introduced me to his guests as the manager of his household—his *Hausdame*.

The house, which was all bedecked in finery, and the bountiful table made an obvious impression on the guests. I served many plates filled with meat and salads and all sorts of delicacies. As dessert for this most luxurious banquet, the guests indulged themselves with nut and almond cakes covered with whipped cream. Sep asked me to pour coffee for all the guests. So I went around the table from guest to guest with the large crystal sugar bowl in my hand and poured for each one, adding one spoonful or two of sugar, as they wished.

I shall never forget the moment when I came to Sep himself to pour sugar into his coffee cup. Suddenly, he jumped up from where he was sitting as if someone had just spilled a large kettle of boiling water upon him and asked whether I had forgotten that he was a diabetic and took no sugar. I was quite surprised at this sudden outburst, but quickly I understood that there was some reason why he had made up this lie. Evidently, he was using this as an excuse to continue evading front-line military duty, for he explained to the general who was present that evening that he had to maintain a very strict diet. I requested his forgiveness for my forgetfulness.

Before I left the room all the guests thanked me one by one for the excellent meal, and they complimented the master of the house on his good fortune in finding such a capable household manager.

I went up to my room, gave Tusia and my daughter some cake and pastries to eat and breathed a sigh of relief that this party had passed without incident. The fact that I had found a home for myself and my daughter in Sep's house was a blessing from heaven, and I was prepared to take on even the most difficult job just so I would be able to stay in the place as long as I could.

For several days thereafter, Sep was in a most happy

mood. He brought home all sorts of special foods and candies for my daughter.

One day, he brought home a package of soap that weighed several pounds. He told me there was no need for me to try to conserve this soap, as he could obtain as much of it as he needed. When I opened the package I found some small, white odorless cubes that did not look at all like the kind of soap that was distributed to the Polish population by ration, just as all other daily necessities were distributed to them. The woman who took care of the apartment building always used to complain to me that the soap that she received according to ration was not enough for her and that she always had to be extremely thrifty, for her little son used to get his clothes very dirty all the time, like any boy his age. I told her that my German boss had brought home a package filled with soap. And then I heard from her something that filled my heart with horror.

"Mrs. Kwiatkowska, have you not yet heard that that soap is made from human fat, from the fat of the many murdered Jews?" she said. "From the skins of these creatures, murdered by order of the Nazis, other Jews, incarcerated in the camps, make all sorts of lampshades and other household items."

I cut short the conversation with her quickly so that she would not sense that I was shocked beyond belief. I did not want her to notice the blood draining from my face, so that she might guess, Heaven forbid, that I was a Jew. I had no idea whether she was also an anti-Semite who would turn me over to the Gestapo for money. I had to be very careful of her and her husband, for many of those who supervised apartment buildings were informers.

I do not know whether anyone will believe me that even before I found out what material the Nazis used to manufacture this soap I had felt a certain revulsion toward it, and whenever I had had to wash my hands I would put it aside as quickly as I could and use the soap that I received for my ration.

One day, as I was serving Sep his lunch, he repeated his offer that my daughter and I take our meals together with him at the same table. Perhaps he was still under the influence of all the compliments that his guests had paid me. Gently but firmly I declined his offer in order to avoid getting any closer to him than I already was. He was obviously disappointed, but he still continued to treat me with much respect.

One Sunday, after I had finished my work, I took my daughter to visit my mother, hoping that my son, whom I missed terribly, would be there too. At that time, he was living with my sister Lydia.

From Lydia I heard about her son Adasz, who was working with some German firm together with a group of Poles. The job involved manual labor. Adasz was a very energetic worker, and his employers were most pleased with him. Lydia, who had been widowed at such a young age—the Germans having killed her husband—made superhuman efforts to keep her two children alive. Her son's job was a great relief to her.

After just a short while, Adasz had come home from the place where he worked and told his mother and grandmother that two of his Polish co-workers had come up to him and told him that they suspected he was a Jew, for he was too industrious and too serious for a boy of his young age. The boy was frightened half to death and tried to turn what they had said into a joke. He told them to stop talking such nonsense. Even though fear was gnawing away at his heart he tried to make his mother and elderly grandmother believe that everything was going to be all right. Nevertheless, both of them begged him to stop working at that place. But he, who loved these two women who were dearer to him than anything else, insisted that if he did not show up for work he would in effect confirm the suspicions of those who were after him. In that case, they would try to follow him home, and the danger to the entire family would only become much greater.

As time went on, Lydia became determined to find another place for her son to work. She knew that my employer hired people for various jobs, and as she had met him before, she approached him about finding work, ostensibly for the unemployed son of a friend. Sep agreed to grant an interview to the boy.

When Adasz came to the house, I, of course, had to pretend that I did not know him. Nevertheless, I arranged my schedule so that I would be setting the table in the dining room during the interview, in order to be able to hear all that went on.

Sep spoke in German and asked Adasz if he understood. Adasz responded briefly in order to leave the impression that his command of German was imperfect (although, in fact, he spoke the language fluently). Sep offered him a job driving a delivery truck, and Adasz agreed.

The interview had seemed to go well, and I thought that Adasz had made a good impression. But at the end of the interview Sep raised his voice to Adasz and warned him that if he did not do everything exactly as he was told he was liable to be thrown out or even shot.

"*Du wirst herausgeschmiessen oder erschossen, verstanden*? (You will be thrown out or shot, understand?)" he asked.

"*Verstanden*," whispered Adasz.

Adasz's father had been a noble man, a shining example of honesty and integrity. His son could certainly be entrusted with goods to transport and deliver. His sad childhood, the lack of security over what the next day would bring, the loss of his revered father and, most of all, the fact that at the time he was growing up he was beset by worries without end—all of these had an adverse influence on his future state of health. Although early in his medical career he specialized in complicated brain surgery, a heart attack he suffered at a young age forced him to limit his surgical practice to simpler operations. He gained a reputation for these operations as well.

He is married to a woman, a bacteriologist, from a good and wealthy Jewish family, and he and his wife have two daughters and a son. Their home is a faithful Orthodox Jewish home.

Back on the Street

A short while after the party at Sep's house, and after I had thanked him for the honor he had granted me in inviting me to dine at his own table, my boss showed up in the kitchen. I was out of the house at the time, so he asked Tusia to make up the guest rooms on the second floor. They had not been used for a long time, but now he was expecting guests from abroad.

Since I had come to live in Sep Wirth's house, Tusia had blossomed. She shed the constant dreadful fear that had plagued her before. The girl became close to me, and I felt toward her as if she were my younger sister. During the daytime I was calm too, for I was engaged in the affairs of running the household and did not have time to think about things. But at night I usually could not sleep. My heart would flinch with pain out of worry for my son. To be sure, Lydia was doing all she could for the boy, but he would cry bitterly and ask why his mother had abandoned him and taken only his sister with her.

I was also deeply worried about my husband, whom I had had to leave behind in Brzezany in a German work detail. Every now and then, he would manage to send a short letter to Lydia's address. In one of these, he wrote that a while before some of his companions in the detail had been called aside and told that they were going to be sent temporarily to work in another place. However, none of them had as yet come back. My husband was deathly afraid that the same fate might soon befall him. Anxiously, he asked if there was any possibility of extricating him from Brzezany and bringing him to us.

I had to find a way to save him. But even I myself was not sure what the morrow would bring. One day, out of the blue, my boss gave me news that hit me like a loud thunder from the sky.

He told me that he had invited his girlfriend from Germany with her daughter to spend several weeks with him. From the letters that she sent to him from time to time I already knew that the woman's name was Erna. Sep had already given Tusia the instruction to clean out the guest rooms upstairs. Since he had given this order to her directly, and since I had confidence in her, I did not feel it necessary to supervise Tusia's work.

The day before the guests' scheduled arrival, Sep stormed into the kitchen, enraged beyond control, and began to literally pummel Tusia with his fists until she bled. I froze where I was standing, certain that I would be next. I had no idea what had happened. Then suddenly he turned toward me, placed the keys to the guest rooms in my hand and told me to see for myself how much dust Tusia had left on the furniture and window sills. It seemed as if some force was preventing him from raising a hand against me. I could only apologize that I had not checked Tusia's work and promise that all would be put in order. First, however, I had to tend to Tusia, who was still bleeding profusely.

Sep stormed out of the house. The moment he left, Tusia resolved that by the time he returned she would already be gone. Her eyes were filled with tears. She packed her belongings in a hurry, left the bundle with the caretaker (as being seen wandering about with such a pack during the day would surely arouse suspicion), gave me a hug and walked out the door. She said that for the time being she would stay with her sister.

After I had locked the door behind her, I felt a great sadness descend upon me. What awaited me when my employer returned and discovered that Tusia had disappeared? I figured that I did not have much time left in this household either.

When Sep returned and did not find Tusia in the kitchen, he demanded to know where she was. This was the moment I had been dreading. I made up a lie. I told him that I had gone out shopping and that when I had returned she was nowhere to be found. I said that I had looked all over for her, but to no avail. He ran into her room and discovered that her closet had been cleaned out. He became furious and nearly lost control altogether.

Sep had always treated me fairly. He looked upon me as a woman of high social origins. As a result, he did not vent his wrath upon me. Instead, he quickly ran outside to the caretaker's hut, thinking that perhaps the girl might be hiding there. The poor caretaker told him that neither she nor her husband knew anything about the girl's whereabouts, but Sep did not believe her. He beat her viciously and threatened that if he found out she was lying he would kill her and her husband as well.

I should like to think that Sep was basically a good-natured man and that he regretted what he had done. I knew that in his heart he felt pity for poor young Tusia, for he knew that she was an honest girl who was beyond reproach. Whenever he would make a request of her, she would look at him with her beautiful eyes, trying to understand exactly what it was he wanted from her.

The caretaker's husband later told me how he had struggled with himself all night not to attack the miserable German who had beaten up his wife. He realized that if he did such a thing he would pay for it with his life; the German could simply take out his revolver and shoot him to death. But he swore to me that he would one day gain revenge, for he believed that the Germans would ultimately be defeated in the war.

The next day, Sep's girlfriend arrived with her young daughter. She seemed quite nice, but she gave every indication of intending to take over the management of the household herself. She was determined to be in control of everything that went on. And indeed, a few days later she politely informed me that my housekeeping services would no longer be required.

With great sadness but still trusting in G-d, I packed my bags and set out once again into the unknown. Somehow, even in the darkest hours, I always managed to find a last shred of hope, a hope that ultimately enabled me to survive and not give in to despair. I know that I owe this to my religious upbringing and to the deep faith in G-d above that my father and grandfather implanted in me.

Now there were new problems I would have to deal with. How would I find a new place to work? What arrangements could I make for my son? What could I do with my daughter? What could I do to save my husband? How could I bring him out of Brzezany?

In these moments, I raised up a prayer to G-d. "O merciful and compassionate G-d! Perform a miracle! Make an end to this awful war and bring about the downfall of the oppressor Hitler. Give him his recompense for his awful crimes. May his hand be stayed from annihilating the entire Jewish people whom You chose from among all the nations of this earth. Grant us, O merciful and compassionate G-d, that we might be privileged to live to see that great day. I promise You faithfully, O Father in Heaven, that I shall raise and train my children to fear Heaven and to keep Your holy commandments. And until the great moment comes, give us shelter and refuge in Your great mercy."

The German Psychiatrist

Several days later, my sister Lydia appeared once
again like an angel from heaven. She brought a
newspaper advertisement from a German family of four
looking for a housekeeper. I literally jumped for joy, praying
that I would get the job. Before I left for the address listed in
the ad I saw my mother, pale with excitement, reciting *Tehillim*. She wished me good luck, and that gave me encouragement.

Dressed like a housemaid, with a colored scarf on my head
and with a frantically beating heart, I rang the doorbell. The
lady of the house opened the door. She was a pretty, young
woman, brunette with brown eyes, wearing a suit that accen-
tuated her good figure. She seemed somehow more French
than German. She looked me over, then asked in German if I

had come about the housekeeper's job.

She took me inside and explained that her family occupied a six-room apartment that took up an entire floor of the building. Her name was Toni Sopp and her husband, Professor Helmut Sopp, was a psychiatrist, a high-ranking officer in the medical corps; director of an institute for the mentally ill and chief physician for the nearby prison. They had two children. My job would be to keep the apartment clean and in good order and to run the kitchen by myself. I could tell that I had made a good impression.

When she asked me what salary I required I told her that although I had not been a housekeeper before the war I was well acquainted with the work; I asked for a modest payment, provided that my little girl could stay with me. Upon hearing this last provision she informed me that she would have to obtain her husband's consent. She asked me to return the next day when her husband would be at home.

I reported the next day, as instructed, full of worry and lacking confidence. This time the master of the house greeted me himself. He was in his thirties, tall, with a commanding, intelligent appearance. When I explained to him that because of my need to keep my daughter with me I was willing to leave the determination of my salary up to him, he told me to return the next morning with my daughter to begin work.

Thus my mother's prayer was answered. My beautiful daughter thoroughly charmed my new employers and their children. The older son Peter and the younger Imo, as his mother called him, took great interest in the girl, and after but a short time, they began to invite her to take part in their games. They were about the same age as my children.

My new employers regarded me as a woman who had come upon hard times on account of the war and who had been forced to work for her daily bread. Both of them treated me with respect, and I did all I could to satisfy them. Once, when my daughter complained that her shoes were getting too tight for her, the mistress of the house gave me one of her sons' many pairs.

I shall never forget the first dinner I prepared for them. Toni brought home some fresh vegetables, a fair-sized portion of lentils and a chunk of lard, and she told me to make a soup according to my own taste. I had never made a soup from such ingredients before, but I added some fried onions, seasoned the broth with salt and pepper and served a full tureen to the table. They ate everything, down to the last drop. I, on the other hand, did not even taste the soup, for I had made a vow that I would never eat non-kosher food. My daughter and I thus made do with bread, butter and cheese. Toni was surprised that I left half a pot of soup over for the next day. Evidently, she had worried that I had a hefty appetite and that my board would cost her dearly.

Later, Helmut came into the kitchen and announced that he had never before tasted such delicious soup. From that time, I was given a completely free hand in the kitchen. Of course, I couldn't prepare them the sort of dishes I was used to, so I had to learn how to cook foods that were completely foreign to me.

I took particular care that the expenses for my board and my daughter's would be small and not impose any hardship upon my employers. In this respect, I was lucky that Helmut, as director of a hospital and as a close friend of the German governor-general of occupied Poland Hans Frank, would frequently receive extra quantities of vodka as a gift. He was able to exchange this sought after commodity for the tightly-rationed butter, cheese, eggs and meat that the peasant women from the surrounding villages would bring to the doctor's home.

After a while, I was placed in charge of the exchanges, and I was able at the same time to purchase milk products for myself with my own money. Of course, I ate no meat. Once, when Toni noticed that I served the family the full quantity of meat I received, she asked me why I didn't set aside any of the meat for myself and my daughter. I explained to her that I was a vegetarian. This seemed to satisfy her entirely.

The master and mistress of the house used to entertain

guests in their home often, and I acquired a reputation for the eggnog I would prepare for their receptions. I would mix egg yolk with milk, sugar and vanilla, bring the mixture to a boil, let it cool and later saturate it with cognac. It was a superb drink. After one party at which I served this beverage, the guests asked who had made it. The answer they received was that the drink was called *kwiatkognac*, after the surname inscribed on my false Aryan papers—Kwiatowska—which they shortened to kwiat.

Polish doctors who worked under my boss's supervision also attended these parties. They would bring him all sorts of gifts in order to maintain good relations with him. They also explained to him that the word *kwiat* in Polish translated into German as *Blume* (flower). Helmut liked this.

Several weeks went by. Taking care of this six-room apartment, the shopping and cooking—all of which demanded a great deal of effort—helped me keep my mind off my worries for my husband and my young son, at least during the daytime. The only difficulty I encountered was in lighting the large furnaces, for never before had I done such a job.

Before the war, I had had two maids in my house, one for cleaning and the second for taking care of the children. Sometimes, I had seen how they used to place sticks of kindling wood in the furnace, covering them diagonally with larger logs and setting a match to them. When the wood began to burn they would put coals on top. But I simply could not manage to get the furnace lighted. I am ashamed to relate how I would stand over the furnace praying that the coals would catch fire. Eventually, Toni rescued me from my embarrassment. Once she came home early from shopping for a party. When she saw how worried I was, she taught me that it was first necessary to spray kerosene on some old newspapers, arrange the logs in appropriate fashion, put some coals on top and, after everything had begun to burn, to add more coals every now and then.

Toni was a good and friendly woman, and I knew she had

pity on me. One day, she informed me that her husband and she decided that from then on one of the hospital employees would come to carry the coals and wash the windows. This made my job much easier.

On Sunday afternoons, I used to have some time off, and I would run to visit my dear mother. She would look with concern into my pale and tired face and beg me to eat everything I could. I should not, she insisted, refrain from eating non-kosher food. She assured me that it was not a sin to eat food not prepared according to the Jewish dietary laws, for during wartime this would be regarded as a life-saving act that any rabbi would permit. But how could I allow myself such a luxury when thousands and tens of thousands of my people were dying every day of starvation and exhaustion? The mere fact that I had managed to find a place of refuge and save myself was an unparalleled act of Divine grace. In the Sopp home I felt myself secure.

Every day, I used to go to buy fresh milk at the dairy store on Lobtowska Street. Even though the store was not far from home, I was always afraid that someone might follow me. More than anything else, I used to dread when Toni would send me shopping at the crowded Szczepanski Market. The peasants brought fresh fruits and vegetables, eggs and all sorts of dairy products there, and the prices were much lower than in many grocery stores. As a native of Krakow, I was afraid of running into one of my former Christian friends. I had to be extremely cautious not to show my face on the street any more than absolutely necessary.

One day, while I was buying vegetables for lunch, I suddenly felt the touch of a hand upon my shoulder. I was so frightened that I froze in my tracks. When I turned my head to look back, I saw Maria, my sister Stella's first voice instructor. She saw that I was afraid and smiled to calm me. She placed her lips close to my ear and whispered, "You shouldn't hang around here. This place is full of suspicious characters. G-d bless you. You know how much I loved Stella, and you too."

Maria squeezed my hand warmly, and on taking leave whispered, "Watch out for yourself, my child."

Christmas was approaching, so I used to accompany Toni quite often on holiday shopping trips; when I was with her I felt more secure.

Toni had a birthday coming as well, so she asked her husband to buy her a dachshund for a gift. Helmut was not very happy with her request, for such a dog was a most expensive item. But still he did as his wife asked. So Toni got the dog, and it fell to me to take it out for a walk every day on my way to the dairy store. Walking a dog was a typical activity of people of Aryan origin, so I felt safer in the company of my mistress's canine.

The dog was not housebroken and left a mess all over the house, and I used to have to clean up after it. This went on for several weeks, until one day, when I served a succulent roast for dinner and Helmut was busy washing up, the dog jumped up on the table and downed a healthy portion of the meat. Helmut became extremely angry and firmly announced that the dog was to be thrown out of the house that very day. All of Toni's protests were to no avail, and she was forced to give the dog to a friend of hers. I too breathed easier, for now I was free of the constant job of cleaning up after the messes the dog left.

Thus Christmas drew near, and the members of the family were doing lots of shopping. They put up a big tree in the living room and decorated it. They also put a small tree in my room and decorated it. I was moved when I found a package under it containing a nightgown that fit me perfectly. My daughter also received a gift.

During those days, I worked hard in the kitchen together with Toni, for high-ranking dignitaries, including top Army officers, had been invited to the home for the Christmas dinner. Among the invited guests was a Mr. Bizanc, who ran a prestigious cafe and restaurant on the corner of Karmelicka Street opposite the university campus.

Before the war, the Bizanc cafe had been known as Cafe

Esplanade, but many of its customers used to call it simply Bizanc's place, after its owner. This cafe was counted among the best and most elegant in town. It was a meeting place for high society, people with money, senior government officials, artists and the like. Ladies and gentlemen used to meet there over a cup of coffee and a piece of cake; it was the "in" thing to do.

When the Nazis conquered Krakow, the Bizanc brothers had declared that they belonged to the German *Volk* and collaborated with the occupation authorities. They changed the name of their cafe to Cafe Kristal as a gesture and sign of identification with the events of the infamous Kristallnacht of November, 1938. The Bizanc cafe enjoyed considerable success. During every hour of the day and the evening it was full of Gestapo agents, army officers and their families, and it was difficult to find an available table.

One of the brothers, a plump middle-aged man of medium height, was a regular guest at the home of my employer. For the holidays, he sent my employers several pounds of carp, which was traditional holiday fare in Poland. I was given the task of cleaning, cooking and serving the fish. Of course, I prepared the fish according to the recipe I had learned before the war from my mother, the same way I used to make it at home—Jewish style, with onions, pepper and salt.

The holiday feast arrived. The tables bent under the weight of all the many dishes laid out upon them. The guests delighted over the bountiful feast and the many beverages offered. But most of all, they liked the fish I made, and they left not a single morsel on the platter.

Nevertheless, those fish caused my heart to pound with apprehension. During the course of the evening, Mr. Bizanc showed up in the kitchen, his face radiating pleasure and satisfaction after the hearty meal and abundant drink he had just consumed.

"Mrs. Kwiatowska, where did you ever learn to make fish Jewish-style?" he asked.

I trembled like a thief who had just been caught red-handed

I searched my brain feverishly for an answer to his question. Quickly, though, I recovered my wits and answered that I had gotten the recipe out of some cookbook or another, I couldn't remember which one.

Indeed, I had good reason to be worried. None of the German guests had asked such a question, but he, a resident of Poland of long standing who had had close business connections with many Jews, had detected something unusual right away. Jewish bankers, lawyers, merchants and suppliers had frequented his cafe in large numbers before the war, and it may well have been that some of his Jewish customers had entertained him in their own homes, serving him fish the way Jews traditionally prepared them for their *Shabbos* meal. Therefore, it was quite possible that he would become suspicious and guess that I was a Jew. After all, it was quite unusual for a Polish woman with a good appearance who spoke excellent Polish and German to consent to work as a housekeeper in a German home. Moreover, Mr. Bizanc, who declared himself a member of the German *Volk*, was liable to want to ingratiate himself to the authorities and let them in on his suspicion. The Germans would never have developed such doubts on their own. It was enough for a person to have regular facial features, light-colored hair and blue eyes, as I, my parents and my entire family had, for them to have no doubts about his Aryan origin.

I spent a sleepless night. But in the end I managed to calm down, because I had heard my employers praise me to their guests so often for my industriousness and absolute honesty. Indeed, they had good reason to be pleased with me. Whenever I used to return home from shopping in the marketplace I would give Toni a scrupulous accounting of what I had spent, down to the last penny. And what is more, I would pay for the things I bought for myself and my daughter out of my own pocket, so that my employers would not feel it was costing them too much to maintain me. Toni was grateful for my ability to manage the household on my own, so that she was free to spend time with her friends. She treated me with such confidence that she used to tell me intimate details about her private life.

Toni was quite fond of me and not ashamed to admit I was better educated than she was. Once, while writing a letter, she asked me the correct spelling of the word *Juwelier* (jeweler)—was it written with a "v" or a "w"? She had not been able to acquire an education, for her husband had started courting her while she was a student in high school, and she had married him at a very young age. But during the first few years of their marriage, after she had had a chance to find out what kind of person he really was, her feelings for him had waned.

Of the two sons she had borne him, the older one, Peter, looked like his father in every respect, whereas the younger, Imo, differed from him both in outward appearance and in personality. The little boy was the apple of his mother's eye.

During the times she was off with the children visiting friends in Upper Silesia, he used to invite guests to the house for wild parties that would last until all hours of the morning.

On one of these occasions, while Toni was absent from the house, Lydia came to see me. She looked like a dog being chased on the street. She was extremely depressed. She told me that Mother was suffering from a bad cold and that she did not look well at all. I told her to bring Mother to me while Helmut was at the hospital. When I saw my mother with her face a waxen yellow color, I felt a twinge in my heart. Immediately, I had her lie down in my bed, covered her with a warm blanket and waited for Helmut to return home for lunch.

Tensely, I listened and heard the click of the key being inserted in the front door. I pulled the blanket up over Mother's head while she lay with her face toward the wall so that she would be able to breathe. I also had my daughter sit next to her on the bed. I thought that in the evening I would ask Mother to join me at the table for dinner and to explain that she was a relative of mine who had just come by for a visit.

But fate had a real shock in store for me. Helmut came through my room as usual, but instead of going straight into the kitchen, he stopped for a moment on the threshold. My poor mother, suffering from a severe head cold and perhaps also because she lacked air, began to cough. The surprised Helmut looked at me with astonishment and walked further into the dining room. Could it be that he suspected that I had taken advantage of his wife's absence with the children and his being at work to bring someone into my room? He could see that the bed was made and that my daughter was sitting on it. How was he to explain the scene he saw and the cough coming from under the pillow? Up until then he had thought me an honest and unquestionably moral woman. What would he think of me now?

Once again, it was Toni who helped me out of my predicament. That evening, she came home and found my mother, whom I introduced as my aunt who had not seen me for many months, seated at the table in my room. I served her a glass of hot tea and homemade jam. When she saw my mother's delicate, pale face, she suggested that I have her spend the night with me in my room and return home the next day. I told her that I had had my aunt lie down in my bed because she was shivering from the cold but had wanted to conceal this from her husband for fear he would be angry at me for bringing a guest into the house without his or Toni's knowledge. I asked her to explain this to her husband, and she said she would.

Thinking about the way Toni always treated me used to give me a certain feeling of security. Nevertheless, I believed that should it ever be discovered I was not a Pole but a Jew she would be forced to turn me over to the mercies of her husband.

Lydia, who used to come from time to time to see me for a few minutes, came by now to see how Mother was doing. Toni knew Lydia as my friend Maria. This time Lydia asked her if she wanted to buy a short-length, fine-quality fur coat from her at a very good price. Toni agreed, and Lydia brought her the coat the next day. Toni was very happy with this acquisition, for the coat seemed actually to have been made just to fit her. Lydia was happy that she had found some money to live on.

The Ukrainian Gestapo Man

One day, while peeling the vegetables for lunch, I cut myself with the knife and received a deep gash in my finger. I was preoccupied at the time with worries about how the other members of my family were getting along, so I didn't pay attention to the way my finger became swollen and filled with pus.

About this time, Toni's father had come from Muenster in Germany to visit his daughter. He was an elderly, distinguished-looking man. He was quite happy when Toni introduced me to him and told him that he could speak with me in German. He told me, while lowering his voice, that he was not happy with the abundance he found in this house, because it had been acquired dishonestly. Who could tell how this war would end for the Germans? He understood that I had not been a domestic servant before the war.

Toni's father noticed my wounded finger and solicitously brought it to Helmut's attention. Helmut immediately took me, over my objections, to the hospital. I asked him just to put some ointment on it, hoping that the wound would heal by itself; but to no avail. Helmut entrusted me to the care of a surgeon and instructed him to take care of me at once. So I was brought into an operating room and operated on under general anesthesia.

It was the anesthesia that scared me to death. What would happen if while unconscious I should blurt out something which would reveal that I was a Jew? Maybe I would recite verses from *Tehillim*, which I knew by heart and which I used to recite during the day even while doing my various jobs around the house.

When I recovered from the anesthetic my first question to the attending nurse was, "What did I say when I was under anesthesia?"

She did not understand what I was talking about, but she reassured me that I had been in a very deep sleep. For that I thanked G-d.

One day, I was supposed to help Toni prepare a big reception for high-ranking visitors, most of them top army officers and Nazis of the uppermost ranks. One of them who used to visit my boss often, especially frightened me. He was a senior officer in the Gestapo.

Helmut had ordered Zofia, a Polish woman who worked at the hospital, to help me with the preparations. Her job was to clean the windows, light the stoves in each of the rooms and help in the kitchen.

The guests arrived and hung their warm coats and hats with the death's-head insignia on the rack in the spacious entry hall, while I felt revulsion and could sense my heart pounding with fear. Zofia, who had been working all day, continued to work alongside me a little while longer, and then she left.

The guests all had a very good time and made merry until

late into the night. When they had all had plenty to drink they joined hands and sang, "Everything's well with us now that we're sitting in the valley of the Vistula."

I, on the other hand, lay in my bed next to my sleeping daughter, and for hours I was unable to fall asleep. I felt my heart torn inside me out of pain and concern for my dear mother, my sister Lydia, my only son and my poor husband. Lately, my worry for my husband had grown even greater. In the latest letters he had sent from Brzezany, he related how the Germans were detaching a work detail of Jews every day and sending them out on jobs from which not a single one of them ever returned. The Moskwa family, who owned the house where he was living in Brzezany, told him one day that he should do everything he could to get out of there and go into hiding in Krakow. This landlady was a devout person, and her advice came straight from the heart. But how could he follow it? She had told him the same story I had heard earlier from Mrs. Zielinska about how the Germans drove the Jews with clubs into the forest and forced them to dig pits into which they would fall after being mowed down by a hail of bullets from the German machine guns. Those that were not killed immediately by the bullets were simply left in the pits and buried alive. These criminals, for whom there was no parallel in history, took care not to waste bullets and were not even willing to put suffering human beings, created in G-d's image, out of their misery.

These thoughts ran through my mind as I lay in my bed listening to the loud drunken noises of the party. The next day, Toni came into the kitchen with a worried look on her face. She told me that one of the guests, a colonel in the Gestapo, had felt when he left the house that night that his revolver, which he kept in his coat pocket, had been stolen. He claimed that I was the only one who could have done so, because no one else had been in the house. The master and mistress of the house rejected his suspicion as out of hand and recalled that Zofia the Pole had also stayed a while in the house after the party began.

Several days later, I was told by Toni that Zofia had been arrested by the Gestapo, and it had been discovered that she was a member of the Polish underground. But worry continued to gnaw away at me for quite some time. I knew I was in the lion's den, and a single incautious word might easily give me away. If, Heaven forbid, they decided to question me about my background, who my parents were and where I had lived before the war, I and my entire family would be doomed.

A short time after these things, the master and mistress of the house had another party. Among the guests at this affair was a Ukrainian Gestapo man, who would make me shudder whenever he came to the house.

Toni and I were in the kitchen arranging the plates and filling them with food, when, this Ukrainian came into the kitchen and asked Toni to keep him well supplied in alcohol while he was there. He had just returned from taking part in an *Aktion*, he explained, and had had a rough day. During the process of selection at the camp, where Jewish women were sent either to work or to death, one of the women had clutched her infant son to her breast and refused to hand him over. The Ukrainian had shot her and the baby to death. Still, he was haunted by the tragic eyes of that Jewish woman, and because of them he could not sleep.

I ran to the bathroom and doused my face with cold water, for my entire body was shaking and I had to get control of myself.

Several days later, the same Ukrainian came to the party. This time Helmut received the guests alone, because Toni had gone with the children to stay with her friends in Upper Silesia for the weekend. Helmut was happy that he could entertain his friends as he pleased. Like Toni, Helmut trusted me to keep a secret; both of them had gotten to know me well over a period of several months. I realized that there were two reasons for their base lifestyle—the lack of respect by Helmut and Toni for each other and the great material wealth that had come to them easily and tempted them to live for pleasure alone.

I cooked a meal for several people, and when it was over I served coffee and cake. Helmut told me politely that I was free to leave the dishes for the next day and to go to sleep. I did not hear what time the guests left that night.

In the morning, Helmut came into the kitchen and announced that because it was so late he would eat breakfast out. I went into the living room to begin cleaning there. When I opened the door my whole body began to quiver. On the couch lay the Ukrainian, half-dressed. I wanted to get out of there as quickly as I could, but he told me to come in, saying that he had lost his wallet with his money. Stiff with fright, I began to search the room, under the couch, behind the chairs and everywhere else I could think of. Suddenly, the man called out with sadistic laughter that he had found his wallet in his pants pocket. I promised to bring him breakfast soon.

When I set the tray down in front of him and tried to get out of the room quickly, he stopped me and told me to sit down. Instead of going to the table to eat, he began to interrogate me about my husband's whereabouts. I told him, shaking all over, that my husband served in the Polish army and had been reported missing in action, and I had no idea what had become of him. He continued to shower a rain of questions upon me. What was my husband's rank? In which unit did he serve?

I was desperate and losing hope, but thanks to the generous and merciful G-d, I hit upon an idea. I rose quickly and begged the guest's pardon that I had to prepare lunch and set the table, for Toni and the children were due home any minute. The man looked straight at me.

"You got out of that very nicely," he said.

Although he left immediately upon finishing his breakfast, I was not able to shake off the fear that he had implanted in me. Why hadn't Helmut told me when he had left the house that someone else had spent the night and was still there? Had this entire episode been planned in advance? Had

Helmut not eaten at home that day so that the Ukrainian Gestapo man would be free to interrogate me? Apparently, in spite of everything, someone had become suspicious that there was a Jew hiding out in the house.

G-d in heaven, answer me, guide me, what must I do? Where should I go at a time when my entire family is in mortal danger? None of us has his own place to live. How would my employers react when the Ukrainian Gestapo man told them about his conversation with me? Maybe they needed me so much and because it did not cost them very much to keep me, either in salary or in room and board, they would ask him to refrain from interrogating me further. I managed to calm down only after Toni had come home.

Upstairs from the Sopp apartment, there lived a German family by the name of Leksa. Mrs. Leksa, who already had four children, was pregnant with the fifth. She was the daughter of a priest from Munich. Her appearance was gentle, and she was most humane in her dealings with other people. Every so often I would help her explain her instructions to her maid in Polish. Mrs. Leksa always treated me courteously and warmly. She frequently remarked on my good breeding and expressed the opinion that were it not for the war I certainly would not be working as a housekeeper.

Returning home after visiting my son one Sunday, I heard Mrs. Leksa's voice calling me from the balcony, "Frau Anna, would you be so kind as to come up to my apartment?"

This time she had asked to see me not in order to borrow an onion or an apple, as often was the case. This time the matter was more serious. Her peasant maid was due to take a vacation for several days, but Mrs. Leksa simply was not able to remain alone with her four children without any household help, especially since she was pregnant. She asked me to try to persuade her maid, in Polish, to cut short her planned vacation. I managed to work out a compromise. The girl agreed to stay away for no longer than a weekend and to return immediately thereafter to her job.

Mrs. Leksa looked at me with gratitude. She could not help

but notice that my eyes were swollen from crying.

"Frau Anna, you are very sad," she remarked. "You look very sad."

At that time, she was bending over a pot of boiling water filled with cheese balls, a special dish she used to prepare only on Sundays. Her words sent a chill through my body.

She continued that she had just returned from the camp at Plaszow, where household utensils manufactured there were distributed to German families. I, who knew the truth about that camp, was able to visualize how thousands of Jews, my brothers and sisters, were compelled to make these utensils as part of their forced labor service, during which many of them died of hunger. At that time, I did not yet know that the Jews in that camp had also been sentenced to annihilation.

Mrs. Leksa became extremely serious; she put her two hands on top of her pregnant stomach and continued, "What fate is in store for this baby of mine who is about to see the light of day for the first time in a world in which Jewish human beings, including innocent children, are slaughtered not for anything they ever did, but just because they are Jews? I am the daughter of a priest. I know the holy Scriptures well, and I remember that when G-d revealed himself to Abraham He said, 'I shall make you a great nation, as numerous as the stars in heaven.' And now my people, the German people, is destroying the very nation that G-d chose as His special treasure."

Hearing those words, I could not help wondering whether she did not suspect that I myself was a Jew. How I wanted to hug this woman and to thank her for her honest words. I wanted to confess to her. If only I could pour my heart out before her and tell her of my suffering and worries over the death that awaited me and my children. But with all my might I constrained myself. The sense of caution I had developed kept me from revealing my identity. I feared she might let her husband in on my secret, and who could know if he would be of the same mind as she? He might be a Nazi, and he might turn me over to the Gestapo. Quickly, I took leave of her, on the excuse that I had to serve dinner to my employers.

One day, Helmut held a party for men only, and he received his guests personally. Earlier, he had asked me to prepare a fancy dinner, explaining that this time he had invited his friend the general, who had just come in from Germany, and several of his officer friends. Obviously, I did as he asked. I set a fine table and served the meal. The guests looked me over with keen interest.

After the meal I asked if I should serve the guests anything more. Helmut replied politely that everything was all right and I could go to my room.

I entered my room on tiptoe and lay down in bed next to my daughter, who was already sleeping the sleep of the innocent. Her soft and tender face, her tiny head with the blond curls, gave me a wonderful feeling of happiness and calm. Looking at this creature, so dear to me, I prayed to G-d to save my children, and I promised to myself that I would raise them to be G-d-fearing, honest and charitable people.

I lay still and began to think. For a long time, I could not fall asleep. During the day, when I was busy with the housework, I did not have time to think. Only at night was I able to search for a way out of the painful problems that beset my soul.

Until late into the night singing voices kept coming from the living room. The hoarse voices gave testimony to the fact that the guests had not spared the alcohol. Suddenly, I heard a knock on the door of my room.

At first, I did not know how to respond, but when the knocking continued, I put on my bathrobe and opened the door a crack. Before me stood a young officer of high rank. I was frightened, but I looked him straight in the eye and asked what I could do for him. He replied, a bit embarrassed, that he wanted to get into the kitchen to make coffee for everyone, and in order to do so he had to pass through my room. I spoke with him next to the open door, but I did not let him into my room. I told him calmly and politely that I would make the coffee myself and serve it to the guests.

The next morning, when I went into the living room to clear out the remaining traces of the party, I became sick to my stomach. I had to get rid of vomit from the floor of the living room and the hall. The representatives of the "Master Race"—as the Nazis presented themselves to the world—had eaten and drunk themselves sick.

After this time, Helmut became extremely polite in his behavior toward me. Once, on a Sunday, While I was busy getting dinner, he came to see me in the kitchen, and with a pleasant smile on his face he began to give me compliments, something he had not generally done before then. He expressed surprise that I, a young and pretty woman, was always so serious and my wardrobe was as modest as could be. After all, doesn't every woman like to get dressed up in fancy clothes?

As he was saying this, he took out his checkbook from his pocket, adding that I didn't have to be so frugal when doing the shopping for the household. He told me to buy myself a nice dress. When he saw that I was completely taken aback by his offer, he became confused and began to stammer. I gave him back his checkbook and thanked him for his generosity and for his lovely gesture. But, I explained that I could not even think about clothes because lately I had been extremely worried about my little boy. Earlier I had told my employers that I had a son, explaining that he was staying with relatives in my village.

Helmut brightened up and asked me if he could do anything to help. This was indeed a most fortunate coincidence. I lied, saying that my relatives had demanded that I take my son back with me, but I did not know where to put him up. He asked how old he was. When I told him that my son was the same age as his younger son Imo he said tersely that I should bring the boy to live with me.

I was overcome with happiness. I took this as a clear sign that the G-d of my fathers was watching out for me and for my children. I felt that this gesture of Helmut's was not the result of simple human kindness. I suspected that he might have another purpose in mind. Perhaps his willingness to put up my son in his home was a sort of insurance policy, that if it should turn out that I was a Jew, he would be able to clear his name—if the time should ever come when he would have to do so—by showing that he had given shelter to a Jewish woman and her two children in his home.

This thinking was not without foundation. I knew that he had had a talk with the Ukrainian Gestapo man, and I had the impression that the Ukrainian Gestapo had made Helmut suspicious about my origins. If, then, he had not changed his attitude toward me and had continued to keep me in his home, and if his wife Toni was just as polite toward me as before, this must be a sign that Heaven had decreed that my children and I would survive.

New Hope for My Son

At that time, my little boy was staying in the home of a Polish teacher. This innocent child somehow sensed the impending danger. In his eyes and in every facet of his behavior, it was possible to perceive an undefined fear, a fear that affected me as well.

My son would cry his eyes out on Sundays when I came to visit him at the home of the teacher who had taken him in. The teacher demanded a high price for keeping him, and she threatened me that she would not be able to hide him any longer unless I stopped visiting him every week. After each of my visits, she told me, the boy cries and begs to be brought to his mother. When he does this there is no choice but to lock him in the cellar so that the neighbors will not suspect that there is a Jewish child hiding in the apartment. I understood her fear that if the boy was discovered, she and her entire family would be in mortal danger as well.

The whole week I would look forward to my meeting with my son on Sunday afternoons, when I would see how his eyes shone with happiness. I used to bring him candy. But when the time for me to leave came near he would become anxious; he would squeeze me, kiss my hand and my neck.

"Mommy, take me with you; why can't I also be with you?" he would beg in desperation.

How could I explain to a four-year-old boy that as a Jew he had been circumcised, and if I took him with me both his life and mine would be in danger? As long as I live, I shall never forget how he begged and pleaded that he would sleep under my bed with two pairs of pajamas and would not cry.

"Whenever you leave me and I cry," he told me, "they hit me and put me in the cellar for punishment."

During long, sleepless nights, I could see his sad and desperate eyes.

One Sunday he clung to me closely, not letting me go, and he begged me to take him with me for just a little while, after which he would return to his place of shelter. Only when I promised that his Aunt Lydia would come to take him to me did he let me go.

I left him with a broken heart, depressed as could be. My eyes were filled with tears. I felt helpless against the cruel fate which had forced me to be separated from my precious son. I poured out my heart in prayer to the G-d of my fathers. I cried to Him to have mercy on the little boy and to save him from the Nazi beasts. For a long while I was immersed in prayer. My supplications went out from the depths of my wounded heart, the heart of a poor Jew pleading for her only son, knocking upon the Gates of Mercy in her hour of great affliction.

And indeed, I kept my promise to my son. Lydia knew how desperate I was on account of the boy, so she took him to her home, in spite of the danger this involved. Fortunately, it turned out that this step saved his life. That very evening

Gestapo agents broke into the teacher's apartment and arrested another Jewish boy who was also hiding in her home. No one had known that this teacher had been hiding two Jewish boys. To this very day I do not know if it was the landlords or neighbors who had informed on the teacher and brought the Gestapo to his apartment. I know only that they had searched for my son all over the house but could not find him. This time, too, G-d had miraculously saved my son.

Lydia was seized with fear and trembling lest Julia trace her, placing the boy in danger once again. It was thus most urgent that another, safer shelter be found for him right away. So my younger sister Bronia had taken him to her home for a few days until a permanent place could be found.

And indeed, as I have already related, once again I was in luck. Helmut gave me permission to bring the boy to stay with me. It was as if the boy had been born again when he came to live with his mother. He behaved politely and quietly, something that impressed Toni. But it is no wonder that children who had felt such suffering grow up before their time.

The transition benefitted the boy greatly. He quickly made friends with my employer's sons, and even though they had difficulty speaking to one another because of the language barrier, they spent lots of time together in group games. Peter and Imo used to invite Danusia and Jasz, as they called my children, to their room and would let them play with their toys.

When Helmut's two sons would take a bath they would invite Jasz to come and join them in the tub. But I would always decline their invitation, explaining that I needed him to help me in the kitchen. On the other hand, whenever I washed my son in the bathtub, he would always ask me to lock the door and not let Peter and Imo see him. Even though he was just a little boy he understood that no one must discover that he had been circumcised.

I must admit that I grew quite fond of Helmut's two boys. Whenever guests would come and bring them candy, they would always save some for me and my children. I used to stroke their heads. Peter's hair was like that of his father, light-colored, while Imo's was darker, like Toni.

It is hard to believe, but in my thoughts I used to try to find some justification for Helmut. I supposed that whatever he knew about Jews consisted of the horrible descriptions he had heard from Nazi propaganda. After all, he had grown up in the Hitler Youth organization, which filled the hearts of its members with the poison of Jew-hatred.

I myself had seen this education in action and how Nazi propaganda influenced the population, especially the youth, in Germany, during the time I had spent in that country in the years following Hitler's rise to power. Even then I had understood that Hitlerism was not simply a passing phenomenon. Even then I had been shocked and fear-stricken with regard to the future. Now, after Helmut had agreed to keep me and my two children in his home, I understood that he had taken into account our behavior during the entire time we had been there. He always used to speak with his guests respectfully and appreciatively about me, and it may be that he had even come to the conclusion that the way his people treated mine was a crime for which there was no recompense. Hitler, that crude, simple, uneducated man, had managed to hypnotize the entire German people, to scream into their ears day and night that they belonged to the noble Nordic race, the master race, the *Herrenvolk*, that would not rest until the bloodthirsty Jewish people was destroyed root and bough. If such a man had succeeded in anesthetizing the brains of an entire people and in bringing about a world war in which, among other casualties, were millions of his own Germans, there was no wonder that a young man like Helmut, no matter how educated, had been taken in by that mass hypnosis.

There was nothing left for me to do but to give thanks to G-d for the grace He had shown me and my children thus far and to pray that He would continue to protect us. I remembered my father telling me that whenever I lit the *Shabbos* candles, I had the right to ask G-d for anything at all.

But how could I keep this sacred commandment to *Shabbos* lights in the home of a Nazi who after the war would be arrested as a war criminal? Still, I longed to keep the commandment of the *Shabbos* lights with all my heart. Then an idea ignited in my brain. When I was certain that Toni and the children would not come into the kitchen, and when it was more or less time to kindle the *Shabbos* lights, I used to cover my head with a kerchief, light two matches with great emotion and say the blessing over them.

"O G-d, hear my prayer and have mercy upon me," I would whisper hurriedly. "Do not abandon me or keep your distance from me." The light of the two matches did not allow me any more than this, for they would go out quickly.

I chose these words, which I remembered from the *Shema Koleinu* prayer of *Yom Kippur* as I remembered the excitement and tears they used to arouse among the worshippers on that holiest of days. Such great and deep content was hidden away in these few words that I believed that G-d would look, see and understand my situation, that I would find favor in His eyes, and He would not forsake me.

An Act of Treachery

I n the meantime, Lydia had been making efforts to bring my husband from Brzezany to me in Krakow. In the process, she had found out that a certain Polish woman, a Mrs. Grochowska, had already successfully transported several Jews secretly from places where they were in immediate mortal danger. This woman had agreed, in exchange for a large sum of money to be paid in advance, to travel to Brzezany and to bring my husband from there, disguised as a railway worker.

My husband had written in his last letter, which he sent to Bronia's address, that his friends from Tarnopol had wished him success from the bottom of their hearts in his efforts to make it over to the Aryan side. They also entrusted him with the jewels and gold coins they had brought from Tarnopol and buried in the ground; they knew us well, and they had not even a trace of a doubt that after the war they would get their property back with nothing missing. And if, G-d forbid, they should not be saved, it would be our duty to turn this property over to whichever of their relatives was still alive or to members of their family abroad. They wrote the addresses of these family members on tiny pieces of paper.

The night Grochowska left for Brzezany, I had a horrible nightmare. In my dream, I saw my husband lying in a pool of blood, and some dark figures were tearing his body apart limb by limb. I ran like a madwoman to my sister and begged her not to let Grochowska go get him. But it was too late; she had already set off. I awoke in a cold sweat.

Before Grochowska had traveled to Brzezany to bring my husband back to Krakow on the night train, it had been arranged that she would bring him to her home, where I would meet him the next morning. From there I would bring him to my sister Bronia's house. Bronia had already managed to find a place for him to stay for a few days.

I was supposed to show up at eight o'clock in the morning with my daughter to pick up my husband. But Toni, who was always good about letting me off if I needed to take care of some personal business and had never refused any request I had made of her, would not let me go this time, even for one hour, until after ten o'clock. She was all flustered because that evening Hans Frank, the governor-general of Nazi-occupied Poland, had been invited to the house together with his entire entourage. Toni insisted that I go out with her to do the shopping and take care of all the arrangements for the reception. She could not understand why I had to get away only at eight o'clock in the morning and not at any other time.

However, as it turned out, it was divine intervention, the Hand of G-d, that made Toni so stubborn and that in the end saved my daughter's life and mine. Never before had I been under such deep emotional stress as I was then. I made the utmost effort not to show it, but Toni saw that I was not behaving as I ordinarily did and asked me if I was sick.

When I approached the Grochowska house, two hours late, I saw a group of people gathered outside. They were talking among themselves about something tragic that had just happened. When I entered the courtyard, I saw Mrs. Grochowska's husband going out of his apartment on the ground floor, walking quickly and carrying in his hand the blue leather suitcase I knew so well, in which during our sojourn in Brzezany we had kept money, jewels and other valuables we had managed to take out of Tarnopol.

With my daughter, I went into Grochowska's apartment, but the moment she saw us she turned pale.

"Saint in Heaven, get out of here! she shouted. "They just this minute took your husband!"

Shocked and wounded, I shouted back, "What have you done? Have you no fear of G-d?"

But she literally chased us out.

Later, I discovered the whole truth. After having travelled the entire night on the train, and after a nerve racking identity check, my husband had reached the Grochowska house. Because there were a few hours left until morning she had told him to lie down and get some sleep so that he would be fresh when I came at eight o'clock with my daughter. My husband was utterly exhausted. He fell asleep right away, and she took advantage of the opportunity and opened his suitcase. When she saw the fortune he was carrying she hid the suitcase and ran to summon the Gestapo. She also told them to wait until eight o'clock when I was due to show up with my daughter, so that they could catch us, too. Had I indeed come at the appointed time, Grochowska would have killed three birds with one stone, and no one would ever have known what became of my husband. She knew as well that my mother and sisters and their children were also hiding out somewhere. She knew that the sadistic Nazi criminals would torture the children before my eyes, and then I would break and disclose the hiding places of the rest of the members of my family. And when she saw me at ten o'clock she warned me off so that she would not have to face me after the terrible crime she had just committed against me.

So it was truly an act of G-d's grace, a miracle from Heaven, that saved me that day from the hands of the Nazi murderers, on the day of my husband's misfortune. Had it not been for that big reception at my employer's house that evening and Toni's absolute refusal to let me off that morning, it is clear what would have happened. The agents of the Gestapo and the Grochowskas had assumed that if I was over two hours late, someone must have tipped me off, so that there was no point in waiting any longer. We had been saved by a hair's breadth. The Gestapo agents had left just a few moments before I had shown up with my daughter.

The memory of those horrible times, the days of the Nazi hell, was engraved upon my heart from many years, but whenever I would think about them I would put off writing them down on paper. Every time I would be shocked anew; the memories would make me physically ill, and I would not be able to bring myself to concentrate upon them enough to set them down on paper.

The ways of G-d are unknown to us. Today, more than in the past, I am aware that it is the duty of every human being who was rescued from the Nazi inferno to tell of his experiences, to keep them alive and to pass them on to the generations to come. May this serve as a historical document, and may G-d grant that it influence the nations of the earth so that such a tragedy as that experienced by my people under the Nazis will never be repeated. May my words serve as an inspiration especially to my Jewish brothers and sisters: "Let not your spirits fail, even in the most abysmal moments of despair. The One who watches over Israel shall not sleep nor slumber. Israel, trust in G-d; He is your help and shield."

Two Tragic Events

T he people in whose home my sister Lydia was hiding, knew one of the guards at the prison on Montelupich Street, and from them she learned that my husband was being held there. After the shock that hit me, I ceased to think rationally. I did not ask anyone's advice, not Lydia's, nor my mother's, but acted according to some deep internal drive. These dear souls saw how I was torturing myself, and in order to comfort me, they told me that the Polish woman in whose home Lydia was hiding had visited my husband in prison and had said that his condition was not bad. I knew that Helmut Sopp was the head doctor of the prison. So I decided to ask him to intervene on my husband's behalf.

I tried desperately to figure out how I could raise the

matter with him. Finally, I hit upon an idea. Thanks to a fortunate coincidence I happened to be alone with him in the house. Toni had gone away with the children for a couple of days to visit her friends. So I made a special dinner for Helmut, and when he had finished eating, I told him that I had a good friend from school who had married a Jew. Someone had informed on him, and he had been taken to the prison on Montelupich Street. My friend wanted to bring him some foodstuffs and money. So I asked him if he could help my friend, and I would be thankful to him with all my soul. I also gave him my husband's original Jewish name. Helmut looked at me with astonishment and promised that two days hence he would give me an answer.

When the time was right, I went to visit Mother, and I found Lydia there, too. I told them about my conversation with my employer. Lydia grabbed her head, and her voice sounded of despair.

"Are you out of your mind?" she asked. "Why didn't you ask us beforehand whether you should go to him? Have you forgotten that your husband was carrying forged Aryan papers with your Polish family name? Don't you know that Grochowska had passed your husband off as Mieczyslaw Kwiatowski? Where can you run now? Desperation has made you take leave of your senses altogether."

I decided, however, that I would run no longer. In such a situation of complete insecurity as to what the morrow would bring, I guessed that I had no other refuge. If the Holy Blessed One, wanted us to be saved, He would save us by a miracle. At this point, when I had a roof over my head, I could not run away any more. Whatever was going to happen would happen.

Two days later, as I was serving Helmut his lunch, I saw that his face was like a stone. His former courtesy had disappeared completely. His eyes were cold as he looked at me inquisitively. I was unable to summon the courage to ask about my husband a second time.

After thinking it over for a long while, he said in a voice cold as ice that he had indeed promised me an answer and that I could give him a sum of money but absolutely no foodstuffs to transfer to prison.

When I approached Lydia with a request to obtain the money so that I could send it to the prison, as Helmut was prepared to deliver it to my husband, neither she nor my dear mother were able to hide from me any longer the bitter truth that my husband was no longer alive. The Gestapo had tortured him for days on end, trying to get him to reveal where we were all hiding. But the murderous methods of the Nazi criminals proved useless. They would break their victims' bones and pull out their fingers with tongs, but to no avail. My husband remained silent until his soul left his body under great suffering, and he offered his life as a martyr who dies for the sanctification of G-d's Name.

Now I had no doubt at all that Helmut knew that when I had turned to him for help I was referring to my own husband. Of course, I did not give him any money, and he never mentioned the incident again. For my part, I fell into a deep depression and apathy. I was prepared for whatever happened. I had no more strength to fight.

My husband was not the last of my dear ones to be devoured by the Nazi murderers. Not long after this tragic event I went through another one, when the Gestapo got hold of my beloved sister Lydia. She, who was always so brave and gave us all encouragement, had been living for quite a while in constant dread. One day, Julia, the daughter of the caretaker of the building where we had lived before the war, approached her on the street. This ugly blond girl with a nasal voice was known as a Jew-hater, and she threatened my sister.

"You Jew!" she said. "You are pretending to be a Christian, wandering around the city. Your children and your sisters are also probably pretending to be Christians. I'll reveal everything and turn you all over to the Gestapo, unless tomorrow you bring me all the money I demand."

Julia knew all of us, and her threats frightened Lydia

terribly. For several days, Lydia was afraid to leave the house. A while later, she came to me and asked me to put Mother up that night, because in two of the houses near where she, my sister Frieda and her two children were living the Gestapo recently conducted searches. Who could tell if they would not come to her house as well?

It turned out that Julia's threats had not been idle. This monster kept her promise; she followed Lydia and discovered where she was living. Lydia was arrested and tortured by the Gestapo in the cellar of the prison on Montelupich Street, as we later found out from the Polish woman in whose house she had been hiding. They had promised to let her go if she would reveal where her sisters and their children were hiding. The criminals tortured her to death, but they were not able to get a single word out of her. In this fashion did she return her sainted soul to its Maker.

Following the tragic events of my husband's death, my employer had become quiet and pensive. In this I saw a clear indication that he knew that my husband had died in the course of unspeakable torture. I got the impression that he said nothing to Toni, for nothing changed in the way she treated me. Could anyone imagine what was going on in my heart, what horrors I was undergoing, what was oppressing me at night when I recalled that nightmare that had visited me the night Grochowska had brought my husband from Brzezany to Krakow? And now the nightmare had turned to reality. In the weeks before he was supposed to come I would spend whole nights awake just imagining how happy we would all be once we had been reunited after such a long separation, how my husband would regain his spirits when he saw his two beloved children again. And now I had lost him.

But I consoled myself that at least my children were alive and well. Was this not the ultimate happiness? Was it not an act of Divine grace that I had been privileged to have my children with me at a time when the Germans were murdering thousands of Jewish children every day? Maybe G-d would continue to help me, and we would be able to go on living in this house. Maybe now that Helmut knew that Germany's political situation had worsened and that Germany was likely to be defeated in the war, the fact that he had kept a Jewish woman and her children in his home would be of use to him, and he would decide, therefore, to keep our secret and allow us to remain in his home.

Still, my mother was deeply concerned; she feared for our lives. She advised me to take the children one day when my employers were out of the house and run away. But my poor mother could not advise me where to run. It was late Friday afternoon, and the time for lighting *Shabbos* candles was approaching. I tried to calm her and told her that after *Shabbos* I would decide what to do. When I left she put her hands on my head and blessed me with tears in her eyes.

That evening, as my children stood beside me and I repeated our ritual of lighting two matches to signify the holiness of the *Shabbos*, my hands were trembling. I whispered a silent prayer, "Our Father, our King, have mercy upon us, for we are alone and poor." But the tears poured ceaselessly out of my eyes, and they doused the flame. Try as I might I could not put a stop to the flow of tears. The children broke out crying, too. They stood close to me, hugging my knees. "Mommy, why are you crying?" they whispered.

Quickly, I dragged them into the bathroom, washed their faces, ran cold water over my own face as well and went back with them into the kitchen, so that no one would be able to sense what was going on in our hearts. I explained to the children that I had been praying that the war would soon come to an end, and we would all be able to live in peace.

The End Draws Near

T he next day, I went out to buy some milk. On the street, the caretaker of the building came up to see me. Her face was radiant, and joyfully she told me that her husband had heard from a reliable source that the Germans were absorbing defeat after defeat with heavy casualties on the Russian front. This was indeed joyous news. Evidently, the Russians had, for the second time in history, repeated the tactic they had employed in their war against Napoleon, when they had sucked his armies deep into the snowbound, frozen Russian interior, where "General Winter" was able to vanquish the invincible French army that had previously conquered almost all the countries of Europe. May Heaven grant, I prayed in my heart, that this miracle repeat itself this time as well, and this horrible war, unprecedented in all of human history, come to an end as quickly as possible.

The reports of the German defeats came not only from the Russian front in the east. One day, when I was in the house alone with the children, I turned on the radio in order to listen to a news broadcast from London. Rumors were already spreading at the time that the Germans were about to be defeated. Several times before, I had turned on the receiver to the station that broadcasts from Britain in order to listen. I had to do this quietly, so that the neighbors in the next apartment would not hear that familiar signal of the secret station from London. Suddenly I heard the wonderful news that the Allied armies had landed hundreds of paratroopers at Normandy. The paratroopers had turned out to be decoys, and when the Germans had brought up their divisions to ward off the invaders, the Allies had landed their major forces on the beach. Thus began the great battle that ultimately led to the final victory over Nazi Germany. Indeed, this was a stroke of genius born of a most sophisticated plan of operation. It heralded the beginning of the end, the downfall of Hitler and even the end of the war.

Listening to this station was a capital offense, but in the excitement of hearing this wonderful news I may have turned up the receiver to make sure that I picked up every detail of the announcement. I wanted to be able to cheer up my downcast family afterwards. The children were with me in the living room, as I had been cleaning at the same time.

Suddenly, I heard a long ring on the doorbell. At first I thought that it must be Adasz, Lydia's son, who used to drop in on me from time to time so that he could go to his grandmother and let her know I was all right. But when I quietly opened the door leading from the living room to the entry hall I froze in my tracks. Through the translucent glass of the front door I could make out three German military helmets. They rang the doorbell a second time.

I told the children to be quiet, and with them I crawled on the floor into the dining room and the kitchen. From there I went down the back stairs into the courtyard and went into the apartment of the caretaker on the ground floor. My entire body was shaking. It took a great effort for me to calm down and not to make her suspicious. I asked her for the recipe for baking cookies that she had once promised to give me. Through the window of her apartment I was able to see into the stairway of the building.

After a few minutes, which seemed like an eternity to me, I saw the soldiers descending the stairs and leaving the building. G-d Almighty had had mercy on me once again. The Gestapo agents must have figured that if no one opened the door for them they must have come to the wrong address, and they went away.

To this day, when I recall this incident, I shake all over, thinking about how I was once again saved from death.

A short while later, Mrs. Leksa, the German woman who lived on the top floor of the building, called on me. She had given birth to a son named Klaus Detlev, but the boy died in infancy and was buried in Krakow. She told me that soon all the families of the German personnel serving in the area were to be evacuated, for there was no longer any doubt that Germany was about to lose the war. "We deserve this punishment from G-d," Mrs. Leksa added. "A people on whose conscience rests the crime of the murder of millions, a people whose soldiers bashed open the skulls of babies against walls, a people that killed the children of G-d's chosen people—that they deserve to be defeated decisively."

She also took this opportunity to ask me to visit from time to time the grave of her baby, who had been born in Krakow and buried there, and to say a prayer for him when she herself would no longer be able to do this. I promised to do as she asked, and on Sunday her husband took me to the cemetery. I brought violets with me, and I placed them on the child's grave. I reflected on the close feeling between the child's mother and me, despite the fact that she was a daughter of the German people, which had annihilated millions of my innocent Jewish brothers.

Several more days had gone by when Toni came to me in the kitchen and told me that in a few days all German women and children would have to leave Poland. The men who held important positions in the administration would remain behind. She managed a lachrymose smile.

"Who knows, Anna?" she said. "Maybe I too shall be compelled to work as a housekeeper after we lose the war."

She assured me that she was very sad to leave me. But now I had new problems and new worries. How would Helmut treat me after his family left? How would he make use of the fact that he knew my secret?

The day of the evacuation arrived, and Toni left the house together with the children. She cried when she said goodbye to me. I reassured her and said that perhaps we would meet again sometime. I was sad after they had gone.

Several days later, Helmut informed me, wearing a most serious expression on his face, that I would have to leave his house, for after his family had left he had no real need for my services. Now I was really desperate. Just when the longed-for hour of salvation was drawing near I was about to lose the roof over my head. That was a real tragedy. Politely, I asked him to allow me to remain with my children in my little room. Well aware of my difficult situation, he thought it over a while and finally said that he himself would go to live at the hospital. But, he said, if he did that he would have to return the disposal of the apartment to the German housing authority, although he had no objection to my remaining in the home with the housing authority's permission.

It was only a few days after this conversation that Mr. Bizanc, the owner of Cafe Kristal, the very same Mr. Bizanc who had once caused me so much anxiety after he had asked me how I had learned to prepare fish Jewish-style—showed up at my door. He asked politely to sit down and explained to me that he had brought with him a most serious proposition. Since Helmut and Toni had so often praised me to him for my honesty and excellent conduct, he wished to offer me the position of cashier at the restaurant and cafe that he owned in partnership with his brother.

During ordinary times such an offer would have filled anyone's heart with happiness. But in the circumstances of those times, and in my situation, it was clear to me that I must not accept this proposition. The last thing I needed was to sit behind the cash register, where hundreds of people would pass by and see me every day. Who could tell if one of the customers would not recognize me and expose my identity? So I explained to Mr. Bizanc that I could not leave my children alone in the house. He was ready with a reply. Both children and I were welcome to take our meals at his restaurant. In addition, he offered me a handsome salary.

At that moment, I caught on to what was happening. Helmut had let him in on my secret and may even have told him the tragic story of my husband. It was practically certain that now Bizanc was in fear of his life, for the whole town knew he had collaborated with the Germans. So it seemed that he was looking for some security, for proof that he had been good to the Jews. His proof would be that he had given shelter to a Jewish woman and her two children.

I turned down his offer politely but firmly. Now, when the Russian front was getting closer by the day, his fears were not at all without basis, but I was not about to let him off the hook. Suddenly, he told me that Helmut had said that he could take half of the coal supply from the basement, leaving me the other half. To this, of course, I could offer no objection.

Liberation at Last

During the final weeks before liberation a young Jewish girl from Lwow, also masquerading as an Aryan, had been hired to work as a housekeeper in the home of the Leksa family. Her name was Janka. At the time, Russian planes were already circling overhead and dropping bombs on the suburbs of Krakow. A stern order was given to take cover in the bomb shelters until the all-clear signal was given. All the residents of the building, including Janka, would hurry down into the bomb shelter, but my children and I used to stay in the house. The truth is that I felt no fear at all. On the contrary, each air raid warning filled my heart with joy. Now I was finally convinced that no ill would befall us.

On the ground floor of our building lived a professor from

the University of Lwow and his wife. They were an elderly couple, well-bred, devout Catholics. When they observed that I alone among all the residents of the building did not go down into the bomb shelter during air raid warnings, they sent someone to warn me that at such a time I must not put my life in danger. So I took the children down into the shelter, mainly in order to avoid suspicion.

There were chairs in the shelter for all the residents of the building, and in the middle of the room was a table with two candles burning next to a statue of a Christian saint. When the professor's wife saw me, she asked me to say a prayer to the saint, as had all the others in the room. So I stood before the burning candles, covered my face with my hands and whispered, "Blessed be You, O G-d of my fathers, who has kept us alive to this great moment." Then I went to sit in the darkest corner of the shelter so that no one would notice the happiness and tranquility that my face no doubt reflected.

After a full day of sitting in the shelter, the building caretaker could no longer endure the confinement. She went out into the street to see what was happening. She did not come back for a long time. Suddenly, though, she burst in like an explosion and told us excitedly that she had seen the Russian Army, with huge tanks, nearing our street. She also related that she had seen how people had already begun looting carpets and other valuable items from the apartments the Germans abandoned. She and her husband decided to join in the activity, so the two of them left the shelter.

I shall never forget how the refined wife of the professor reacted when she heard the news that the Russians were already in the streets of Krakow.

"What a blow for us," she said. "If the Russians come, they'll bring the Jews with them." And in a voice that tried to imitate the accent of simple Jews she added, "Now we're back to petty trade and artisanry."

Hearing this, I whispered to myself the passage from the *Pesach Haggadah*, "Pour out Your wrath upon the nations that have not known You and upon the kingdoms that have not called upon Your name."

Could it really be that at this exalted moment of liberation from the greatest criminals history had ever known, this respectable woman, a member of the elite of Polish society, had forgotten that not only millions of Jews had been murdered at the hands of the Nazi oppressor, but thousands of Poles as well, and that the Germans had deported thousands upon thousands of Poles to forced labor? Did she really have nothing better to worry about than whether the Jews would come back and deal in trade? This woman and those like her knew full well that in pre-war Poland the Jews had been denied access to government jobs and that thousands of Jews in the cities and small towns subsisted from petty commerce in poverty and destitution, working by the sweat of their brow to earn their daily bread and to purchase two candles to light every *Shabbos* eve. Didn't these devout Catholics know that this was not the first time Poland would be called to account for anti-Semitism, for spewing heaps of contempt and derision upon our people? For all that they had done to us they deserved to have the Russians in their home now. Now they would have to do as the hated Russians ordered.

When we finally left the dark shelter we saw the caretaker and her husband carrying a valuable carpet into their apartment on the ground floor. Previously they had already managed to bring all sorts of expensive silver flatware and serving utensils, crystal and many other valuable items. I returned with my two children and Janka to our apartment. Janka asked to stay with us so that she would not be left alone in the apartment that had been abandoned by her employers, the Leksa family. For the first time in a long while we sat down together at the table to eat a light meal in a relaxed atmosphere.

But this idyll did not last for long. Someone rang the doorbell. I opened it and saw standing before me two Russian soldiers wearing helmets. Their faces were full of dust. They were unshaven, and their uniforms were wrinkled and neglected. I was not surprised at this; they must certainly have been on the march or in combat for many days and not had time to rest. They asked for water. I remembered a little Russian from the days when I had lived under Soviet occupation at the beginning of the war. I gladly served them glasses of water.

The days that followed were filled with incidents. People related gloatingly about seeing the two Bizanc brothers hitched like horses to a wagon laden to the brim, while people chased after them, beating them with whips. Later, after a long search, the two of them were found cowering in an abandoned cellar and were shot to death. Helmut and many other Nazis like him escaped this fate by managing to get out of Poland in time.

One day, a man calling himself Professor Jablonski showed up at my door. He introduced himself as the former owner of the apartment, which the Germans had confiscated. With great theatricality he knelt on the carpet and asked that I return the apartment to him and his family. I told him that I was a Jew, that the Germans had murdered my husband and that I had been left alone with two children and wished nothing more than to leave Poland for good as soon as I could. I promised him that as soon as I found another place to live I would let him have his apartment. Satisfied and excited, he left.

Another time, a Jewish woman named Mrs. Halberthal appeared at my door. She was a widow, and she requested to be allowed to stay in my house for at least a few days. She became very emotional when she saw my two children, among the few Jewish children left alive after the war. I had plenty of beds at my disposal, but I had only enough sheets for myself and the children alone; Toni had not left me any more. Still, Mrs. Halberthal looked very trustworthy, so I suggested that she take a warm bath, and at night I let her sleep together with me in my bed. She stayed in my house over ten days and ate together with me and the two children at the same table. When she left she could not thank me enough for my hospitality. She promised never to forget my kindness.

BOOK FIVE

The Aftermath

34

Recalled to Life

Immediately after the fighting around the city died down, a committee was organized to take care of the few Jews remaining in the area. The authorities gave the committee a house on Dluga Street, which was used for offices, a kitchen that distributed meals to the needy, a small hospital and dispensary and, perhaps most important, a bureau for registering everyone who lived in town or passed through, so that those interested could locate friends and members of their family who had survived the war.

The first *Pesach* following the war was approaching. Now I was able to visit my mother every day. My dear mother continued to live on Karmelicka Street, in the same apartment where she had lived during the war. My sister Frieda and her three children were living with her. Poor Lydia was no longer among the living.

My children were as if recalled to life by liberation. The chance for them to live close by their beloved grandmother and to play with cousins their own age, to talk with them in their mother tongue as they had been accustomed to do earlier—all this gave them unimaginable joy.

One day, a man knocked on the door of Mother's apartment. I opened the door and saw a Jew dressed in the striped uniform of a camp inmate. He was emaciated and looked like a skeleton, nothing but skin and bones. The man asked me if Mrs. Rachel Marcus lived here. He had obtained the address from the offices of the Jewish Committee on Dluga Street.

I confirmed that this was indeed Rachel Marcus's apartment, and I asked him to identify himself. He replied that Mrs. Marcus knew him well. I led him into Mother's room. She looked him over but did not recognize him. She asked who he was and how he knew her. His eyes expressed boundless love, and he broke down.

"Auntie, dear Auntie, don't you know me?" he cried. "I'm your sister's son. Don't you know who I am? I am Shachne Raby."

It is difficult to describe what happened at that moment. None of us was able to believe that a person could change so completely that no one would recognize him.

For many years before the war Shachne Raby had been a frequent guest in our house. Hardly a *Shabbos* evening went by in which he would not come to spend time with us and to sing *Shabbos* songs with the family. The warm family atmosphere that prevailed in our house drew many family members to us; they used to drop by our house after eating their own *Shabbos* meals. The wonderful feeling our family displayed, drew the others like a magnet. We used to have very exciting evenings.

Shachne Raby used to come by our house regularly, even during the winter when the weather was harsh and rainy. My mother's sister had died before the war, and he regarded my mother almost as his own. Even now, when my mother saw him in his awful condition, her heart was broken.

Shachne sat down at the table, and Mother quickly cooked some cereal and served it to him. None of us had ever before seen anyone so starved. He swallowed everything in the bowl at lightning speed. This cousin, whom we had known as a person of impeccable manners, was not ashamed to lick out the remnants of the cereal from the bowl with his tongue until not a single drop remained. It was not easy for Mother to cook for him every day and to feed him. It was difficult to obtain enough food. But my mother loved him dearly, and she was delighted when after a while he began to recover his strength and look like a human being again.

One day, Shachne asked Mother if she had heard anything from her son Aharon? What did he write? At that point, I made a terrible mistake for which I could not forgive myself for many years thereafter. I told her that Aharon was no longer alive. My thinking was that now that Lydia was also no longer alive there was no longer any point in continuing to deceive Mother, especially since she always used to ask where he was and why he did not return from the concentration camps in Germany, as so many were then doing.

The great Polish poet Juliusz Slowacki wrote, "Not knowing is like a thorn, but reality is like iron; it wounds and kills." Telling Mother the truth about her precious son Aharon brought great suffering upon her. She began to complain of heart pains. At every opportunity, she would repeat how terrible it was that she had remained alive after losing such a young and exceptional son. Of course, not only I, but Frieda and her children as well did everything we could to make her sorrow go away. Frieda and her children lived with her, and when she saw those fine children, she understood that G-d had been gracious with her and had let them live.

From Shachne she found out that like many others with whom he had been imprisoned in the death camp at Auschwitz he had been saved by a miracle when the Germans had fled. Hundred of thousands of Jewish children had perished in Auschwitz alone. After hearing this Mother used to repeat time and time again, "Please G-d, forgive me for the sin that is upon my tongue. You rescued my daughters and grandchildren for me at a time when from so many families with so many children not a single one remained alive, like my sister Miriam Engelberg and her husband Saul and their eleven wonderful children, all of whom perished except for one son and two daughters."

Another incident that occurred around the same time also shocked Mother and all the rest of us. One day, Mother's cousin, who before the war had been living in a small town where he managed a successful business, turned up. The man cried bitterly over the loss of his wife and children, who had perished in Auschwitz. He had a brother in the United States who had invited him to come to him. So he decided to sell his house in the town where he had lived, along with his furnishings and all his valuables, which his Polish neighbor had promised to keep until his return after the war.

My mother was completely opposed to his returning to the small town. She wanted him to stay with us for *Pesach*, so that he could take comfort in the family atmosphere together with his relatives. But this poor, proud man saw how difficult it was for us to get along with the limited means at our disposal, and he did not wish to become an extra burden upon us. Thus he did not accept Mother's invitation and decided to return to the town where he had lived previously, in order to effect the sale of his property as quickly as possible. Still, he hoped that if he could take care of this in time, he would return to us for *Pesach*. He went off hungry into the cold, broken in spirit.

He never came back to us. Only a while later did we find out what happened to him. A delegation from the Jewish Committee that had set out to track him down found out that the Pole who had been entrusted with looking after his property had taken his entire family to live in our relative's house. When he turned up suddenly in town, the Pole could not hide his anger over the appearance of this unwelcome guest. Nevertheless, he fed him and made a bed for him in his own house, and that night, he murdered him in cold blood.

Neighbors had heard this Pole shouting, "Hitler promised to destroy all the Jews, but he didn't keep his promise." The same neighbors, who looked askance at the one who had gotten rich at the expense of a poor Jew, had reported this to the representatives of the Committee, and they had also pointed out the place in a nearby field where the murderer had buried his victim that same night.

This dreadful incident made it utterly impossible for us to rejoice in the first holiday that we spent together after the war. If I had ever dreamed that after the war an end would come to all our troubles and worries, I knew now that this was an illusion. When I found out that the murder of mother's cousin was not an isolated incident but that such things had happened in many places in Poland, I came to believe with all my heart that one day the hand of G-d would reach out and punish all of these cold-blooded murderers. No one, not the Germans, not the anti-Semitic Poles, would ever eliminate the Jewish people from the earth. I believed with all my being that after the Holocaust, the greatest of all catastrophes that ever beset our people, G-d would raise us up to the peak of glory, for He had chosen us from among all peoples, and a new light would shine forth from Zion; our eyes would behold His return there in mercy, and His glory would fill the entire land.

As we were busy getting ready for that first *Pesach*, solitary people who had lost all their relatives during the war began to show up at Mother's home. Mother would see all of these emaciated bodies with their sunken, waxen faces and huge tragic eyes, and she would invite them to celebrate *Pesach* with us.

We ran around looking for potatoes, beets and other assorted vegetables for the traditional *Seder* meal. We had very little *matzoh* at our disposal, certainly not enough for the fifteen hungry people we had invited. But fortunately, we managed to get hold of a fairly sizeable amount of cabbage, vegetables and fat. When word got around that Mother was preparing a *Seder* meal, even more guests showed up without having been invited. Sad, embarrassed and frightfully poor, they would pull a few miserable potatoes out of the pockets of their tattered garments, asking us to cook them for them and let them sit down at the table to eat. All of them were completely exhausted, worn out from running around, looking for relatives they had not found.

I shall never forget that *Seder* as long as I live. About twenty-five people sat around the table. As one of the guests, a scholar, read from the liturgy for the evening the passage, "And G-d brought us out of there with a mighty hand and with an outstretched arm," he found himself unable to finish reading; he broke down crying like a baby, together with all the guests. He was unable to calm down.

We sat crammed together, for the table was not large enough to accommodate so many people. But this crowding made us all feel close together, and it gave us an important emotional release. We sat together until late into the night, satiated and excited. Even though some of the guests had found places to stay at the shelter run by the Jewish Committee, not a single one wanted to get up. All of them preferred to spend the night sitting up in a corner of our apartment, in order to remain together in a home atmosphere, as if they were in their own homes with their own mothers. Somehow, we made places for all of them on the floor and gave them blankets we borrowed from neighbors. Some covered themselves with their own clothes. They fell asleep murmuring words of thanks and blessings to Mother and to all of us.

Towards an Unknown Future

I n those days, my greatest dream was to leave
Poland as soon as I could. I needed to watch out for
every penny, for I had no means with which to support
myself and my children. So I decided to look for a job. In the
meantime my sister Frieda's eldest son, an intelligent, good-
hearted boy of eight, promised me that if I would bake good
cakes and package them in cardboard boxes, he would distribute them at the grocery stores and split the profits with
me. Jozek (Jozef), the handsome blond-haired boy, whose
father had been a well-known lawyer in Lodz, did indeed
keep his promise. He would run around the city for hours in
his short pants, and he used to return happy when he managed to sell his wares.

This state of affairs did not continue for long. G-d, the

judge of the widows and the father of the orphans, came to our aid. One day, a good friend of our family, a neighbor from the building where we had lived before the war, found us. This man told us that when he had returned to Krakow from the camps he had found his apartment, in which he had also maintained a wholesale cloth business. Before the Nazis had expelled him from his apartment and from his business he had managed to hide his valuable woolens and silks in one of the rooms and to build a brick wall to hide the treasure. No one would be able to guess that there was something hidden behind that wall. He had known us since we were little children. When he heard how badly we wanted to leave Poland, he offered from the bottom of his heart to loan me money for expenses. He knew that we had been well-to-do before the war. He had also known my late husband, and he was certain I would repay my debt.

Now that I had money to pay for my journey, I learned that I would have to wait a long time to obtain a transit visa through Germany, the point from which I could continue to any other destination abroad. Many who had long since submitted an application for a transit visa were still waiting for a reply. There were rumors that women with children who travelled by night train could manage to cross the border without having their transit documents checked.

My cousin Shachne Raby, who was certain that I was about to leave Poland, asked me to let him have the apartment in which I lived together with my children. Unfortunately, I had to disappoint him. My response was that this was utterly impossible, for I had promised to return the apartment to its former owners. I also explained to him that it was immoral for him, a single man with no family, to occupy an apartment that took up an entire floor in an apartment building, especially since the apartment's owners were a family with children. But Shachne did not calm down until I persuaded him that there was no longer any place in Poland for Jews and that he ought to try to obtain an exit visa and leave the country.

But suddenly the matter began to become complicated. Adasz, my sister Lydia's son, asked me to take him abroad with me on his own responsibility. I loved that precious boy who had lost both his father and his mother in the war as if he were my own son. His sister, who during the war had been known by the Polish name of Jadzia, had decided to remain behind with my mother, who needed to be taken care of on account of her heart condition, which had become particularly aggravated after she found out about the tragic death of her son Aharon. I could sense that when she heard that I was planning to leave soon, she became sad. Still, she understood that after I finally managed to reach Palestine I would be able to assure a livelihood for myself and for my children, for in Haifa I had the house my husband had purchased before the war.

One day, my cousin Henia Kluger and her brother Shmuel showed up at my home and told me that a friend of their late parents had reached Hanover in Germany and had been appointed to a respected position on the local Jewish Committee that had been organized there. This man had let them know that if they could manage to get to Hanover he would help them establish themselves. The two of them thus asked me if I would take them along with me when I left for Germany. Of course, I consented gladly. In Germany I knew no one, and with their help I, too, might have an easier time getting along.

Before leaving Krakow I decided to visit my father's grave for the last time. I wanted to ask him to intervene on our behalf before the Heavenly Throne that we might succeed as we set out toward an unknown future. I did not tell Mother that I was going to the cemetery, for I did not want to touch the wound in her heart that had not yet healed and to remind her of her beloved husband and of her son, who she could not forget.

But as I was riding the streetcar to the cemetery I noticed Mother in the same car. I turned red like a thief caught in the act. I explained to her that I was going to take care of a few last details before I left the country. Mother looked at my face with worry and great love. She could tell that I was sad, and she understood that the reason for my sadness was my anxiety over the upcoming journey into the unknown. I shall never forget how she encouraged me.

"Remember, my child, that this difficult situation of yours will pass," she said. "Where there was once water, there will be water again. You were once a fine lady, and you shall be a fine lady once more."

"You will see, my beloved mother," I whispered in her ear. "Once I reach Palestine I shall do everything in my power to bring you to me, so that we shall be together once again."

When I reached the Jewish cemetery of Krakow I was shocked. Everywhere I looked there were broken tombstones. I looked for someone who could show me where the grave of the Rabbi of Wielopola was, for I remembered from before the war that my grandfather Aharon Marcus and my grandmother had been buried nearby, and that near them my father and brother had been laid to rest. As time passed my sadness and disappointment grew greater and greater. The graves were destroyed, the tombstones shattered; the beautiful and dear markers of carved marble had vanished without a trace. The ground was muddy following a recent rain, and it was easy to stumble. I had to skip over open trenches, and I feared lest I fall and break a leg; for who would know where I was and what had happened to me.

I looked around, and my eyes filled with tears. When I could not find the graves of my dear ones, I lifted my eyes toward G-d. "Our Father, our King," I pleaded with Him fervently. "Grant us Your blessing for the journey on which we are about to embark. Let us leave this accursed place quickly and safely. Grant my dear mother health and long life and a little joy from life after all the terrible suffering she has endured."

An Important Position

Finally, the long-awaited day arrived when we were to leave Krakow. One evening, all of us boarded the night train that was to take us to Berlin. In Berlin the local Jewish Committee was to help us reach Hanover. We reached the border crossing at Szczecin. The train stood on a bridge over the Oder River while border inspection went on.

The tension among the passengers was unbearable. It seemed that time did not move forward at all. Every now and then, we heard the inspectors calling out the names of various passengers and taking them off the train. My nephew Adasz and my cousin Shmuel Kluger became very nervous, because they had no papers permitting them legal passage. So they locked themselves in the lavatory.

Henia Kluger, wan and worn after all she had gone through

in Auschwitz, sat next to me, and we lay the tired children over our laps, where they immediately fell asleep. We, too, pretended to be asleep. The inspectors passed by us several times and shone a flashlight into the poorly-lit car, but they did not disturb us. Perhaps the sight of two women with their children did not arouse suspicion that we might be travelling without the proper documents.

At last we were on German soil. But that was not the end of our worries. After all, we did not know what happened to the two boys. But after the train had pulled away from the border a safe distance, they turned up, their faces beaming with happiness. They told us with great animation how the inspectors had knocked forcefully upon the locked door of the lavatory, but when they heard no answer they told each other that the door had been locked intentionally in order to prevent anyone from hiding there.

When we arrived in Berlin, we were met at the train station by a group of people from the United States, mostly representatives of the American Jewish Joint Distribution Committee who greeted all the refugees from Poland. My children were delighted with the chocolate the Americans gave them. From the station we were brought to a transit camp, where we met many other Jewish refugees. The Americans wrote down our names, assigned us places to sleep and gave us food in the camp's large mess hall. During registration we gave our destination as Hanover, except for Adasz who stated that he wished to go to Frankfurt. We had to wait in Berlin until a transport to the Western parts of Germany could be arranged.

Because I knew Berlin from before the war, I left the children with Henia and went out to tour the city. The destruction and devastation I saw cannot be described. Thousands of houses had been reduced to rubble. The enormous department stores, the great and famous coffee houses on the Kurfurstendam, all the other grand old buildings, were now in ruins. Even the Memorial Church was partially destroyed. I simply could not believe my eyes when I saw men and women, old and young alike, wandering through the streets filling sacks a nd blankets with all sorts of refuse they found among the ruins, mainly door and window frames, and carrying them off to their apartments for use as fuel for heating and cooking. Absolutely nothing survived of that vibrant, exciting city, of the elegant stores whose display windows used to be illuminated all through the night. An atmosphere of sadness and depression pervaded the city.

I returned to the children who were waiting for me at the camp. The atmosphere was pleasant there. Refugees from many different places struck up acquaintances at the common dinner table, mainly by asking each other if they had heard any news of their relatives. When the bell rang announcing mealtime, everyone would push and shove in order to get a good place at the table. I did not like all this pushing and crowding, so I would enter the mess hall after everyone else had already gone in, sitting down with the children wherever there was room.

After Berlin, Adasz went with a group of refugees to Frankfurt, where he hoped to study medicine, while I went with the children to Hanover. My cousins Shmuel and Henia Kluger were fortunate that a family friend worked for the Jewish Committee in Hanover, and he obtained permission for them to reside in the city permanently. For me he was able to arrange only temporary quarters in Hanover.

In Bergen-Belsen, near Hanover, a special camp had been set up for children who had survived the war. In the meantime all of us were housed at the refugees camp at Windhorst, which had served as a military hospital during the war. There we met a number of people from Poland. Everybody took to my children immediately, since except for them there were no other children in the Windhorst camp.

Among other people we met a young girl from Krakow named Halina. After talking with her for a while it became clear that her grandfather was my mother's cousin. Halina was engaged to be married to a Jewish man from Lodz who was a member of the Windhorst camp committee. From then on, we took our meals at the camp in addition to sleeping there. We were especially pleased to be together with relatives.

A few days later, Halina's fiance told us that we would have to move to Bergen-Belsen, as a direct order had been received from UNRRA (the United Nations agency in charge of the displaced persons' camps in Germany) not to take any children into Windhorst but to send them on to Bergen-Belsen. Halina wanted to help me because she loved the children, but she had no influence in such matters. For my part, the very name of the place to which we were to be transferred sent me into depression.

I decided to try my luck, so I applied to UNRRA directly in order to obtain permission to remain in Hanover. I left my children with Henia and Halina and went to UNRRA headquarters on Lindenerbergstrasse. I told the director that the Germans had murdered my husband while I remained with my children with no means of support, and the very name Bergen-Belsen frightened me.

The man looked me over carefully. My good German impressed him, and he asked if I knew English as well. When I responded in the affirmative, he began to speak to me in a more friendly tone, and on the spot, he offered me a job with UNRRA, registering all of the arriving refugees, no matter what their origin or nationality. There was no limit to my joy when he handed me a letter containing an order to assign me and my children double food rations as an UNRRA employee.

It is hard to describe the impression this letter made on the director of the camp at Windhorst. He had never expected something like this. At once, he understood that I outranked him, for it was my job to assign him the food and clothing ration coupons for the camp population. I had been appointed his superior. He was so polite. He did not know what to do to make me and my children like him.

My new job was like a gift from Heaven for me. The fact that I would be able to help my Jewish brothers and sisters, who like me had passed through all the fires of the Nazi hell, gave me a great amount of satisfaction.

When I began to work at my job, I found a Mr. Enises, who introduced himself as a former Lithuanian consul in Germany, sitting at an adjoining desk. In the corridor, refugees, mostly Jews, waited to be registered. My new co-worker used to watch me carefully as I registered the people who came to me. During breaks, when we would be brought strong English tea, Enises would engage me in conversation with keen interest. From what he had to say I came to the conclusion that he was a thorough Jew-hater. A while later, he complained to me that I was showing favoritism toward people of my own religion. Calmly, I explained to him that I probably did do so unconsciously, but he had to understand that the Jews had suffered much more during the war than any other people. The Jews had been sent to the death camps in enormous numbers, where entire Jewish families had been burned in the ovens; the Poles and other peoples had not.

Two young Lithuanians were in charge of the clothing warehouse that was located in the same building as my office. They would distribute jackets, coats, pants and shoes according to my instructions. These were used clothes that had been collected in America and sent for war refugees.

I must confess that I did show bias in favor of Jews, for whenever I saw a sick Jew, broken in body and spirit, who had lost his entire family (some had lost five, six or even seven children) and had been left all alone in the world, how could I not show him favor? I would ignore Enises's inquisitive looks and take such a poor man into the warehouse myself, selecting the best items for him. Those in charge of the warehouse did not look kindly upon what I was doing, but they kept quiet, because they were interested in remaining on good terms with me. Still, I tried not to be absent from my desk for too long in order not to hold up those waiting in line.

Enises used to take his time handling the correspondence for which he was responsible. One day, as the end of the workday was approaching, someone showed up, out of breath from running, and asked me to register him. I sat down at my desk to take care of the man. At that point, Enises handed me a note, on which he had written in German, *"Die Ruhe sei dem Menschen heilig, nur die Verrueckten haben es eilig"* (Rest should be sacred to man; only crazy people hurry.) Even so, he showed me respect, and when he heard that my daughter had a birthday coming up, he asked me to invite him to the party. Sure enough he came, and he brought me flowers and my daughter a present. He never handed me notes accusing me of bias toward my own people again.

The trip from the camp at Windhorst, where I lived, to the place where I worked took up a lot of time each day. Thus I was grateful to the director of UNRRA for helping me obtain from the local housing authority a large room with kitchen privileges in the home of an elderly, childless German couple named Sagers, at 13 Podbilki Street. This was one of the long streets that led to the town of Celle and to Bergen-Belsen. I took Henia Kluger in with me to live.

Unfortunately, I did not have the good fortune to enjoy the peace of mind that had begun slowly to come to me for long. My children fell ill. The lack of vitamins during critical stages of their growth, combined with the emotional trauma they had undergone during the war years, had taken their toll. The doctors suggested that I take them for a rest at the health spa at Bad Pyrmont, where they could enjoy fresh air. I took a leave of absence for two weeks and went there with them. I stayed with a German family that maintained a small hostel.

I tried to get the children some additional fruits and vegetables, so that they could get more vitamins. Every day I would also take them for a walk in the public park so that they could enjoy the fine air. In the park we would run into people who had been crippled or maimed during the war, people with amputated arms and legs who supported themselves on crutches or canes. Sometimes some of them would sit down next to me and, not knowing, of course, that I was a

Jew, would brag about how they had been high-ranking officers. They were victims of the war.

Cigarettes and coffee were rare items at the time, and they were accordingly extremely expensive. It astonished me to see how they would bend down to pick up a cigarette butt, light it, and inhale the smoke with gusto. One day, while I was walking with the children in the park, a heavy rain suddenly began to fall. I took cover with the children under a tree. I could not believe my eyes when I saw how these war heroes began to race with one another to pick up the cigarette butts off the ground. I thought to myself, "G-d in Heaven, so this is Hitler's Master Race!" American soldiers stationed in the area used to throw half-smoked cigarettes at them and look on mockingly, or perhaps with pity, as those who had until recently been soldiers of the greatest of their enemies, raced for them.

Incidentally, like all UNRRA employees I received weekly two cartons (twenty packs) of American cigarettes. I used to use the cigarettes as money; with them I would buy all sorts of things that I needed. I hoped that when the great day came and I reached Palestine with my children, I would not arrive entirely empty-handed. I also used to exchange my coffee ration this way.

When we returned from our stay at Bad Pyrmont, a doctor examined my children and sadly determined that my daughter's lungs were in danger. A chest x-ray had shown a serious inflammation. My son was also diagnosed with the disease, but his case was not quite so advanced.

Once again, it became clear to me that I had been mistaken when I thought that once I left Poland all my suffering and worries would be over. In accordance with the doctors' instructions my children were sent, at UNRRA's expense, to the hospital for lung-patients at Bad Rehburg, several hours drive from Hanover. I was despondent when I realized that now, after the war, my sick children would be in an altogether foreign environment.

But in this trying moment as well, someone turned up who

made my burden easier to bear and who gave me the feeling that despite everything I was not alone and dependent entirely upon myself. I had acquired a good name among the Jews who had settled in Hanover after the war, because the leaders of the Jewish Committee knew that I helped anyone who needed the assistance of UNRRA wholeheartedly. I did more than I was allowed for them. One of the members of the Committee, a native of Warsaw, who had lost his entire family, had shown special affection for me and my children ever since we had first come to Hanover. So he offered to drive us to the hospital in the car that the Jewish Committee had placed at his disposal. His German driver knew the route well, and he brought us quickly to Bad Rehburg.

This was an extremely difficult period for me. I could visit my children only once a week, on Sundays. The children lay covered with a thick blanket on an open porch all day every day, no matter what the weather. Since at the time it was quite difficult to obtain food, all the patients were fed a bowl of barley and milk twice a day, together with a slice of bread and margarine. They received no fruits and vegetables at all. So I used to bring them fruit every week, but I was never certain if they received it. I feared that hospital officials distributed the fruit among all the patients. I used to return home in a downcast mood and utterly exhausted.

We Meet Again

T he Jew from Warsaw who had helped me with my
children was a fair and honest man. He used to
take care of various matters with the British occupation
authorities, even though he did not know any English. He
heard from me and from Henia that I had survived the war
together with my children in the home of a Nazi. When I told
him that I would not leave Germany without first locating
the employer in whose home I had found shelter during the
war, he made me promise not to go unless he went with me.

I knew that Helmut's father was a doctor in Bielefeld, and I
was able to find the address without much difficulty. So on a
Sunday morning we went to Bielefeld. I rang the doorbell. A
middle-aged woman, who looked like Helmut's twin sister,
opened the door. She asked who I was and what I wanted.

When I introduced myself by my Polish name Kwiatowska she immediately asked me to come in. I told her that I had managed the household of her relative in Krakow.

It turned out that she was Helmut's older sister and that she had heard much about me—all good—from her brother. When I asked if it would be possible for me to meet her brother and sister-in-law, she told me sadly that Helmut was in prison in the city of Fuerth in Bavaria. Because he was a Nazi he had been sentenced to ten years imprisonment. In the meantime, Toni and the children were staying in a small town. My hostess defended her brother Helmut, claiming that he did not deserve such a harsh punishment. He was charged with castrating thirty thousand mentally ill Polish men during the time when he was the director of the hospital. She took hold of my hand and begged me to intervene on his behalf with the prison authorities, for having been in his home I was in a position to know that he was really a good man.

I decided to locate Helmut in the prison for war criminals in Bavaria. I hoped I could receive information from him about the date of my husband's death, so that I and the children could observe the *yahrzeit* on the proper anniversary every year.

One Sunday, I went with the man from Warsaw to the prison in Bavaria. Here, however, a disappointment was in store for me. When the prison authorities saw I was an official of UNRRA and that my companion was a member of the Jewish Committee in Hanover they permitted us to enter the prison yard, but from there we could see only barbed wire fences all around. When I explained that we had just undergone a long and tiring journey, a high-ranking official came forward. He quickly found Helmut's name on the list of inmates but told us that we could not see him because he was not just an ordinary criminal but a war criminal convicted of crimes against humanity. When he saw how disappointed I was he agreed to give Helmut the chocolate and cigarettes I had brought him and promised to deliver letters from me.

And indeed, I received an answer to a letter I sent him, thanking me heartily for the chocolate and cigarettes. Every now and then I used to get short letters from him, full of excitement, in which he wrote that he had always regarded me as a woman of distinguished character and that even now he could not thank me enough for the cigarettes and sweets I sent him.

During the next several weeks I would call the hospital at Bad Rehburg often, asking how my children were getting along. I asked the authorities to take care that the fruits and vegetables I brought the children did in fact reach them. Sometimes, I managed to visit the children during the week and to bring them cookies I baked for them. The children were especially happy on such days. I used to return from these visits altogether exhausted, but I was happy they were getting better and gaining weight.

One Sunday, I took my travelling companion, the member of the Jewish Committee, and went to see Toni. My companion showed great interest in hearing about my employer's wife and wanted to meet her so that he could find out if she had known that I was a Jew. We went to the small town where she was staying, to the address that her sister-in-law, Helmut's sister, had given me. I also wanted to ask her if her husband had told her while they were still in Krakow, or after the war, how he had found out that my husband was a Jew, and whether she knew how he had died. Since Toni had always treated me as a friend, I hoped she would not hide anything from me now. I must confess I was not happy about meeting Toni in the company of a third person, but the man had almost pleaded with me, and I could not turn him down.

When I rang the bell of Toni's apartment, she opened the door herself. She hadn't changed at all. But when she saw I was accompanied by a man wearing a hat and carrying a briefcase, she evidently suspected that he might be a police detective, for she turned pale and whispered to me, "*Kommen Sie zu mir als Freund oder als Feind?*" (Are you coming to me as a friend or as an enemy?) I hugged her and told her with a smile on my face that I had come as her friend, for in those trying days she had been good to me and to my children. Only then did she invite us in.

Inside, at the table, her two sons were sitting eating breakfast together with an American army officer. Toni introduced him as Major White. My appearance together with my companion made a great impression. They immediately invited us to sit down to the table with them and join them in their meal, but we made do with a cup of coffee. The children greeted me happily; they recognized me right away.

After they had finished eating I asked to speak with Toni privately. When we sat down alone in the next room, I asked her if she had known I was a Jew. When she heard my question her eyes widened in shocked surprise and a strange pallor crept into her face. Then she embraced me and began to cry loudly. I believed she was telling the truth, but I could not understand why she had been so frightened when she had seen me. She hugged me and kissed me over and over again.

"Poor Frau Anna," she said. "How you suffered so! It's a good thing Helmut didn't know, because as a devoted Nazi he would certainly have turned you over to the Gestapo."

Toni added that he deserved to sit in prison for the things he had done during the war. She did not know that I already knew what had become of her husband. I looked at her in wonderment when I heard the way she talked about her husband, the father of her children. How loathsome!

She sat with me on the sofa and confessed to me that she was engaged to Major White, he wanted to marry her and take her and the children with him to America. She asked how my children were, and I told her that both of them were suffering from lung disease and were in the hospital and that I hoped they would recover soon and return to me.

She began to recall the war years and asked how my friend Maria was doing. She told me that she still had the fur coat she had bought from her, the coat that she used to wear when she went with her husband to receptions at the home of Governor-General Frank. The coat made such an impression on the wives of all of the dignitaries, who wanted to know where she had found such a fine coat at such a low price.

I could feel the wrench in my heart as she said these words. I told her that Maria was really my sister Lydia, who had been forced to sell the fur that she had received from her husband as a gift when she had nothing else to exchange for food, and that she and her husband had been murdered by the Gestapo. Toni broke down in tears when she heard this, and I truly believed that her tears were of genuine sympathy for my deep personal pain. I knew that although she was a flighty person, she was fundamentally a good person.

When we parted she asked if she could come visit me and see my children. I invited her to come and gave her my address and telephone number so that she could call me in advance.

A very short time later, Toni got in touch with me and arranged to come for a visit. I was exceedingly surprised to see that she had brought Major White with her. She asked to see the children and gave them presents for which they thanked her.

Later, when we were alone, Major White explained his presence in fluent German. He told me that after I had left Toni had told him all about me. He said that he and Toni were engaged and that he wanted to marry her and take her to America. His superior officer had told him, however, that he was not permitted to marry a German woman unless it could be proven conclusively that she had never been a Nazi. The fact that her husband had been imprisoned as a war criminal only complicated matters. Therefore, both of them had come to me to ask my assistance. As long as Toni had no document that could clear her of the charge of Nazism, they could not be married.

Toni turned to me with her hearty smile and said, in words which shocked me, "You know how I took you and your children into my home even though I knew you were a Jew!"

"What hypocrisy!" I thought to myself. I was perplexed. But the two of them did not even wait for an answer but asked me to swear before their attorney that this was true.

At first, I refused. I explained that I also owed my life to Helmut and that I would be doing him an injustice if thanks to me his wife was able to marry someone else and his children were taken away from him while he was sitting in prison serving out his sentence.

The discussion between us continued for quite a while. I was upset. I very much wanted to get out of the situation. But I recalled that Toni had told me more than once that she did not have a marriage with her husband. I thought that if I helped her now she would be able to open a new chapter in her life and that it would be best for her and for her children if she married a man for whom she cared. So in the end I acceded to their pleas and made a short statement before the notary that Toni had known from the first that I was a Jew.

For a long time afterward, I had a bitter taste in my mouth over what I had done. I know that the two of them got married, but I never tried to see them again.

Palestine Beckons

Several months later my children came back to me from the sanatorium. It was time to begin to arrange our immigration to Palestine in earnest. I wrote again to my husband's relatives there, asking them to approach Mr. Klibanow from Haifa, the attorney who had been managing the apartment house my husband had bought before the war, and ask him to send us an immigrant visa based upon his affidavit before the British mandatory authorities that since we owned property in Haifa we would not be a public charge. I also asked that he stress that I had been widowed and was left with two children.

A long time went by before I received an answer from my husband's relatives. I was mortified when I read in their letter that the British regarded the house as abandoned property, because such a long time had passed without the appearance of an heir in Haifa to make a claim upon it. They had decided, therefore, to sell the house for several thousand Palestine pounds. I consulted the representatives of the Jewish Agency for Palestine who were in Bergen-Belsen and Hanover including some who were involved in organizing illegal immigration into the country. They advised me to write immediately to my attorney that under no circumstances would I consent to the sale of the house in my absence.

A few weeks later, I received the lawyer's reply. He was very sorry that he had not known for so long that I had survived; my husband's family thought that we had all perished. Nevertheless, he would do everything he could to obtain immigration visas for us. He also informed me that, Shmuel Kluger, Henia's brother, had managed to get safely to Palestine on one of the ships that ran the British blockade.

At that time, the Jewish community in Hanover was like a seething cauldron. Two young Jewish men had been apprehended and charged with planting a bomb under a British military train in protest of Britain's refusal to allow Jewish holocaust survivors to emigrate to Palestine. A farmer who had been working his field and had been hidden from the young men's sight had seen what they had done from afar and informed on them. They were arrested and sentenced to death. One of them was named Yaakov Redlich. He was engaged to a girl from the camp at Windhorst named Henka whom I knew well. Leading figures in Palestine, England and Germany interceded on their behalf, trying to get their death sentence commuted to a term in prison.

After this tragic episode, I redoubled my efforts to reach Palestine. My nephew Adasz had already managed to pass the entrance exams and to be accepted to medical school in Frankfurt, and I decided to visit him before I left for Palestine. I let him know in advance that I was coming.

When I reached the place where he was living, the German landlady opened the door and politely invited me into his room. She asked me to wait, saying that he would return shortly. In the meantime, she introduced me to her daughter, a young and pretty girl. The woman did not stop singing Adasz's praises to me; again and again she repeated how proud I should be of my nephew. She had been renting rooms to university students for a long time, but she had never before had such a polite and sensible boarder. In her opinion, he was too serious for his age. He was constantly running around doing all sorts of jobs to support himself, and when he came home tired he would lock himself in his room and study, sometimes even until dawn. I was surprised to hear from her that she would gladly consent to his marrying her daughter, even though she knew he was a Jew and he had also told her explicitly that he would only marry the daughter of a well-bred, religious Jewish family.

Soon after, Adasz came home and greeted me cheerfully. He brought with him a package of kosher food, which, considering his financial situation at the time, was an extravagance. We ate dinner together in high spirits and continued to talk for a long time, for since we had taken leave of each other we had each gathered much to tell the other. I rejoiced as if I had been his own mother when he told me how well he had done on his exams and what an excellent job he was doing in his studies. He asked the landlady to draw me a warm bath after my long trip and to offer me a bed in one of the rooms in her house. I was moved to tears when she went into the bathroom and poured an entire bottle of bath fragrance into the water, wishing me good night. Early the next morning, we bid each other our final farewells and knowing in my heart that I would not see my nephew again for a long time, I returned to Hanover.

When my nephew completed his course of studies and received the M.D. degree, he went to the United States for post-graduate work. He did not wish to remain in Germany. After a while, relatives introduced him to Carla, a bacteriologist from a fine family, and they were married. Theirs is a strictly Orthodox Jewish home. They have two daughters and a son, who have been brought up like their parents, as Orthodox Jews.

When I visited them in New York many years later he told me that he continued religiously to take part in Jewish study and that he was taking a course in Talmud by correspondence with a rabbinic scholar. His work as a doctor had always taken up so much time that he had not been able to complete his Jewish religious education while he was young. Only now could he attempt to make up what he had missed earlier by studying in his spare time at home.

A Strange Offer

During this time, I continued to receive occasional short letters from Helmut from prison. One day, out of the blue, I received a letter from him, in which he told me that he was awaiting a retrial, as the Polish doctors who had worked with him in Krakow had testified on his behalf and were constantly endeavoring to have him released. They argued in his favor that he was polite and sociable and that he had been forced to perform the castration operations on the orders of his superiors.

A few weeks later, I received an additional letter from him, this time not from prison but from Bielefeld. Helmut wrote that he had been released and would be most grateful to me if I would invite him to visit me, for he wished to make me an important offer. I was very surprised and curious to know what he wanted from me. I also wanted to see what he looked like after having spent two years in prison. The sight of him getting dressed up to go to a party at the home of Governor-General Frank was engraved in my mind. He used to put on an expensive fur coat that looked just like the one my late husband wore. Every time I would see him in this coat, I would feel a twinge in my heart. Among the wealthy Jewish families of Poland it had once been the custom for fathers to give their sons a fine fur coat before their marriage, and I knew that those furs worn by high-ranking German officials in Poland had been stolen from the Jews, who had been forced to turn them over to the murderous occupiers under penalty of death.

I responded affirmatively to Helmut's request and invited him to come to me on a Sunday when I did not work. Together with Henia, I prepared a fine meal, for I knew that he was something of a gourmet. I set the table for the entire family, including my children, who had already returned from the sanatorium.

When Helmut arrived and entered my house, I beheld a very tall, thin man. It turned out that he had lost fifty-five pounds. This made him appear taller than he had appeared previously. He was glad to meet us under such greatly altered conditions. Once he had been my employer, who provided me with my livelihood and shelter. This time I was hosting him in my home. It was important to me to receive him well, for I had not forgotten that it was because of him that I had survived the Holocaust. I had thought a great deal about whether to ask him details about my husband's death, but now that he was my guest I could not bring myself to ask him such questions.

Following the meal, which he enjoyed very much, he exchanged a few words with my cousin and my children. When Henia took the children into another room and we were left alone, he explained to me the real purpose of his visit. To begin with, he pointed out that he had always valued me highly, and my conduct during the time he had been

imprisoned had greatly moved him. Now that he was free
and trying to rebuild his life for the future, he wished to make
me a proposition. Although he had been freed from prison,
he was forbidden to engage in the practice of medicine for a
period of ten years. As a result of the war, many people in
need of a good rest to recover their health were interested in
becoming patients in private sanatoria. As a doctor and a
doctor's son he could open such a private sanatorium, but
because of the prohibition on his practice of medicine he
could not be listed officially as the proprietor or director of
such an institution. Therefore, he was asking me to present
myself officially as the director of the proposed institution.
He had no doubt that as a victim of the Nazis I would have no
difficulty obtaining a license to open such a business, which
many sick people were anxious to see established.

Helmut was quite animated while he was talking to me; he
did not stop smiling for a second, and he was certain I would
accept his offer happily. I began by addressing him as "Herr
Professor," in order to soften the blow my reply was bound to
bring him. I confessed that his offer was quite attractive, but
not for me, for I hoped that soon I would be able to immigrate
to Palestine.

This news hit him like thunder from heaven. He had not
expected to hear something like this. He began to explain at
great length and with great patience that I was making the
wrong move. What was the point, he asked, in moving to a
backward and poor country like Palestine with two sick
children? How would I make a living there? What future was
in store for me? Again and again, he tried to persuade me to
change my mind. If I accepted his offer he would split the
income with me equally, and there was every prospect that
the business would be quite profitable. In a few years, I could
go to Palestine as a wealthy woman with my financial future
assured. However, all his entreaties were to no avail. I would
not accept his offer.

"I am sorry," I told him. "I cannot change my decision. No
money and no words can hold me back. This German soil,

this country, will always remind me of the murder of millions of my innocent brothers."

His face became very grave. He understood that there was nothing he could say that could make me change my mind and that each additional word he spoke on the subject was wasted.

During his entire visit, he did not mention his wife Toni at all, and I did not ask about her, either.

When he left, he said, "*Sie sind eine lautere Natur.*" (You are pure by nature.)

After this encounter, I waited with increasing impatience for the moment when I would be on my way to Palestine. But lately my thoughts had been with Mother. My sister had written to me that her health had taken a decided turn for the worse and that the doctor had become a regular visitor to the house. In the end, my dream of being together with Mother in Palestine never materialized. She died in Krakow at the end of 1946.

A short time later, I learned that with the help of the Joint Distribution Committee, Frieda's children, and later she herself, had managed to reach Belgium. I was overcome with joy, and soon after, joy upon joy, I received a letter from my attorney in Haifa containing the immigration certificates I had awaited so long.

Voyage to Haifa

The happy moment finally arrived. In the spring of 1947, we left with a group of prospective immigrants for the port of Marseilles, from where we were to set sail on the French vessel *Providence* for the shores of the Promised Land.

At the port, I stood together with the children some distance from the vessel and watched as the people crowded and pushed one another, everyone wanting to be the first aboard ship so as to get a comfortable berth. Among the passengers, I saw a group from the transit camp at Berlin, including a woman named Paulina, an elderly spinster. Suddenly, I noticed two sailors standing on deck looking at me. A few minutes later, they came down off the boat, and without saying a word, they took my suitcases and the children onto the boat as I followed behind.

On deck, there was an officer who registered the passengers and assigned them to their cabins. He asked me several questions in French, including how old the children were. I was able to answer him in his language, which I had studied, along with English, as a young girl. I also told him that the Germans had murdered my husband.

A short distance from us stood a rabbi who made a great impression on me. He was standing on deck while my children and I waited to be assigned to a cabin. I remembered figures such as him from before the war; he was the image of the great rabbis of glorious countenance. His entire being aroused in me a feeling of reverence, his long black coat, his beard and sidecurls, the black velvet skullcap atop his head and, most of all, the sight of his noble expression.

My happiness was great when I was assigned a cabin with four berths and the captain ordered my luggage brought there. There was even a porthole in the cabin. I left the suitcases and went up again on deck. I asked the fine-looking Jewish rabbi if it were possible to obtain kosher food on board ship. His answer was that if I made a request in the galley in time, I could receive kosher food. When I asked him whether he too ate in the galley I did not receive a clear reply.

On my way back to my cabin, I heard complaints all around from the passengers who had been assigned to berths in the ship's hold. The beds were crowded together, and there were no windows in the entire dormitory. Chaos reigned. Paulina, who had been in such a hurry to get on board, complained to me that she did not know how she would manage under such conditions. I told her quietly to take her suitcase and come to my cabin, which had an extra bed she could use. Her joy knew no end, and I too was happy that I could help her.

In the dining room an unpleasant surprise awaited us. Most of the passengers sat down to the table and enjoyed a full meal, as usual. On the other hand, those who had requested kosher food were given the same fare for lunch and dinner every day—hard-boiled eggs, potatoes boiled in the jacket and sardines. This was not the fault of the ship's crew. Their previous sailing had been during*Pesach*, and the food they now served was the same menu the Jewish Agency ordered then. The man in charge of the galley thought that this was what people who asked for kosher food wanted.

I did not see the rabbi with the noble face in the dining room at all. I imagined he ate his own food in his cabin.

From one of the passengers in our group, I found out that we were about to celebrate the first day of the holiday of *Shavuos*. In the ship's lounge, a worship service for the holiday had been arranged. When I entered the lounge I saw the rabbi standing on the platform, leading the prayer. The room was filled with worshippers.

What happened on that occasion is something I shall never forget as long as I live. The rabbi gave a sermon for the holiday and reminded the worshippers that on the holiday it was the practice to pray for the souls of our dear departed parents and relatives, so that they would rest peacefully in heaven. Now, after the war, after all of the horrors and terrible suffering, after the tragic holocaust that had engulfed our people, we were about to return to the land of our forefathers. On our way we were accompanied by the sacred souls of millions of our brethren who had met a martyr's death just because they were Jews. They would stand before the Heavenly Throne and intercede on our behalf, so that we could rebuild our lives.

"Trust in G-d, my dear brothers and sisters," the rabbi concluded. "He has not forgotten His chosen people. He will be with us."

I cried when I heard those words. My entire body began trembling. I was so excited I simply could not calm down. All the worshippers shared my tremendous excitement; all of them cried like babies. The rabbi began to pray aloud for the souls of the martyrs, the sages of the Torah, for the innocent men, women and children, for the millions whose death had sanctified the Name of G-d.

At the conclusion of the prayer, I asked several people who the rabbi with the wondrous face was, but no one could tell me. Only later, after I had settled in Haifa, was I to meet him again under most curious circumstances.

The day for our landing drew near. Before I had set sail, while I was still in Germany, I had written to my relatives in Haifa and told them when I was scheduled to arrive in Palestine. However, I did not know which of them would come to receive me at the port. As it turned out, my husband's young nephew, seventeen-year-old Chaim, was waiting for us. His parents had come to Palestine several years before the war, bringing with them their four children, of whom Chaim was the youngest. I was to find out later that his father had been murdered by Arabs only a short time before.

Unloading all of the baggage from the ship was scheduled to take several hours. Since the children were extremely tired and needed to rest, the purser advised me to come back the next day to pick up my suitcases. Chaim helped me with this as well. The British, who controlled traffic into and out of the port, checked his papers and gave him permission to look for our suitcases and to remove them from the port.

As we came off the ship, I saw a most disconcerting sight. I had no idea that the British regarded the Jews of Palestine with such great enmity, and I was shocked, therefore, when I saw British soldiers facing the ship with rifles and bayonets at the ready. Apparently, life in Palestine would not be without its problems as well.

The Rebbe's Advice

We stayed with Chaim and his family for several days, during which time I sought out the attorney who had been managing my building. I wanted to ask him to find us a place to live. I was certain he would give me the rent money he had been collecting from the tenants over the years. I expected that money to support me and the children while we got settled in our new homeland. I did not anticipate the disappointment that was in store for me. I found out that the lawyer had turned over the rent collection to a relative of his, and this relative, who was also entrusted with taking care of maintenance and municipal tax payments, had turned out to be irresponsible. He had gambled away the rent money, and finally, he had died of a heart attack. The amount I actually received in cash was hardly enough to purchase a few pieces of furniture.

My attorney implored me to sell the building, as he had done even while I was still in Germany. A relative of my husband's who had arrived from America also advised me to sell. I protested that my children were sick and that I was just emerging from years of suffering and hardship. I worried that whatever money I would receive would slip away quickly, and I would be left penniless. When they heard this they both advised me to get a job. I did not like this advice either, because without knowing the language I would have no choice but to perform menial labor, and who would look after the children while I was out working? To be sure, I had worked as a housekeeper during the war, but then I had been fortunate to have been able to keep my children with me. But if I went to work, who would buy food? Who would clean my apartment? Who would take the children to school? What would happen to them in this strange new place whose language they did not know?

Several days later, a real estate broker came to me. He knew my situation well and announced that he had a potential buyer. He promised to try and persuade the buyer to offer a higher price in consideration of our difficult circumstances. If that was the case, then the first thing I had to do was to arrange some shelter for me and the children.

All the apartments in my own building were already rented for a pittance, and the chances of evicting one of the tenants was virtually nil. Nevertheless, I decided to approach one of the tenants, who was not a full-time resident of Haifa but merely stayed in the apartment on those days when he was at the port on business. His permanent residence was in Netanya, where he had his own house.

The man was rather old, so I expected that he would look upon our situation with understanding. I told him that I had sick children who had lost their father and that we were uninvited guests in the home of relatives, while he was a well-established head of a household.

I saw that my words made an impression on him. He

admitted that he indeed knew, from reading and hearsay, what had happened to the Jews of Europe, but he also had to apologize for not immediately acceding to my request. He opened the door to the room that opened onto the balcony, which was itself the size of a room, and there before my eyes was the glorious view of Mount Carmel. In the distance, it was possible to see the ocean, while a soft breeze brought with it fresh and refreshing air.

The man told me that he had been suffering for years from a heart condition and that for this reason he came to Haifa every week for several days in order to rest after work in the fresh air. The summer heat was not especially oppressive here, and he felt that by staying in Haifa he was actually increasing the length of his life. But after hearing about my situation, he agreed to seek other quarters for himself.

One day, not long afterwards, an old woman who had known my parents well came to see me. She had come to Palestine with her family from Berlin immediately after Hitler had taken power in Germany. When she found out that we had survived the war, she felt a strong urge to see us. I told her of the difficult straits into which I had suddenly fallen after all the suffering and pain I had endured during the war years. Since she was an extremely religious woman, I was not surprised when she advised me to travel to Jerusalem to consult with one of the rabbis who was universally regarded as a saintly man.

This was my first trip ever to the holy city. I had to wander about for over an hour until I found where the rabbi lived. He had a tiny house in one of the neighborhoods on the outskirts of town.

It was a summer day, and the rabbi was sitting in his garden underneath a tree next to a table piled high with sacred books. He was deeply immersed in study. The rays of sunlight filtered through the branches of the tree. When I approached him I saw his handsome, splendid face filled with spirituality. Suddenly, I began to tremble with excitement. Before me sat the great rabbi of Husiatyn, who had blessed me so many years before and all of whose blessings had thus far come true.

I cried and was unable to get a word out of my mouth. I told him who I was, and he looked at me with his good and gentle eyes like a merciful father. I told him that everyone was pressuring me to sell my building, which was my only property. We had always lived in the hope that we would someday come to Palestine and together make a future for our children, but sadly the Germans had murdered my husband, the father of my children. Now I could not sleep at night for fear of not knowing how I would surmount all the difficulties that stood in my way.

The words I heard from that great man had the effect of a healing balm. Just as before, years ago, so too now I heard him say, "The Holy Blessed One will help you my precious daughter, and your children. Do not sell your building. It will be for you and for your children."

I am unable to express in words the divine power that is hidden in this man, so great was the confidence and the faith he implanted in my heart that G-d would not forsake us. Before giving me his parting blessing he reminded me that my grandfather Rabbi Aharon Marcus was known not only for his great deeds of charity and for the way in which he fulfilled the commandment to "love your neighbor as yourself," but also as a G-d-fearing man of unshakable faith. The deeds of the fathers are an indication of what the children will do, and the deeds of such a father bring blessings upon his children and their children for generations to come.

I returned home feeling as if I had been reborn. When the real estate broker came to me again to tell me that his client was prepared to raise his original offer if I would only agree to sell him the building, I was already more collected. I asked him what the client's address was. The broker's answer was evasive. From what he said I gathered that he was speaking for a relative from America. So I told him succinctly that for the moment I had decided not to sell the building at all. I was surprised when I saw that he accepted my response quite willingly. This broker turned out to be an honest man. He confessed that after he heard that I had lost my husband at such a young age and remained alone with my two children, he no longer wanted to serve as a broker in this transaction.

When he got up to leave he said to me, "Don't sell this building to anyone."

Now it was clear that the building was to remain mine, I had to find a way of supporting myself so that I could take care of the children properly but still have an income. I enrolled the children in school and decided to look for employment, even in manual labor and even part-time. I also decided to study Hebrew intensively, for I could feel the lack of the language at every turn. I learned that as a new immigrant I could obtain part-time employment at a daycare center for children of immigrants, provided I could produce a recommendation from some influential person. I asked my attorney to write me such a letter. He did, and I got the job.

I would get up early in the morning, prepare a meal for the children, bring them to school and run to catch the bus that would take me to the place where I worked. I used to cook for the infants and toddlers in the daycare center, serve them their meals and help feed them. I found a certain fulfillment in this job, for most of the children were children of parents who had survived the Holocaust. With great patience and love I tried to nurture these children, who were very thin and did not look healthy at all.

When I returned home after work I would have to worry once again about preparing lunch and dinner for myself and the children. After taking care of all these things, and cleaning the house as well, I used to be so tired that I would sometimes fall asleep in my clothes.

Several months went by. One day, when I reported to work and went into the kitchen to begin my chores, the supervisor from the Jewish Agency, which ran the daycare center, came up to me and told me that as someone who owned property I had no right to take a job away from some other woman who had nothing at all.

I did not deny that I owned an apartment building, but I told the man that I had taken this job because the income from the building was not sufficient for me to support myself and my children in even the most modest fashion. This argument, however, was to no avail; the next day I found myself unemployed once again. Still, I did not lose hope that G-d would come to my aid.

My Daughter's Eyes

My life continued to present me with new surprises. One day Hanka, the young girl I had met in Hanover, came to see me. By chance she had found out where I lived. She begged me to help her. Like all the Jews who had lived in Hanover after the war, she knew that I had worked for UNRRA, and she had great confidence in me. She was an orphan who had lost not only her parents but almost all of her relatives as well. When she had come to Palestine, she had nowhere to go. She implored me to allow her to stay in my house, in return for which she would do housework and help me take care of my children. I immediately consented. Both of us were happy.

At that time, it was a major problem getting things to eat, as foodstuffs were severely rationed. In order to obtain an extra portion of the most essential items, like meat or milk which were rationed in the smallest portions, or even fruits and vegetables, it was necessary to have a lot of money and connections with one of the *kibbutzim*. I had neither. For this reason I suffered greatly, for the children were not receiving enough food. I remember standing outside the grocery store owned by an Arab from Syria who lived in the neighborhood, watching jealously as he sold his English customers the gorgeous red apples he displayed in his window, apples that I could not obtain for my children. Sometimes, I would go to one of the surrounding villages with my relatives to buy a few eggs, a little butter, some onions and potatoes. But on my way back from these expeditions on the bus I frequently witnessed British police officers conducting searches among the passengers and confiscating these foodstuffs as "contraband." Once, someone had managed to purchase a live chicken and hide it in a basket, only to have it begin clucking at the very moment the British officials boarded the bus to conduct a search. Those caught "smuggling" in this way had to pay a stiff fine.

The severe lack of vitamins had a deleterious effect on my daughter's health. She began to complain of a stabbing pain in her eyes. On her way to and from school she used to be blinded by the strong sunlight. I was frightened and worried, for in Israel there are many days of strong sun all year round. An opthamologist ran a series of tests on her and discovered strange spots on her pupils, but he confessed that he had never seen such a case. She had to wear heavy dark glasses, and every day she would be given eyedrops at the local dispensary. Still, her condition did not improve. More specialists examined her, but they told me that this condition was unknown in Israel. They had heard of it in Europe, especially among undernourished people who lived in unsanitary conditions, without sunlight. Sometimes it occurred in people who were recovering from lung disease.

This misfortune hit me hard. All my other troubles and worries were insignificant beside it. My daughter stopped attending school. When I took her to the dispensary for treatment, people on the street would look at us and shake their heads. The doctor did everything he could. He would give her shots of milk, which hurt her very much. I went to the famous Dr. Ticho in Jerusalem, but even he could not help.

My daughter would spend hours next to the radio listening to music. She could always answer the questions on musical quiz shows, and I used to send in the answers in her name. One day she heard her name broadcast as a winner of a contest. She was delighted. Her name also appeared in the newspaper, and I read it to her. But concern for her condition did not leave me for a moment.

I know that a person must praise G-d for the bad things that befall him just as he praises Him for the good, for all things come from G-d. Only someone who has suffered physically can understand the sufferings of other people and is willing to extend succor to the poor, the sick and the childless. We must remember that every one of us is destined to die, some sooner than others. The pursuit of wealth and glory shortens life. The rich man, like the poor, will take nothing with him to the next world.

If we would only think about this a little more often there would be fewer misers in the world, especially among the elderly, who suppress thoughts of their approaching death and become stingier and stingier from year to year. We must never forget that our only chance for heaven lies in the performance of good deeds. Above us is a seeing eye and a hearing ear and an open ledger in which the Divine hand is ever writing, and only through our good deeds now will our children benefit in the future. Where medical knowledge ends, only G-d can help. And indeed, in this case He helped me and my daughter.

One day, my daughter came down with a high fever and flu. I called the doctor, who gave her a prescription for penicillin. Penicillin was still something of a novelty in those days. I gave her an antibiotic for several days. And a miracle happened.

At one point, as I was bending over her to give her something to drink, she whispered, "Mother, I can see you fine."

I saw the hand of G-d in this event. It was He, praised be His Name, who created this drug in order to save my daughter from blindness and millions of other human beings all over the world from their diseases. After only a short while, my daughter went back to school without her dark glasses. On one of her eyes the spots remained, but they vanished over a period of several years, and she did not suffer any pains in her eyes at all.

In later years, I was able to observe how suffering helps to make for a gentle soul. As my children grew older I was proud to see how willing they were to help others.

In the meantime, my income from the rent my tenants paid was quite small. The building was already an old one, and the manager had to retain a portion of the rents for making structural repairs. He would also take his own salary off the top. No wonder, then, that little was left for me. I decided that as soon as I was able to function in the language of the country, I would take over managing the building myself.

There were other difficulties as well. Some of the tenants were late in paying their rent, which was low in any case. They asked to be treated with patience and understanding, because they were unemployed or had to care for a large family in which the husband was the sole breadwinner. I had to plan each and every expenditure.

I shall not forget a certain incident that brought me to tears. The entrance to the building was off a courtyard. When the building had been built years before the courtyard was at the front of the building, and opposite this side was a row of houses belonging to wealthy Arabs. The neighborhood was known as Wadi Salib, which became famous in Israel during the 1950's after a series of civil disturbances there. The front of the building opened onto HaNeviim Street, which in the course of time has turned into a commercial center. Nearby was the beginning of Hechalutz Street, with its shops and apartment buildings. One day, I was standing, as usual, next to the window, waiting for my son to come home from school. I was impatient and worried whenever he came home late, because there was much traffic in the streets at that hour and crossing the street required considerable caution. After a while, I saw my son walking barefoot over the asphalt surface of the street, which was melting under the heat of the midday sun. In his hand he held the shoes he had been given at the UNRRA warehouse before we had come to Palestine.

When he came in covered with sweat, I asked him why he had taken off his shoes. The boy answered that his feet hurt when he wore the shoes, because they were small on him. "I know, Mother," he added, "that you don't have money to buy me new shoes. I've been going barefoot now for a while, and I'm already used to it."

I hugged his precious head and covered his face with my tears. If his dear father had only been able to see his beloved son now, in such a state, he would no doubt have cried, too. He would not have believed that things could ever come to this.

Every night, before going to sleep I used to recite the *Shema* prayer and thank G-d that he had saved my dear children and brought us to the shore of our long-sought homeland. I felt confident, as if I were still together with my mother. A still small voice inside me told me that better days would come.

Under Arab Attack

One day, my cousin Shmuel, who had come to Palestine earlier as an illegal immigrant, came to see me. He was looking for a job in Haifa, and I gave him a bed and a corner of his own in my apartment. I felt great relief at his presence in the house. At that time, the fighting between Jews and Arabs that preceded the War of Independence had broken out, and Arab snipers had begun to shoot at Jews indiscriminately. Their bullets claimed many victims on the city streets.

Such incidents grew in frequency toward the end of 1947, in connection with the resolution of the United Nations General Assembly to partition Palestine into a Jewish and an Arab state. I believe completely that everything happened in accordance with G-d's will and as a result of G-d's concern.

After two thousand years of exile, persecution and wandering, the homeless Jewish people were privileged to receive a refuge of its own, where it could build a homeland with its own hands for all of its children, scattered over the face of the globe and bring them all together in their own country. An outpouring of joy swept over all Jews everywhere, and here in Palestine there was rejoicing such as I had never seen. Strangers came up to one another and hugged and kissed each other on the street. People cried from happiness, as old and young alike danced in the streets. For those of us who had survived the Holocaust, who had lost everything we had had in life, it was a sign of the grace of G-d that we had managed to reach this great and joyous moment. At the same time, we noted with sadness that without the awful sacrifice of six million of our brothers and sisters, the nations of the world would not even have given a thought to granting a homeland and refuge to the Jews. To our great misfortune, it had taken such a terrible sacrifice, a tragedy unprecedented in human history, in order to strike the conscience of the world.

As events developed it became clear that the formal decision by the United Nations was not enough to establish the Jewish homeland; many more sacrifices of life and limb would be necessary before a semblance of peace would come to the land. The Arabs of Palestine refused to abide by the United Nations decision, even though they too had been granted the right to establish their own state in a part of the country. Not only did the neighboring Arab countries support them in their refusal, but they themselves began to make preparations for war against the Jews, in order to receive a slice of the spoils. The British, who still ruled the country, encouraged them in this. Even though they were out to relinquish formal control of the country they continued to stir things up so that the partition resolution would not be carried out and the Arabs would conquer the Jews.

Some of the things I saw during those days ought to shock anyone with basic human feelings. One afternoon, I was sitting on the balcony of my apartment, where there was a breeze and I could cool off from the terrific heat. I shuddered when I looked across the street and saw that on the roof of the opposite building, which was owned by an Arab, stood two British soldiers instructing a group of Arabs how to place sandbags on the roof, leaving spaces between them to serve as slots for their rifles. This sight did not bode well for us. I quickly went inside.

A short while later, a terrible tragedy occurred. On the first floor of my building lived the Biton family, with many children. The eldest daughter Hannah, who was married and had three children, was staying with her parents in their apartment because she was pregnant. Her children used to play in the courtyard.

One day, when I saw my daughter coming home from school, I ran toward her to hurry her inside. As I was going in, Hannah ran out to call to her son and almost bumped into me. At that very moment a shot was fired from the Arab house across the street; it struck Hannah in the heart and killed her instantly. To this day I cannot shake the feeling that that bullet had been meant for me, for the attackers knew that the building belonged to me.

From that day on I was afraid to step out of the house even to buy food. Nor did I allow my cousin Shmuel to go outside either. But we were hungry, and we had to do something to stock up on food. Here Shmuel displayed great ingenuity and agility. He climbed down to the street from our balcony on a rope. It was a dangerous stunt, but with G-d's help it worked. Shmuel returned with a basket full of food, tied it to the rope, and I pulled it up into our apartment. Shmuel returned the same way he had gone down, climbing from balcony to balcony.

The British, who were supposed to defend the inhabitants of the country and to protect them from criminal acts, continued in their treacherous ways. I was filled with great sadness whenever I saw British soldiers patrolling the streets of the city in big tanks, looking apathetically as innocent people fell victim to the bullets of the Arab marauders. I was unable to understand how Great Britain, that same power that knew so well how six million of our people had perished, and that saw how we Holocaust survivors, physically and emotionally broken, were prepared to labor with all our might in order to build this poor and tiny country and to turn it into a home for our people, could allow the Arab murderers to run rampant and complete the work Hitler had begun. Among the tens of millions of Arabs we were like a drop in the ocean. If they had only consented to live with us in peace and allowed us to build the country quietly, they would have gained greatly from living close to us; they could have shared in the achievements of modern science and technology and brought culture and progress into their lives. Even today I still hope that the time will come when they will feel and understand that the two nations are both descended from Abraham our common father, and that the spirit of true brotherhood will be awakened in their hearts. That day peace will be a reality.

Tears poured down my cheeks every time I saw Hannah's poor orphaned children. But she was not the last victim of the Arabs. They continued firing from their hiding places in broad daylight. I was an eyewitness to another shocking incident. I was standing next to the window as my neighbor, an engineer from Vienna named Mr. Pauli, was coming home from work. As he was entering the building a bullet struck him, and he fell to the ground, bleeding profusely. I saw him lying on the pavement in a pool of blood, but no one dared go out to help him.

After a while, a man passed by in his automobile. When he saw Mr. Pauli prostrate and bleeding, he thought he was wounded, and he stopped to see what he could do. At that moment, two shots rang out, and the motorist was killed on the spot. He was a young doctor, thirty-one years old, who left a widow and three young children.

The most tragic shock was the death of my nephew Chaim. We were always afraid to go outside. I would stand by the window to see what was happening. One day, I saw Chaim passing by our building. I called to him. He looked up and waved, as was his custom. I asked him where he was going, and he told me he had to do an errand in the neighborhood. When he finished, he said, he would come to visit me. I had an uncomfortable feeling. I waited for him a long time, but he did not come. Later I found out that on his way he had been killed by an Arab bullet.

The death of this gentle soul, eighteen years old, the apple of his mother's eye, shook me to the very depths of my soul. His mother fell into a deep depression and had to be hospitalized. Doctors watched her constantly to keep her from losing her mind altogether. She never recovered. Oh G-d, avenge the spilled blood of these pure and innocent souls who were killed though they had done no one any wrong!

I went through yet another tragic occurrence, and from this one I was not able to recover for a long time. Arab marauders continued to fire from behind the sandbags on the roofs of the building across the way, as the British had instructed them. Even though I desired very much to sit with the children on the balcony to get some air and to air out the bedsheets, I had to give up the idea. One morning, as I was passing next to my son's bed, I found, to my horror, a rifle bullet lodged about an inch away from him head, and the glass door that led from the bedroom to the balcony was shattered. Only G-d's guardian angels had protected him and saved his life.

The next *Shabbos* I went to the great synagogue on Herzl Street and asked the rabbi to say the *Birchas Hagomel*, the special prayer that is recited upon being rescued from danger, in my son's name. I gave thanks to G-d for the miracle He had performed for us. Since that day not a *Shabbos* has gone by, no matter what the situation outside and no matter the weather, without my going to pray in the synagogue. I was so grateful to G-d for all of the goodness He had so mercifully shown me throughout all the years of suffering and hardship. I asked Him to continue to guide our lives and to influence us for good.

As time and events rushed ahead, what had begun as riots quickly became a full-scale war. The Jewish defenders began to fight back. Needless to say, the Arabs had not expected this. They were certain that within a short time they would be able to annihilate the Jewish settlement. But the very opposite came to pass. The Haganah got the best of them day by day, and quickly Arabs began to flee the country in large numbers.

The day finally came when the Jewish forces took control of Haifa. Suddenly, I heard our people proclaiming in Arabic and English over loudspeakers in the streets that the Arabs had nothing to fear, as we sought peace and wished to live with them in peace. They were in no danger from us. But they did not believe these words and fled in panic.

Those were the great days of Haifa. The city was free under Jewish rule, and its joyful inhabitants breathed their first sigh of relief for many months. Life began to return to normal.

It was also during this time that a very wonderful thing happened, which I must mention here. One day, someone rang my doorbell. I opened the door and saw a young man standing before me. He asked if a girl named Hanka lived with me, explaining that they had been engaged to be married. I let the guest into the living room and called Hanka. The meeting of these two young people turned into an extraordinary experience.

The young man was Yaakov Redlich, the same young man who, together with his companion, had ambushed a British military train in Germany near Hanover and who had been sentenced by a British military tribunal to death. The daring deed performed by these two young men had been intended as a protest against the treacherous policy of the British to close the gates of Palestine before the survivors of the Holocaust. Those same people who had come from the camps and deportation centers without a possession to their names, who had lost their near ones and dear ones, and who wandered over land and sea under inhuman conditions, hungry and cold, with but one goal in mind—to reach a safe haven and to rebuild their lives in their ancestral homeland. But the British hunted down the creaky old shops filled with young and old men, women and children that endeavored to run the blockade of Palestine and deported them back to the displaced persons' camps in Europe or interned them in detention camps in Cyprus. There were also ships that sank on the way.

In Palestine and abroad superhuman efforts were made in order to save the lives of Yaakov Redlich and his companion and to have their sentences commuted to life imprisonment. Finally, after many strenuous attempts, they were set free in exchange for some British officers that had been taken prisoner by the forces of the Jewish revolt and held as hostages. Now one of these heroes, Yaakov Redlich, stood before me, in order to meet his betrothed Hanka, an orphan, in my home. Anyone with the slightest imagination can picture the joy and happiness of this young couple.

Proposals of Marriage

L ittle by little life returned to normal. One day, Paulina, whom I had invited to share my cabin on the boat with which we had come to Palestine, came to visit me. Excitedly, she told me that for quite some time the man who was in the transit camp in Berlin together with his son at the same time we were there had been looking for me. Since Paulina had recently learned my address and telephone number, he had asked her for this information and told her that he would be contacting me directly. And sure enough, a short while later the man called me on the telephone and asked to see me.

When he arrived, I saw that he was tall, handsome and well-mannered. He had arrived in the country before us and had become well established, as was evidenced by the fancy clothing he wore. During our short conversation, he told me that I had caught his attention when I had walked into the dining room in the Berlin camp with my children and instead of pushing my way forward like the other refugees had taken a place that I had found vacant. We went on talking with great animation. It turned out that he, too, was a native of Krakow, and we had many acquaintances in common.

On his second visit to my house he showed great interest in my children. He told them that he, too, had a boy who was going to school and doing well in his studies. Following this visit, he asked me to marry him, but I remained skeptical and critical. Something about him disturbed me. Perhaps it was his fancy appearance. I would have preferred him to be dressed more modestly. Nevertheless, my friends and neighbors encouraged me to accept his proposal. I knew that if I married this man I would make my life easier, but a person's heart is so sensitive, so delicate, that it is difficult sometimes to put a finger on the reasons for a lack of response. I did not know myself what was really keeping me from consenting.

At that time, there was a flu epidemic, and I contracted the disease. The children spent the morning hours at school, while I, suffering from high fever and pain, did not have the strength to get up and go into the kitchen to make a cup of tea or to prepare a wet compress to drive down the fever. While I was ill, the man called me and I mentioned that I was not feeling well. To my great surprise, he showed up the next day, took off his coat, rolled up his sleeves, went into the kitchen, did the dishes, served me tea with lemon and prepared cold compresses. Then and there I decided that I would marry him. Taking so long to make up my mind was doing neither of us any good.

He had frequently mentioned that he knew my cousin Shachne Raby well. When I got over the flu I wrote to Shachne, who was living in New York, where he had married a widow with a child. I told him of my plan for marriage. His reply came quickly. He told me that the man I had decided to marry was indeed quite well educated and talented and likely to make a favorable impression. Nevertheless, Shachne advised me not to marry him. The man had been together with him in Auschwitz in the same barracks. He had managed to obtain preferred treatment for himself from the German camp officials, including extra food rations, but he had never shared these benefits with any of his fellow prisoners, even though many of them died from hunger. Shachne had learned that the man was highly egocentric and concerned only for himself. This was why Shachne had written to me so promptly, hoping that his letter reached me before it was too late. I invited my suitor to come to me, and I explained to him, delicately and with restraint so as not to hurt his feelings, that I had decided not to get married until my children were grown. I advised him not to wait for me but to take a different wife, for he had everything required to be a good husband. There were many other women, without children, who would be delighted to accept a proposal from him. I wished him well in life and asked him not to visit me any more.

Time passed, and again an event occurred in my life that proved to me beyond any doubt that everything in life comes from Heaven.

Every now and then, the woman from Berlin, who had given me the address of the Rebbe of Husiatyn, would call on us to see how we were getting along. On one of her visits, she told me that from time to time a tourist from Zurich came to visit her children. He owned an import firm in partnership with a resident of Haifa, and he came to Israel often on business. He was well-educated and refined, divorced, and observant; he attended synagogue every day. I knew that this woman's intentions were serious and that she was interested only in my welfare. I also relied upon her opinion that this would be a good match for me. So I consented to meet the man.

The man did, indeed, make an excellent impression on me. He was learned, fluent in several languages, with fine European manners. After a few short meetings, he began to talk about all sorts of plans for making profit out of my building. He said that if I married him he would invest the necessary funds in an addition of two floors to the building, for Haneviim Street had in the meantime turned into the commercial center of the Hadar Hacarmel neighborhood. Actually, I was surprised that he was interested in me at all, for as far as I could see he was younger than I and had quite an impressive appearance. When I confided my doubts to the woman from Berlin, she advised me to go to see the rabbi in whose synagogue the man worshipped during his visits to Israel.

One afternoon, I went to the address the woman had given me, and when I saw the eyes of the rabbi, which exuded extraordinary spirituality, I gasped with shock. This was the same rabbi I had met on the ship to Palestine, the rabbi who had held the memorial service on *Shavuos* for the six million victims of the Holocaust and had moved all the passengers to tears! I reminded him that my children and I had come to Palestine together with him on the same ship and that I had even asked him about obtaining kosher food on board. He remembered the incident and asked my name. When I told him that I was the granddaughter of Rabbi Aharon Marcus, he told me that we were indirectly related, for my cousin, my father's brother's son, had married his niece Lotte Hager. Lotte and her husband had been frequent guests in our home in Krakow. She bore my cousin a son. Unfortunately, she, her husband and her child all belong to the ranks of the six million whom the Nazis murdered for the sole crime of being born Jewish.

The rabbi introduced me to his wife and daughter, who looked quite a bit like Lotte. It turned out that the rabbi was a descendant of the famous rabbinical family of Seret-Vizhnitz. He himself was the Rebbe of Seret and lived in Haifa, while his brother, the Rebbe of Vizhnitz, lived in Bnei Brak.

After meeting the rabbi's wife and daughter, I told him why I had come and asked for his advice in this decisive matter. The rabbi's face became extremely serious; he cast me a fatherly glance and asked me if I had spent much time in the man's company. This question gave rise to many thoughts. The rabbi asked in addition what doubts I had about this man. For a long time, he was silent. Finally, he told me that he had known the man in question for a long time. He knew that he was well established materially. Even so, he advised me not to see him for the time being until I could obtain more information. He suggested that I contact this man's partner to find out more about him.

I was very moved as I listened to the rabbi's sensible advice. I had heard more than once that in matters of marriage rabbis would use all their influence to bring two people together in matrimony. Here, however, the rabbi had advised me not to go on seeing the man but first to ask his partner for information about him. The rabbi waited for my answer. I realized that if he had been in favor of my marrying the man he would have said so without hesitation. So I told him that I would not even bother going to see the man's partner and that I would cut off the relationship with him altogether. In the rabbi's face I could see that he was pleased with my decision.

Some time later I found out that the man had left his wife and two children for no reason and treated them most unkindly. Again I learned how great the rabbi's wisdom had been. He had gained his wisdom and his knowledge of life from our holy Torah, which he studied night and day. Indeed, the rabbis, who afflict their bodies with fasting and devote their time to studying Torah, manage in this way to maintain a clear head and to remain close to the Creator of the Universe, so that they can help others with advice on matters of importance. I praised the rabbi with all my heart for the advice he had given me.

This, however, was not my last visit to this rabbi. Several months later I had the occasion to visit him and to ask his fatherly advice once again. One day, when I was visiting the home of a cousin, I met a widower from Krakow who had lost his wife and child in the holocaust. After the war, he and his brother had come to Israel with absolutely nothing. His brother, who had also lost his wife and children, had developed heart disease and had died. His brother's death had broken his heart. He told me, in addition, that from time to time he used to visit a friend of his in Haifa. This was a friend from his youth in Krakow who was dying of leukemia, and he asked me whether he might visit me once when he came to visit his friend. I agreed.

When I met this man at my cousin's house I had noticed that my cousin's children, who slept in the same room would toss and turn and throw off their covers. It was quite cold in the room, and the man would bend over every time to pick up the blankets and lovingly cover the children again, as if he were their father. I could tell that he was a very sensitive man. Later, when he met my children, he immediately found a common language with them; he asked them how they were doing in school and whether they had already managed to learn Hebrew. I saw that he liked my children. He was very impressed with my ten-year-old son, who asked me not to call a plumber to open a clogged drain because he knew that plumbers charge a lot of money. Instead, he volunteered to borrow a wrench from a neighbor and do the job himself. My guest did not have words to describe his amazement. The boy went into the kitchen, and when he came out a short while later, his eyes were beaming—he had fixed the drain himself!

From that day, the man visited me whenever he came to Haifa. I used to accompany him on his visits to his sick friend, where I would see him take food out of his satchel and leave it in his friend's kitchen, so that his friend would not know that he had given him the gift. Out of modesty, he also did not want me to see the good deed that he was doing.

On one of his visits, he told me that his friends were urging him to take a wife, but he could not dream of doing such a thing, for he could not possibly support a family. But the more I got to know him the more I liked him, and I preferred to live modestly with him than to hitch myself to a wealthy person for whom I felt no sympathy. The next time he visited me, he indicated that he had always loved children and hinted that he would be happy to be a father to mine.

I made up my mind to marry him. I told him of my decision but informed him that first I wanted to ask the advice of my rabbi and to receive his blessing. He agreed to go with me to the rabbi, without knowing which rabbi I had in mind.

When we entered the rabbi's house I saw an unforgettable scene. The rabbi stood up, embraced my friend, kissed him and looked at me as if to ask me what I was doing here. I told him that we were virtually engaged to be married and that we would be married if the rabbi gave his blessing. The rabbi was truly happy and told his wife to bring refreshments.

I was curious how the rabbi knew the man. The rabbi explained that during the war he and his family had been in Cernauti, where he had met the two brothers. He had also known their grandfather, a respected scholar and benefactor from Krakow. The rabbi gave us his hearty blessing, and a few weeks later, we were married in a modest ceremony for friends.

The Final Correspondence

Many years passed. My children grew up and married, and my husband and I moved to Tel Aviv. Life in Israel was full of meaning and experiences, both personal and general, but it could not make me forget what had happened to me during the war. Nor could it make me forget the people who had had an influence on my fate during that tragic time. I continued to correspond with the Nazi doctor Helmut Sopp. No matter how revolted I was by his Nazi past, I felt that to a great extent I owed him my life and my children's. And I had another reason for corresponding with him. I hoped that I could find out details of how my beloved husband had died in the prison where Helmut had served as the chief doctor. Of course, I could not ask him this directly, but I hoped that one day he would take the initiative and bring up the subject.

When, with G-d's help, I was finally able to afford it, I made several trips abroad. Among the places I visited was Germany. While I was in Frankfurt I phoned Helmut, who lived in a small town called Neuss, and I spoke with him. He suggested that we meet in Duesseldorf. I suppose that because of his Nazi past he did not want me to come to him, so that the people in his town, who knew him well, would not begin to take an interest in his connection with me; after all, such an interest could damage his standing. But because of various reasons, the meeting never took place.

When I returned to Israel I continued to correspond with him, and I even invited him to visit Israel. He accepted the invitation gladly and thanked me for it. He added that he had heard good things about the country from many German tourists, but on account of his health he would have to put off the visit for the time being. He hoped that in the future he would be able to visit Israel together with his son. Between the lines, though, I could sense his hesitations because of his Nazi past. No doubt his conscience was not clean.

Here are two of Helmut Sopp's letters to me:

Helmut Sopp, M.D.
404 Neuss
Im Jagdfeld 43

Neuss, 6 April 1973

My dear Frau Anna,

I was extremely glad to receive your generous letter. It arrived as a most precious gift precisely on my sixty-eighth birthday. But most of all, I was glad that you are well and that your children have grown.

Two years ago, my wife came here from America and stayed three months. We spoke often about Frau Anna and about our fears. Those difficult times oppressed our memory greatly, and we are glad that all seven of us are now living in peace. Peter and Imo are married, and each of them have two charming children. Imo is with me and asks to send you special regards and to thank you for the invitation. He intends to write to you himself.

I did not remarry, and I am very lonely. My practice is doing well, and work helps me to overcome many things. Age is beginning to show, and that is not always pleasant. But I can be satisfied that I am still completely fit to work.

If you come to Europe again you must certainly visit me. Distance is no longer a problem. Neuss, where I live, is, to be sure, a desolate industrial site, but the Rhine River is not far away, and the surrounding area is quite pretty.

Imo and I are considering whether to spend the holidays together and to fly to Israel. From all those who visit we hear that it is a most beautiful country.

For many years I have not been able to take a proper vacation. It is difficult to get away from my practice, especially when the practice is a specialized one. I work as a psychotherapist, and for the most part I handle cases of depression. I cannot leave my patients without care. In any event, we have firmly decided, Imo and I, that we shall visit you in Tel Aviv. We hope to be able to get away for a few days in the summer.

Dear Frau Anna, I was so glad to receive a sign from the common course of our lives, and I wish you and your children all the best and, most of all, good health.

> Many heartfelt greetings,
> Yours,
> H. Sopp

Helmut Sopp, M.D.
404 Neuss
Im Jagdfeld 43

My dear good Frau Anna,

The sudden death of my eldest brother has upset my plans for the near future. A mountain of extra work had piled up in connection with his will and the disposal of his medical practice. Most of all, it disturbed me that I had to lay all of my personal affairs aside.

Imo has made a major change in his job; he is the manager of a large commercial house, and this has placed a great burden on him. He begs your forgiveness that he has not yet answered the part of your letter that relates to him.

I suggest that we put our travel plans into abeyance for the time being, also because it is already late. In any case it is a bit difficult for me at my age to undertake a long journey by air, even though quite a few friends my age have returned from flights to Israel thoroughly impressed.

Dear Mrs. Banet, your letters are full of friendship and heartfelt kindness, so that it is truly difficult to decide not to take the next plane to Israel. I wish you and your beloved children all the best from my heart, and I conclude with warmest greetings.

Yours,
H. Sopp

After these letters, our mail contact came to an end. Still I did not give up on the chance of finding out the truth about my husband through him. On another visit to Germany I tried to trace him. On the train to Karlsruhe I met by chance Dr. Waldemar Kroenig of Hanover, and during our conversation about various matters I told him of my interest in Helmut Sopp and the main reason for it. Dr. Kroenig offered to help me. About a year later, in April 1981, I received the following letter from Dr. Kroenig:

Dr. Waldemar Kroenig
Director College of Information Systems, Ltd.
3000 Hanover
Goseride 9

Hanover, 22 April 1981

Mrs. Anna Banet
Hadassa Street 13
Tel Aviv, Israel

Dear Mrs. Banet,
You will recall our discussion in the train when you were on your way to Karlsruhe. I hope that your journey was pleasant and not too tiring and that in the meantime you have returned safely to Israel. I had promised you that I would locate Dr. Helmut Sopp. As I have learned today, he died on January 6, 1976. I am enclosing the information from the Hall of Records of the City of Neuss.

I am very sorry that the only possibility to find out more about your husband's death has vanished. I understand that you wanted to know exactly what happened in that terrible event. Now this must remain denied to you. I regret much that I could not help you and will always gladly recall our conversation.

Be well,
Dr. W. Kroenig

Thus, the only source from which I could have learned about my first husband's death had vanished, and I felt a terrible and profound sense of loss and finality.

The Yom Kippur War

In writing this book, I would not see my mission as fulfilled, if I did not devote a few pages to the Yom Kippur War and to the things I went through during those difficult days for the people of Israel and for Jews throughout the world.

As I did every year, I went that *Yom Kippur* to the beautiful Hechal Meir synagogue on Main Street in Tel Aviv. In the middle of the prayer, a young officer came into the synagogue. He asked to stop the service and announced that the Egyptians had started war and that all young men of military age were to report immediately to their units. It is difficult to describe the sorrow and desperation of the fathers as they embraced their sons. Some fainted, and ambulances had to be called to take them to the hospital. On this holy day, when we pray to the Creator of the Universe that He may inscribe us in the Book of Life, we recall our loved ones who have passed away, and when we recall the memory of our martyrs who gave their lives in order to sanctify G-d's Name and the souls of the six million of our brothers and sisters who were murdered by the Nazis and their henchmen, the synagogue is filled with bitter crying and screams of despair. There is not a single house of worship in Israel in which there is not at least one family among the worshippers who does not mourn a loved one. And now, on this holiest of days, the treacherous Egyptians dared to attack us, knowing full well what sort of day this was and hoping we would not be ready for a surprise attack by the Egyptian army.

This news of the war hit us like lightning from heaven. But some voice inside me whispered that this time too the Rock of Israel would not forsake us. Was it possible that on a day when millions of our people were fasting and praying with broken hearts and with deep fervor from sundown to sundown, G-d would forget his people? Egypt, the largest of the Arab states, armed with the most modern weaponry, rose up against tiny Israel, whose entire population, including old people and children, hardly reached three million. Nevertheless, our faith was strong that the Egyptians would be defeated this time as well. We trusted in G-d that He would not abandon His people even as He rebuked them for their sins.

At this time, I was a widow living alone; my husband passed away after a long illness. At night, following the service, I went home by myself. The streets were blacked out in accordance with emergency orders. On my way home, I saw young soldiers directing traffic with darkened flashlights. Their faces were almost the faces of children, and they were frightened and sad. Every one of them was dear to me as if he were my own son, my flesh and blood. Even though I was still fasting I felt no hunger. The soldiers looked at me in amazement when I went up to them and said, "Dear children, trust in G-d, we shall win this war as we have won all the others."

Unfortunately, this war cost our people many needless casualties. When I got home I heard voices coming from the cellar, which served as a bomb shelter in wartime. The tenants were all sitting there by candlelight. I entered and wished everyone a good new year. They were surprised that I had not yet had any food after the fast, but I was calm and helped improve their spirits. I asked them to believe me that G-d would help us win this war. Just as Hitler had been defeated, so too would the Egyptians be defeated. I was the only observant Jew among the residents of my building. My neighbors all surrounded me and told me with great emotion that I had appeared before them like an angel from heaven and had planted hope in their hearts. Their sons had all been called up to the army, and they were all worried for them.

I went into my apartment, pulled down the blinds, and by the dim light of a candle ate some food and drank some water. Afterwards, I phoned my children and tried to reassure them that with G-d's help we would win the war. I finally lay down to rest following the fast and the events of the first day of the war.

Sad days were in store, days of deep sorrow, of mourning and bereavement. Every day we heard of dozens of casualties. Young men, fathers of young children, fell in battle. I would walk in the street and could not stop myself from crying when I saw the young men, actually boys, with their heavy field packs that their mothers had filled with food, carrying rifles. I would go up to them, and they would look at me bewildered and pale-faced as I wished them a safe return to their mothers. I would reassure them, "You will see that we shall win the war."

I prayed with all my heart that there would be no more casualties. Wasn't it enough that we had lost six million of our brothers and sisters? I prayed to G-d to hurry and put an end to this war and to grant us victory.

The fasts and prayers of our people were answered. We sacrificed some of the finest of our young people, but G-d sent us the victory. Our enemies and oppressors have left the stage of history, and their names shall be cursed forever. But we have remained strong in our faith that the peace we long for will come and understanding will unite all.

The tragedy of the war touched all of us, directly or indirectly. The only son of some friends of mine, who also had a daughter, was an army officer and commanded a division during the war. I knew that my friends were very concerned for him, like all other parents whose sons were fighting on the front lines. Unfortunately, his name turned up on the casualty lists. I went to pay a condolence call to the parents. I shall never forget this visit.

The father's hair had turned white, and when I saw his face frozen with grief, I hid my head in my hands so that he would not see my own tears.

I heard the father say words that are difficult to forget. He asked me not to cry. His son had fallen in battle like hundreds of other young people in an unequal struggle against the enemy in order to defend our homeland. He had fallen so that his parents and the coming generations would survive. In every war young men die. Nowhere is it written that the sacrifices will all be someone else's and never our own.

The father's great character was revealed in these words. He is not much different from our father Abraham, who did not withhold his only son and was prepared to offer him as a sacrifice to G-d.

The response of the mother was entirely different. Her usually cheery face had changed completely; her deep sorrow did not leave it. I visited her every day. One day she whispered to me (so that her husband and daughter would not hear) that she prayed to G-d to give her the strength to get over this blow, if only for the sake of her daughter and husband, who had been so weakened by it. But she never recovered. A short time later she died of a heart attack. This was a tragic loss for all of us. How awful that she did not live to see her daughter married only a short while later! The daughter took care of her father with a devotion that amazed all who knew her. She did everything to fill the void that had been left by the deaths of his son and wife. Only after she bore him grandchildren did a bit of light render his morose life.

I am writing all of this in order to remind all the enemies of our people that their evil designs will not succeed. Never will they destroy us, for G-d wills it so. After every setback our strength and security grow stronger. The time has come for our enemies to consider making peace with us. They will learn that peace with us will bring them nothing but benefit and will regret that they took so long to do so. Were it not for their stubbornness, countless human lives could already have been saved.

Even though we are a tiny people we have earned a good name for ourselves throughout the world. All the nations of the world have learned that we are industrious, talented, intelligent people and that above all we pursue peace diligently with all other nations. Our enemies' plans shall always be foiled, for G-d is with us.

"Who is like You among the gods, O Lord, glorious in holiness, awesome in splendor, working wonders?"

A Note to the Reader

As you have gathered from reading my book, I am an old woman who has had an arduous life, but I am still young in spirit and I feel strongly for my people and my homeland. At this stage in my life, as I reflect back on everything that has happened to me and how I was spared from the terrible fate that befell so many of my brothers and sisters in the Holocaust, I feel I would like to do something worthy and charitable, something that would benefit others. Therefore, I would like to take the opportunity of the publication of my book to convey to my readers my great distress at a recent development here in Eretz Yisrael and to ask them for assistance.

Unfortunately, because of the economic difficulties in Eretz Yisrael, many thousands of our young people are emigrating to seek their fortunes elsewhere. Many of these young people are not religious and do not necessarily seek out a strong Jewish center in which to live. Instead, they settle wherever they find most convenient, in Europe or in the United States, often in places where there is no Yiddish- keit at all. Not surprisingly, this leads to a shocking rate of intermarriage, a rate which is increasing constantly, reach- ing into many thousands. It is a frightening thought, and I feel it is the responsibility of the entire Jewish community to do everything in its power to stem this terrible tide.

For my part, I would also like to make a modest contribu- tion towards the solution of this problem by bringing into actuality an idea which has been in my mind for many years. Specifically, I would like to establish an organization which will offer material assistance to young people who would like to get married and raise families but cannot do so because they lack the resources to buy apartments. I would like this organization to be called *Chupah Vekedushin*, and I feel it should have centers in Jerusalem, Tel Aviv and Haifa, the three major cities of Eretz Yisrael. I myself own an apartment in the center of Tel Aviv, which I have dedicated to charitable purpose in memory of my grandfather Rabbi Aharon Marcus *zal*, and I would turn this apartment over to the organization as a modest beginning. Furthermore, I would also be willing to donate all my royalties and earnings from this book towards this important charitable cause. Indeed, it would give me the greatest pleasure to know that whatever this book will earn for me will be used for *chesed*, just as my father and grandfather were always involved in acts of *chesed*.

However, I realize that I no longer have the strength and vigor to accomplish much singlehandedly, and I pray fer- vently to the Lord who protected me in my times of greatest danger to send me good and honest people who would be willing to get involved in this project. First of all, the organi- zation would arrange weddings for young couples at the minimum expense possible, including food for the wedding *seudah* and wardrobes for the young couple. The young couple would then be offered a rent-free apartment in one of the outlying districts for one year or until they are able to find suitable work and living quarters in one of the larger cities. Hopefully, by easing the financial pressures during the time when they are trying to get on their feet, they will no longer feel driven to seek their fortunes in foreign lands among foreign influences and environments. Moreover, by offering these services to young people, especially those who have not had the benefit of a religious upbringing, the organization will develop a personal bond with them, and in this way, they can be introduced to the great wonders and truths of their Jewish heritage and brought closer to the *Ribono Shel Olam* and His holy Torah.

It is my fervent hope that my book reach many people in all corners of the world, because this is the only way I have of publicizing my ideas for this organization. I invite all those readers of generous spirit who care deeply for our people and our land to write to me about how they can lend their assistance towards the fulfillment of this goal. My address is: 13 Hadassah Street, Tel Aviv 64513. Your warm response is eagerly awaited. And if through this appeal I can help put together a group of dedicated and capable people who can help turn the tide of emigration, I will have the satisfaction of knowing that this book has served a very great additional purpose besides my testimony of my experiences during the Holocaust and the unbelievable Divine Providence through which I was saved, and I will have accomplished something truly important in my life.